MASTERING Writing at GREATER DEPTH

MASTERING Writing at GREATER DEPTH

A GUIDE FOR PRIMARY TEACHING

ADAM BUSHNELL
ANGELA GILL
DAVID WAUGH

FOREWORD BY ROB SMITH

CORWIN

A SAGE Publishing Company

Corwin
A SAGE company
2455 Teller Road
Thousand Oaks, California 91320
(0800)233-9936
www.corwin.com

SAGE Publications Ltd
1 Oliver's Yard
55 City Road
London EC1Y 1SP

SAGE Publications India Pvt Ltd
B 1/I 1 Mohan Cooperative Industrial Area
Mathura Road
New Delhi 110 044

SAGE Publications Asia-Pacific Pte Ltd
3 Church Street
#10-04 Samsung Hub
Singapore 049483

Editor: Amy Thornton
Senior project editor: Chris Marke
Marketing Manager: Lorna Patkai
Cover design: Wendy Scott
Typeset by: C&M Digitals (P) Ltd, Chennai, India
Printed in the Great Britain
by Bell and Bain Ltd, Glasgow

© 2020 Adam Bushnell, Angela Gill, and David Waugh,
Rob Smith, Kate Allott, Christina Castling, Lucy Davies,
Michaela Oliver, Pam Vennart, Megan Stephenson,
Dan Hughes, Kulwinder Maude, Lisa Baldwin,
Catherine Reading.

First published in 2020

Library of Congress Control Number: 2019948810

British Library Cataloguing in Publication Data

ISBN 978-1-5264-8734-6
ISBN 978-1-5264-8733-9 (pbk)

At SAGE we take sustainability seriously. Most of our products are printed in the UK using responsibly sourced
papers and boards. When we print overseas we ensure sustainable papers are used as measured by the PREPS
grading system. We undertake an annual audit to monitor our sustainability.

CONTENTS

About the authors   vii

Acknowledgements   x

Foreword   xi
     Rob Smith

Introduction   xiii

1   What is greater depth writing?   1
     Adam Bushnell

2   Developing deeper writing in EYFS and KS1 through a play-based approach   18
     Angela Gill

3   Developing deeper writing in KS1 through the use of high-quality picture books   39
     Megan Stephenson

4   Deeper writing at KS2   62
     Adam Bushnell

5   Developing understanding of language and deeper writing   81
     David Waugh

6   Non-fiction writing   98
     Kate Allott

7   Deeper writing through writing for children   112
     Dan Hughes

8 Deeper writing through drama   126
   Christina Castling

9 Deeper writing for EAL pupils   141
   Kulwinder Maude

10 Engaging pupils through the use of different materials   158
   Lucy M. Davies

11 Developing reasoning to encourage deeper writing   173
   Michaela Oliver

12 Using classic texts to develop deeper writing skills   190
   Pam Vennart

13 Reporting in science at a deeper level   207
   Catherine Reading

14 Deeper writing: a creative mastery approach   224
   Lisa Baldwin

Index   241

ABOUT THE AUTHORS

Adam Bushnell is a full-time author who delivers creative writing workshops in the UK and internationally in both state and private education to all ages. His books have been selected by the School Library Association for the *Boys into Books* recommended reading list. Previously a teacher, Adam now also delivers CPD to teachers and others working in education on how to inspire writing in the classroom. His app, 'Sentence Samurai', was launched in February 2019 and was created in partnership with Vocabulary Ninja. This app was developed as an aid to both teachers and children's understanding of how sentences can be effectively expanded towards greater depth writing.

Angela Gill is Assistant Professor at Durham University. She leads the primary English team, working with undergraduate and postgraduate students. For more than 20 years Angela taught in primary schools in Durham and Somerset, during which time she was subject lead for English and phonics. She has written a number of books and articles, including several about teaching phonics.

David Waugh is Professor of Education at Durham University. He has published extensively in primary English. David is a former deputy head teacher, and was Head of the Education Department at the University of Hull and Regional Adviser for ITT for the National Strategies from 2008 to 2010. He has written and co-written or edited more than 40 books on primary education. As well as his educational writing, David also writes children's stories and regularly teaches in schools. In 2017, he wrote *The Wishroom* with 45 children from 15 East Durham Schools and recently completed *Twins?*, working with twelve Year 5–6 pupils.

Rob Smith is the creator and curator of the award-winning website The Literacy Shed (www. literacyshed.com). After a 12-year career as a primary teacher, Rob now delivers writing workshops to students and professional development for teachers across the UK and around the world. Rob was a contributing author for *Beyond Early Writing* and is now writing his own English ideas website as well as creating a range of apps for teachers.

Kate Allott is a senior lecturer in primary English at York St John University. She has also worked as a literacy consultant for North Yorkshire County Council, and as a regional adviser for the National Strategies Communication, Language and Literacy Development programme. Kate has written extensively on primary English and is co-author of *Language and Communication in Primary Schools* and of *Primary English for Trainee Teachers*, and author of *Assessing Children's Writing*.

Christina Castling is a playwright, drama facilitator and teacher trainer based in County Durham (www.christinacastling.co.uk). She has been delivering drama and creative writing projects within schools for ten years and is the founder of Off The Page Drama CIC. She regularly works with a variety of cultural and educational organisations, including Live Theatre, New Writing North and The Forge, and particularly enjoys helping teachers develop their confidence in using creativity in the classroom.

Lucy Davies is an Assistant Professor at Durham University working with undergraduate and postgraduate students at the School of Education. She has taught in several primary schools in the North East, and continues to work in schools and nurseries across England carrying out research for both her own projects and for organisations such as the Centre for Evaluation and Monitoring. Lucy's main research interests lie in engagement and creativity, and she is currently part of the research team for the Durham Commission on Creativity in Education in partnership with Arts Council England.

Michaela Oliver is an ESRC-funded PhD student in Education at Durham University. She is particularly interested in exploring and developing reasoning in primary education. A former primary school teacher, Michaela now teaches on several modules within higher education alongside her doctoral studies.

Pam Vennart taught English for 35 years and is now a full-time teaching fellow at Durham University lecturing on both the undergraduate primary and PGCE English courses. She has worked on the ITE programmes for both Newcastle University and Durham in a part-time capacity for several years. More recently, she was Head of English at a Northumberland secondary school as well as an SLE for North Tyneside. She has also produced material for use on a National Exam Board website for both GCSE and A Level English.

Megan Stephenson is a senior lecturer in English and Academic Partnership Lead for primary education at Leeds Trinity University. She leads the English team, and oversees both the undergraduate and postgraduate students. She has taught in six primary schools in Leeds and Bradford over the last 20 years, where she has led both the reading recovery and phonics teaching, including the training of staff within the local education authority. She has presented at a number of conferences on her approach to developing 'inspirational teacher education', and is currently writing for a publication identifying the benefits of vocabulary-rich early years settings.

Dan Hughes is a Senior Lecturer in primary education at the University of Worcester. He is PGCE Primary Course Leader, working with both undergraduate and postgraduate students. Before joining Worcester, Dan worked in primary schools in Herefordshire and Worcestershire. As both an English subject leader and member of leadership teams, he has worked to develop the English curriculum in different schools and has delivered training to schools on phonics, teaching writing and developing communication skills. He also lectures in PE and outdoor education.

Kulwinder Maude recently took up a post at Durham University as a lecturer in primary English, after five years as Senior Lecturer at Kingston University, London. She has over 20 years of experience working in different sectors of education, including extensive experience of teaching and learning in primary schools (England and India), as well as the UK higher education. She teaches English on undergraduate and postgraduate Initial Teacher Education programmes, along with teaching on Master's level modules. She has written articles and chapters on many aspects of primary English for ITE and primary practitioners. She is also a co-author of two study guides for educational studies students.

Lisa Baldwin is Senior Lecturer in primary English at the University of Winchester. She leads the PGCE Primary Programme and teaches both undergraduate and postgraduate students. Previously, she taught in Dorset and the London Borough of Brent before becoming an English advisory teacher in London. She has recently published *Leading English in the Primary School: A Subject Leader's Guide.*

Catherine Reading is an Associate Professor at Durham University with a specialism in science education. Catherine is a chartered science teacher and has taught in secondary schools in London and the North East. At Durham, she has contributed to the science provision working across the undergraduate primary and PGCE science courses. She delivers professional development opportunities for teachers in science education, nationally and internationally.

ACKNOWLEDGEMENTS

We are grateful to Lorna Rosie for producing a case study of her work with Bella Winter of Sherburn Primary School, Durham, and to Bella and her parents for allowing us to publish her writing. We would also like to thank Erin Goldsborough of Our Lady and St Joseph's, Brooms RC and her parents for letting us publish an extract from Erin's contribution to the book *Twins?*.

We would like to acknowledge the support of *Busy Bears Children's Day Nursery*, Durham,

Many thanks to all of the staff and pupils at *St Thomas More RCVA Primary School*, especially to Tom Hunt; *Thornley Primary School*, especially to Jenny Watt, Oliver Johns and Jaymie Tateson; *Ox Close Primary School*, especially to Daniel Harrison, Lisa Payne, Leah Curry, Laura Smith and Jessica Todd; and *New Silksworth Academy*, especially to Debra Ridley. Your support has been greatly appreciated.

Special thanks also go to Liam Taylor from *St Thomas More RCVA Primary School*; Tia Orton and Luke Wilson from *Thornley Primary School*; and Ella Horner and Ted Fisher from *Ox Close* plus their families for letting us publish their work in this book.

We would like to acknowledge all the support and expertise of the staff at Baildon CE Primary School; especially the contributions of the Year 2 teacher Rebecca Firth. Many thanks to Sam and his parents for letting us publish his work. Special thanks also go to Cathy Brooke from East Morton CE Primary School for her excellent case study and examples of best practice. Your help and support have been greatly appreciated.

The section in Pam Vennart's chapter using Richard III is written in memory of Alan Currie a colleague at QEHS who died in 2017; an inspirational person and English teacher.

FOREWORD

With the advent of a new English curriculum in 2014 came a rise in expectations and a substantial change in the way that those expectations would be measured. Assessment was overhauled and levels were abolished. They had often been blamed for gaps appearing in learning due to the pace at which some children moved from one level to the next in order to demonstrate progress. Levelling, it was felt by some teachers, could demotivate children due to the 'pigeon-holing' of their achievements. A shift was needed. The DfE wanted greater flexibility in the way that teachers planned for and assessed pupils' learning. In the post-level climate, teachers are now required to develop effective and reflective teaching in order to meet the expected standards for all pupils. Within this curriculum, described as a 'mastery curriculum', it is hoped that all children will achieve the expected standard and that some students will demonstrate that they are working 'at greater depth within the expected standard' (DfE, 2018).

However, the question that has been raised by teachers within this new framework is, 'What does greater depth look like?' The official guidance from the STA is quite vague, and is condensed down to four bullet points and three adjoining footnotes. Those greater depth bullet points require students to 'exercise . . . assured and conscious control' which they can achieve by manipulating vocabulary and writing structures for a range of purposes. I often summarise it as 'write, write well and write often'.

In this book, the authors seek to clarify the guidance of the updated Teacher Assessment Frameworks and what this means for the teaching of writing. The authors have brought together the knowledge and experience of thirteen contributors who demonstrate their expertise through the various chapters. The readers are led through a range of practical ideas, and examples from the classroom through case studies underpinned by research and theory.

The book reminds me of the Maurice Young quote: 'To become a master at any skill, it takes the total effort of your heart, mind and soul working together in tandem.'

In *Mastering Writing at Greater Depth*, the authors discuss the need for engaging stimuli from the early years of schooling, where mark-making emerges through play and reading develops through picture books and early reading books enabling students to develop early writing skills. Throughout the book, reading for enjoyment is recognised as key to writing. Sharing high-quality texts across the school, from Early Years to Year 6, allows children to experience the 'masters at work' and emulate their writing techniques. This emulation will lead children on a journey of self-discovery, through the trialling of new skills and strategies, while responding to a variety of stimuli. Once they develop their own voice, they are able to share their thoughts and feelings coherently with the world through the written word.

We need to remember that 'mastery in writing' is not just utilising a range of punctuation or squeezing in a few colons and semi-colons in order to meet some spurious target, nor is it choosing words from the top of the 'wow-word' pyramid. Mastery in writing should be about children being encouraged to get their words and thoughts down on paper in a way that sings to the reader and ignites something inside them.

The ethos behind teaching to mastery reminds me of my final teaching practice where I was trained under an inspirational headteacher Paul Rangecroft at Studfall Junior School in Corby. On his door, Paul had the following quote from the poet Guillaume Apollinaire:

'Come to the edge,' he said.

'We can't, we're afraid!' they responded.

'Come to the edge,' he said.

'We can't, we will fall!' they responded.

'Come to the edge,' he said.

And so they came.

And he pushed them.

And they flew.

As teachers of writing, we constantly need to take children to the edge of their own skill set, let them stand on the precipice safely with some support if needed and then, when they are ready and fully equipped, 'push them' and allow them to soar.

Rob Smith
The Literacy Shed

References

DfE (2018) *KS1 English Reading Exemplification – Working at Greater Depth Within the Expected Standard*. London: Standards and Testing Agency. Available online at: www.gov.uk/government/publications/ks1-english-reading-exemplification-working-at-greater-depth-within-the-expected-standard

The Maurice Young quote can be found at: https://www.goodreads.com/author/quotes/1784959. Maurice_Young

INTRODUCTION

This book focuses on what greater depth writing looks like. It also looks at how to inspire and encourage greater depth writing. All age phases in the primary school are involved, from beginner writers in the Early Years to experienced writers in Key Stage 2.

We begin by examining exactly what greater depth writing should look like and what it contains by using guidance from the DfE and also examples of children's work in the primary school. We then look at what forms of writing work best to show a greater depth content. By exploring writing through physical activities such as drama and play, we examine which teaching techniques work best to encourage writing at greater depth. We also look at mastery of writing and how to maintain creativity in the classroom while achieving writing at greater depth.

The contributors have been drawn from schools, universities, organisations which are strongly involved in education, and educational consultants. All have in common a passion for sharing good practice and a keen desire to develop children's ability to express themselves in writing at greater depth.

Each chapter provides research focuses, critical questions, activities and reflections to encourage you to consider your own practice in the light of what you have read. There are also case studies to demonstrate how teachers and trainee teachers have helped children to work towards and achieve writing at greater depth.

In Chapter 1, Adam Bushnell examines the misunderstandings in primary education of greater depth writing and looks at clarifying exactly what the term means. Through examples of good practice, the chapter examines how to achieve greater depth writing, building from the EY into KS1 and on to KS2.

Chapter 2 examines how writing is developed in classrooms and educational settings where the focus is on play and free choice of a range of activities. Examples include indoor and outdoor play opportunities, role-play settings, construction, and small word and art and design areas, where writing can be encouraged and developed through a range of media and medium. Angela Gill discusses early writing and how it might develop, from pictures and mark-making to recognisable writing for different purposes. She also shows how young children's confidence and independence in writing is encouraged.

In Chapter 3, Megan Stephenson makes a powerful case for the use of high-quality picture books that engage children and develop the love of reading that then helps them to become better writers throughout KS1. In particular, this chapter focuses on how experiences such as drama and outdoor learning can be used to scaffold young children's learning in order to enable them to demonstrate depth in writing. The mastery approach is also examined in giving children a sense of ownership in their writing for a range of purposes and audiences. All of this is linked to high-quality texts and multisensory experiences used as stimuli.

Greater depth writing at lower and upper KS2 is explored in Chapter 4 by Adam Bushnell. He looks at how to teach effectively towards greater depth writing through case studies of classroom practice and real examples of children's work. Writing opportunities that best exemplify greater depth writing are explored, including the power of writing short stories to show a vast range of descriptive detail and how dialogue can be used to reveal character and plot.

In Chapter 5, David Waugh looks at vocabulary and deeper understanding of language, both within children's writing and for discussing writing. The chapter discusses the challenges involved in expanding vocabulary in order to enable children to write at a deeper level, and considers strategies for developing children's vocabularies. He maintains that a deeper understanding of language leads to greater depth writing.

Kate Allott maintains in Chapter 6 that greater depth writing in non-fiction depends on secure knowledge of the topic being written about, but also depends on critical reading, as exemplified by the National Literacy Trust's 2018 report on fake news and the teaching of critical literacy. The chapter argues that cognitive skills such as reasoning are also significant in non-fiction writing, and that developing a written voice depends on oral classroom activities such as presentations and debates. It also emphasises the teacher's role as expert practitioner.

In Chapter 7, Dan Hughes looks at teachers as writers, and how writing for pupils can have a powerful impact on pupil progress, as well as leaving a lasting impression on the teacher. The chapter discusses some of the challenges faced by teachers when writing for pupils, and gives a powerful argument as to why becoming deeply involved in the writing process can empower teachers. Strategies to support teachers with creating and modelling texts are provided, and Dan shows how having a deeper knowledge of the writing process can lead to more effective writing pedagogies in the classroom.

In Chapter 8, Christina Castling explores ways in which drama can be used to lay the ground for greater depth writing, primarily through enabling creative freedom and building positive experiences of 'play'. She argues that drama is a powerful tool for unlocking creative potential and can be particularly beneficial when working with underconfident or reluctant writers. The drama-based activities outlined in the chapter show how to stimulate story-writing ideas, provide deeper understanding of character and empower the development of new worlds.

Kulwinder Maude looks at greater depth writing with EAL pupils in Chapter 9. She maintains that these pupils need the freedom to 'draw on their resources' from both their learning worlds. The chapter also looks at how the EAL children's range of literacy resources from both their language and cultural worlds can be drawn upon effectively to write in many modes, forms and styles that all contribute to becoming a greater depth writer.

In Chapter 10, Lucy Davies discusses the multidimensional concept of engagement. She argues that engagement encompasses pupils' behavioural, physical, cultural, social, intellectual and emotional state. The chapter also explores how using a variety of materials, other than fiction books, can foster these different dimensions, resulting in children producing pieces of writing across a variety of genres. Practical ideas on how to use films, music, artefacts and picture books are included, along with how and why these improve engagement levels, leading to high-quality pieces of writing.

Michaela Oliver shows in Chapter 11 that developing teacher understanding of how to promote deeper reasoning within English lessons can lead to greater depth writing. She outlines what reasoning looks like in English and how to explicitly model and teach it. Practical strategies and task structures that facilitate development of reasoning are provided too, accompanied by examples from real-life case studies illustrating responses to the strategies discussed. She then considers how promoting reasoning about texts created by others can encourage pupils to make more reasoned decisions when creating their own texts, thus leading to deeper writing.

Pam Vennart examines multiple creative ideas for using classic texts in the primary classroom in Chapter 12. She considers the role that 'classic' texts can have in improving writing at greater depth, and reflects on how teachers can develop grammatical and vocabulary choices in children's writing, as well as increasing both pupil and teacher confidence in using texts that are perceived to be more challenging.

In Chapter 13, Cath Reading explores the benefits of promoting a deeper approach to writing in science and looks at ways of developing a range of strategies that support the development of science writing at a deeper level.

In the final chapter, Lisa Baldwin explores mastery in English and what it means in practice. Drawing from the rich body of research into mastery of mathematics, the chapter begins to define mastery in English and helps teachers to understand what mastery might look like in the classroom.

This book was created by people who are not only passionate about primary education, but who are also leading experts in their own particular areas. They have made use of their wide experience to offer practical guidance on greater depth writing, while underpinning this with theoretical understanding.

We hope that reading this book will help you to reflect on what greater depth writing looks like and how we can encourage children to write at greater depth. We hope, too, that you will draw upon the suggestions for teaching lessons that encourage children to write at greater depth.

Adam Bushnell, Angela Gill and David Waugh

1

WHAT IS GREATER DEPTH WRITING?

Adam Bushnell

TEACHERS' STANDARDS

This chapter will help you with the following Teachers' Standards:

2d. demonstrate knowledge and understanding of how pupils learn and how this impacts on teaching;

3a. have a secure knowledge of the relevant subject(s) and curriculum areas, foster and maintain pupils' interest in the subject, and address misunderstandings;

3b. demonstrate a critical understanding of developments in the subject and curriculum areas, and promote the value of scholarship;

3c. demonstrate an understanding of and take responsibility for promoting high standards of literacy, articulacy and the correct use of standard English, whatever the teacher's specialist subject.

KEY QUESTIONS

- What is the definition of a greater depth writer?
- How is greater depth writing assessed?
- What is the best way to achieve greater depth writing?
- How can we move pupils from working towards greater depth to become a secure greater depth writer?

Introduction

If a child can write pages and pages of well-punctuated and perfectly spelt text, this does not mean that they are a greater depth writer. This chapter will explore exactly what writing at greater depth looks like. According to Roach (2018), greater depth writing needs to include these three components:

> *Aside from the teacher assessment framework, there are a few critical indicators of a 'greater depth' writer.*
>
> * *Concision is key. The old adage 'less is more' can be applied to greater depth writers. We've all taught pupils who – as wonderful as their writing might be – could never seem to reach the end of their story. This can reveal their neglect of forward planning. Excellent writers will instinctually vary the length of their sentences when the writing calls for it. They'll have the confidence in their short sentences to leave them be; they don't just write the next thing that comes into their heads. The ability to self-edit their writing and remove extraneous content or exposition should not be underestimated.*
>
> * *Punctuation should be precise and controlled, but also used for effect rather than a conspicuous opportunity to shoehorn some semicolons into proceedings. Commas and parentheses allow the writer to inject carefully considered clauses or deft asides. Dialogue gives pupils scope to demonstrate their mastery of a great range of the punctuation prescribed by the national curriculum and beyond, such as the dash and ellipsis.*
>
> * *Thirdly (and arguably the most influential factor), the evidence that they draw from reading quality literature – literally spelled out in the framework as 'drawing independently on what they have read' – discloses the writer to be a prolific reader. A pupil's wider vocabulary and its appropriate use; the use of fitting metaphors; other imagery; their intuition for dialect or realistic speech patterns; the way their writing 'flows': these elements illustrate a young writer's appetite for absorbing books and emulating the original authors' styles.*

To put it another way, greater depth writers manipulate grammar and vocabulary for effect and do so with assured and conscious control. These children draw on the style of the authors they read. They do this independently, but do not rely on a particular technique all of the time, but rather use a whole range of different techniques for a wide range of audiences and for a wide range of purposes. Children select their own form and use it with flair.

However, how do we, as teachers, identify the potential for greater depth writing and encourage these children to meet their full potential? This chapter will explore some of the resources necessary to inspire children to write to their full capabilities. It will also look at how to encourage independence in writing.

Finding the right resources to inspire independent writing

It takes time to identify a greater depth writer. To find out if a child can truly write independently, this must be achieved by gathering evidence from a range of pieces of work. Most children use what has been modelled by the teacher and, with some alterations and tweaks here and there, produce structured pieces of writing. However, a greater depth writer will interpret something in their own way. They will use the input from the teacher as inspiration but will independently produce something original using their own written voice.

The Standards and Testing Agency (STA) (2018, p. 14) state that:

Writing is likely to be independent if it:

- *emerges from a text, topic, visit, or curriculum experience in which pupils have had opportunities to discuss and rehearse what is to be written about*

Finding a text that inspires children is important. If a class is not motivated by what they are reading, then they are less likely to want to write about it. A curriculum experience could be a visiting author, historian, scientist, etc., but it could also be exploring an app, website, object, animation, movie clip, or even just an image. In the case study below, a selection of images are used to inspire independent writing with a Year 6 class. The teacher prompted her class to make their own choices, which is important as the STA go on to state that:

Writing is likely to be independent if it:

- *enables pupils to use their own ideas and provides them with an element of choice, for example writing from the perspective of a character they have chosen themselves*

- *has been edited, if required, by the pupil without the support of the teacher, although this may be in response to self, peer, or group evaluation*

- *is produced by pupils who have, if required, sought out classroom resources, such as dictionaries or thesauruses, without prompting to do so by the teacher*

Writing is not independent if it has been:

- *modelled or heavily scaffolded*

- *copied or paraphrased*

- *edited as a result of direct intervention by a teacher or other adult, for example when the pupil has been directed to change specific words for greater impact, where incorrect or omitted punctuation has been indicated, or when incorrectly spelt words have been identified by an adult for the pupil to correct*

- *produced with the support of electronic aids that automatically provide correct spelling, synonyms, punctuation, or predictive text*

- *supported by detailed success criteria that specifically direct pupils as to what to include, or where to include it, in their writing, such as directing them to include specific vocabulary, grammatical features, or punctuation*

(STA, 2018, p. 14)

So, to encourage independent, greater depth writing it is essential that the correct stimulus is used with the children. A stimulus that engages you as a teacher is perhaps even more important than how much it engages the children. If you are passionate about a text, a music video or a painting, then that passion is exuded when you talk about it.

It is a passion that is contagious. If you don't enjoy talking about a particular stimulus, children can perceive this and it disengages them as well. Finding the right resource is not only about finding the right one for the children, but also finding the right one for you as a teacher.

In the case study below, the teacher used *The Mysteries of Harris Burdick* by Chris Van Allsburg, which was first published in 1984. It is a creative writing resource 35 years old, yet can still be used to great effect in the classroom today. Van Allsburg, the author and illustrator of *Jumanji* and *The Polar Express*, writes in the introduction that the mysterious man named Harris Burdick went into the office of a book publishers with fourteen illustrations saying that he had written fourteen short stories to go with them. The publisher was very intrigued by the haunting style of the illustrations and wanted to read the accompanying stories. Burdick left the illustrations with the publishers and arranged to return the following day. However, he was never seen again. The publisher then released the book with an introduction by Van Allsburg in the hope that its publication would lead to finding Harris Burdick, but he remained missing. Then, in 1994, ten years after the original publication, a dealer of antique books found a fifteenth Harris Burdick illustration hidden in a mirror with a frame carved with characters from *Through the Looking Glass*. This led to the republishing of *The Mysteries of Harris Burdick* with a new introduction including the fifteenth illustration.

Interest in who this mysterious Burdick character was increased dramatically and led to people wanting to write the stories themselves. Stephen King chose the illustration titled *The House on Maple Street* and included it in a collection of short stories called *Nightmares and Dreamscapes* in 1993.

Thousands of short stories using the images as inspiration have been written and submitted to the publishers. In 2011, *The Chronicles of Harris Burdick* was published with fourteen short stories written by best-selling authors, including Louis Sachar, Lemony Snicket and Chris Van Allsburg himself.

It is likely that Van Allsburg created the whole narrative behind Harris Burdick himself and that Burdick was never a real person. What *The Mysteries of Harris Burdick* does is to inspire people of all ages to want to write. The illustrations are so intriguing that possible storylines are almost instantly created and they are all unique. The illustrations have been used in the classroom for 35 years and can still inspire independent writing that could be at greater depth, as in the case study below.

CASE STUDY

YEAR 6 CLASS WRITING 'MYSTERY NARRATIVE STORIES' USING *THE MYSTERIES OF HARRIS BURDICK* AS A STIMULUS

Lisa, a Year 6 class teacher, showed her class all fifteen of *The Mysteries of Harris Burdick* illustrations on a PowerPoint and read them the titles and accompanying sentences.

She then let the PowerPoint continue on a loop and the children discussed each one with each other in talk partners.

The class were then asked to choose one of the images to plan a short narrative story independently. As well as having the illustrations on a PowerPoint, Lisa had the portfolio edition of the book so each illustration was loose-leaf and could be photocopied. Many children selected the same images as their friends, but one child chose the image of 'Captain Tory' that had the accompanying sentence of 'he swung the lantern three times and slowly the schooner appeared'.

Figure 1.1 The Chronicles of Harris Burdick by Chris Van Allsburg – 'Captain Tory'

Lisa gave each child a photocopy of their chosen illustrations and a template for a story plan which included sections on character, setting, introduction, build-up, climax and resolution. Ella, a Year 6 pupil, completed each section with her own ideas.

(Continued)

(Continued)

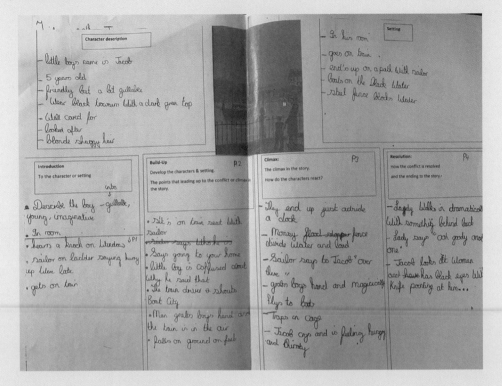

Figure 1.2   Y6 Planning Sheet

Ella went on to write a short narrative with this success criteria:

- I can use capital letters, full stops and exclamation marks.
- I can use a colon and brackets in my writing.
- I can organise my writing into paragraphs.
- I can begin my sentences in interesting ways.
- I can use a range of sentences for effect.
- I can add tension and build up suspense in my writing.
- I can use figurative language in my writing.

Ella used the photocopied illustration, check list of success criteria and her plan to produce the short narrative seen in Figure 1.3.

Lisa then spent a further lesson asking the children to edit and improve their work. The children worked back in their original talk partners to share their stories with each other and discuss their chosen Harris Burdick illustration.

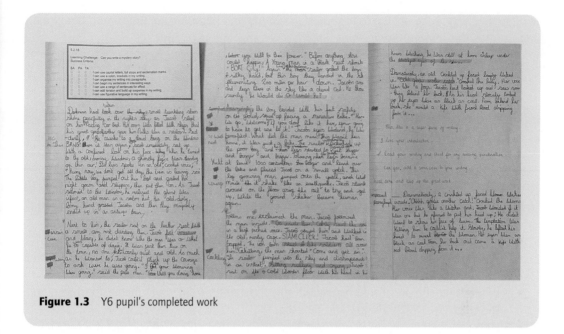

Figure 1.3 Y6 pupil's completed work

In the case study, the teacher gave her children a firm scaffold to work within. Ella's work contained some good vocabulary and punctuation choices. The writing contained some elements of working at greater depth using the following criteria identified by the DfE (2018, p. 6).

Working at greater depth

The pupil can:

- *write effectively for a range of purposes and audiences, selecting the appropriate form and drawing independently on what they have read as models for their own writing (e.g. literary language, characterisation, structure)*

- *distinguish between the language of speech and writing and choose the appropriate register*

- *exercise an assured and conscious control over levels of formality, particularly through manipulating grammar and vocabulary to achieve this*

- *use the range of punctuation taught at key stage 2 correctly (e.g. semi-colons, dashes, colons, hyphens) and, when necessary, use such punctuation precisely to enhance meaning and avoid ambiguity.*

[There are no additional statements for spelling or handwriting]

However, in order for children like Ella to become a greater depth writer, the writing must also be independent and created with less scaffolding techniques. Lessons like the case study above work really well in empowering children to become independent writers. It gives them all of the tools necessary to then find their own written voice and create their own narratives in their own way. Lessons that follow success criteria and planning are important, but equally important is the opportunity to write individually and independently.

ACTIVITY 1   USING IMAGES TO WRITE INDEPENDENT NARRATIVE STORIES

Go to The Literacy Shed website (see Recommended websites at the end of the chapter) and select The Images Shed. Select a series of images such as *Friend or Foe, Winter Landscapes* or *A Pathway to Where?*

- How will you ask the children to select the image they would like to use? How can you make this an independent writing activity?
- Will this be written in the first or third person? Are any other characters involved?
- Will this be the only setting the children describe? Do they have to remain in this setting throughout the narrative?
- What other stimulus could be used in the classroom? What could music do to inspire the children? Which music could be used?
- How can the five senses be incorporated into the description? Also, how will the children show how the characters are feeling?

FOCUS ON RESEARCH

Websites such as www.onceuponapicture.co.uk are a popular way of finding images that inspire creative writing. The images are divided into collections such as the *Character Collection, Prediction Collection, Inference Collection*, and many more. But why use images instead of film or text? According to Bushnell et al. (2019, p. 60):

They [images] can be especially helpful when you are describing an unfamiliar object or setting. They can also be a stimulus for children's own writing and can provoke discussions about descriptions and vocabulary.

Greater depth in the Early Years

The DfE have given examples of children's writing that explicitly show what greater depth writing should look like. For KS2, the pupil 'Dani' is working towards the expected standard, 'Morgan' and 'Leigh' are working at the expected standard and 'Frankie' is working at greater depth within the expected standard. For KS1, the pupil 'Jamie' is working towards the expected standard, 'Kim' is working at the expected standard and 'Ali' is working at greater depth within the expected standard.

But what does greater depth look like in the Early Years? How can we encourage children to become greater depth writers when they have only just started to write? By immersing children in experiences, then we give them fuel for talking. If children can talk in detail and describe something that they have done, then this is a good foundation to be able to write about it.

Learning through play can produce some high-quality and descriptive vocabulary, too. By exploring role play, corners set up inside and outside of classrooms such as restaurants, shops, garden centres or kitchens, children can be onlookers to experience other children at play in these areas; they can imitate what others are doing in these areas; or they can play independently or co-operatively – all of which can develop their own use of language and communication. This form of dramatic play can help children to imitate the world they have seen, but also create new scenarios by interacting with one another.

Areas such as playing in sand and water can do the same as they involve a level of co-operation. Learning through clay or dough and table-top play, such as building jigsaws, shape puzzles, threading and weaving, may perhaps be seen as independent tasks, but often children interact with one another while they explore these activities.

Construction, too, can be done independently or with others. The use of communication and language skills are essential when explaining constructions. However, perhaps the best way of developing not just language but also imagination is through small-world play. Small-world play involves children using puppets or toys to create an environment such as a farm, under the sea, African plains or a frozen landscape. Storytelling with figures feature too, and they are a good way to help children to remember and retell stories shared. But, when small worlds are combined, this is where children can really play imaginatively. Rather than the teacher setting up a jungle environment of trees and animals for the children to explore and play with, the environments can be created spontaneously by the children. If boxes of farm animals, sea creatures, traditional tale characters, jungle animals, space characters, dragons and monsters are made accessible, then children can create their own independent narratives using multi-genre cross-overs. So, a child may have a knight riding on an octopus who comes under attack by a cow that can shoot fire from its udders, only to be rescued by an alien who takes them to meet a mermaid.

This form of utterly creative and independent play is to be encouraged because it will lead to children not only simply following suggested play patterns, but rather thinking and creating independently. The more that this kind of play is encouraged in the Early Years, the more that children can begin to apply their own independent, creative ideas in their writing throughout their time at school.

The outdoors also has the potential to stimulate in the same way, from making potions, wands and spells out of natural materials to identifying trees and cooking on open fires. All of these experiences can mould the imagination and help children to achieve their full potential as writers. In the case study below, the outdoors is used to generate experiences that lead to initial mark making and early writing.

CASE STUDY

RECEPTION CLASS USING THE OUTDOORS AS A STIMULUS FOR EARLY WRITING

Laura, a Reception class teacher in a two-form entry school, took her class to the school garden. In it was a woodland area, storytelling circle with logs for seats, pond, decking area with wildlife viewing platform, vegetable beds and a wild flower area with bug hotels. There was also an outdoor classroom with heating, tables and chairs. Inside was a variety of equipment including pond-dipping materials, mini beast-collecting kits and gardening tools.

Laura explained to her class that they would be going to explore the school garden looking for mini beasts using plastic pots for collecting, plastic tweezers, magnifying glasses and plastic trays. The children had done this several times before and they were at the end of their mini-beast topic, so had a sound knowledge base.

The children explored the garden with their equipment and after ten minutes gathered back together to show each other what they had found. Some children worked in pairs, but most were in small groups. One group animatedly held out a bird's nest that they had found on the floor. This took up most of the discussion that followed involving how it had ended up out of a tree, what had happened to any eggs that may have been inside and where the mother bird was.

Laura discarded her original plans of writing about mini beasts and went with the interest of the children to explore what had happened with the nest. The discussion continued and then the nest was taken into the outdoor classroom. Laura asked the children to draw a picture of what they thought had happened to the nest. All of the children wrote their

Figure 1.4   Reception pupil's work

The bugs liked the nest

5

The Bugs Were very quiet

6

The eggs have hatched in The nest

7

Daisy Was happy to See the chicks

8

Figure 1.5   Reception pupil's work

names, most independently, then they went on to draw their pictures. The more able were encouraged to label their pictures with words to explain what had happened. Laura annotated the less able children's pictures with their ideas.

After the children had returned to school, had snack and went to choose where they wanted to play, some continued to discuss, draw and write about the nest.

The following day a boy named Ted brought in a book he had made at home with his grandmother. She had supported him with the spelling of the words, 'Daisy' and 'friends', by sounding out the phonics. The rest had been created independently.

For a Reception class child to be inspired to want to continue to write at home is what most teachers would want for their class. Ted is clearly a gifted child who has the potential to become a greater depth writer as he progresses through school. But the experiences we offer children in the Early Years is what shapes their writing and gives the potential for greater depth writing. When this is supported in the home environment, this can encourage children to achieve their potential much faster.

ACTIVITY 2   OUTDOOR LEARNING FOR WRITING

Take the children outside and into the school grounds. Ask them to find any natural materials from the ground, ensuring that they are not snapping branches from trees, flowers from the ground or leaves from bushes. Ask them to choose their favourite object that they have found and hold it carefully in their hands. Then ask the children to hold it next to

(Continued)

(Continued)

their ears and listen carefully to the object. Ask the children what the object had been doing yesterday and the day before.

- Can you model a narrative about a selected object such as a leaf, stick or petal? What could it have been doing other than blowing around in the wind? What animals might it have encountered? Where else may it have visited?
- How will you encourage the children to develop their ideas? What other objects could be used to expand the imaginary narratives?
- How will the ideas the children have be recorded? What writing opportunities are there back in the classroom?

FOCUS ON RESEARCH

Using the outdoors has been encouraged by the DfE for some time. In 2006, the document *Learning through Landscapes, Learning Outside the Classroom Manifesto* recommended that children should use the outdoors as a stimulus for learning. According to Gyöngyösi-Wiersum (2012), research identifies that the benefits of learning through games is important, as it leads to increased levels of motivation, a positive attitude and increased learning. This is in comparison to more formal learning that takes place indoors. She maintains that the high level of interaction between players results in good opportunities to test intuitive ideas and problem-solving strategies.

These are all positive outcomes and can be something that helps with writing, too. When working outdoors, children can be given opportunities to discuss writing ideas collaboratively. By sharing ideas and strategies, children can motivate and stimulate one another. This, too, can lead to greater depth writing.

The importance of reading traditional tales

Bruno Bettelheim explains how fairy tales educate, support and liberate the emotions of children in his book *The Uses of Enchantment*. He argues: 'It offers meaning on so many different levels, and enriches the child's existence in so many ways' (1975, p. 15). Fairy tales are powerful developmental tools for children and adults alike. They can have a dark side to them, but generally good overcomes evil. They frequently contain moral messages, too, and are useful devices for promoting oral storytelling. They follow themes and structures still seen in modern writing. For example, *The Gruffalo* feels like a traditional fairy tale.

It has the rule of three, just like *Goldilocks, The Billy Goats Gruff* and countless others. The rule of three can be three characters, or visiting three settings or three major events happening. In *Goldilocks*, all of these are featured as there are three bears, the main character visits three settings and three major events happen in those settings: Goldilocks sits at the table to eat the porridge in the kitchen, sits on a chair in the living room and sleeps in the beds upstairs. This is known as a triadic structure. *Percy Jackson and the Lightning Thief* follows all the rules of the fairy tale, too, with its triadic structure and themes of good versus evil.

Modern books still follow the structure and themes of the fairy tale because they are of everlasting appeal. The themes can be dark, but children still adore them as they excite and inspire. Fairy stories are not just for children, though. In Angela Carter's *The Bloody Chamber*, she describes her stories as *reimagining the fairy tale*. We meet familiar characters from childhood in an adult context. We view the stories in a whole new way.

Fairy tales appeal to all ages essentially because human beings are story animals. We thrive on them in all of their forms, whether news articles, stories in the pub or experiences at work that we share at the dinner table. We communicate through story and we express our inner selves in the retelling of the story. However, fairy tales have been manipulated in the past. The Nazis understood the importance of the fairy tale. One of the first things they did upon rising to power in Germany was to make fairy tales into films and broadcast them in movie theatres across the country. In the Nazi film version of *Puss in Boots*, Puss is seen standing at the end on a raised platform wearing a swastika armband. The crowd gathered around all chant, 'Hail Puss in Boots! He is our Savour! We will live again!' This was a deliberate attempt to compare Puss to Hitler, with a strong suggestion to children in the audience that only a hero should be hailed.

Shortly after the invasion of Poland, the Nazis turned *Little Red Riding Hood* into a film, too, where the heroine is rescued at the end by a swastika-armed, SS uniform-wearing man holding a knife. This film was put on for free in movie theatres so that audiences across the country could view the propaganda without any cost. At that time, most households in Germany had a *German House Book* containing the Brothers Grimm fairy tales. These were often shared beside a fire with the whole family. The Nazis rewrote, reprinted and redistributed the book to all households in Germany, but this new edition had sinister and subtle changes to the text. For example, in one story there is a magic fiddle which makes people dance. The fiddle is used to make Jewish people dance themselves to death in thorn bushes. Hitler wanted to warp young minds into thinking that this was the work of a hero.

Fairy tales are powerful developmental tools for children and adults alike. As such, the Nazis used it to their own evil ends. Hitler knew of the power of these stories and knew that children were influenced by them. He knew that if he manipulated them, he also manipulated children's minds.

Fairy tales are critically important in schools and at home. The more we share them in their untarnished form, the more they help children, and adults, to understand the way of the world. They contain tragedy, comedy and hope. They are also an essential developmental tool for children as writers, as they help the children to understand narrative structure. It is this understanding of how to narrate a good story that leads to effective writing. Character, setting, plot and dialogue can all be developed once the basic storytelling tools are firmly in place. A good example of this is how Dreamworks took William Steig's picture book *Shrek!* and developed a basic, short text into a successful film and musical franchise. *Shrek!* follows the traditional fairy tale genre, but blends storylines and characters together with multiple modern references. The teacher in the following case study also uses her class's firm understanding of fairy tales to teach shifts in formality through dialogue.

CASE STUDY

YEAR 4 CLASS USING TRADITIONAL TALE CHARACTERS TO CREATE DIALOGUE WITH SHIFTS IN FORMALITY

Lyndsey, a Year 4 teacher, asked her class what a traditional tale character was. She wrote a list on the board that included Cinderella, Little Red Riding Hood and the Big Bad Wolf. She then asked the children to list traditional tales in partners to see how many they could think of. These were shared and then she asked them if any of the children had heard of the song and the story *Little Rabbit Foo Foo*. Most of the class had, and recalled hearing the story when they were in Reception. Lyndsey then read her class Michael Rosen's *Little Rabbit Foo Foo*. The class laughed throughout as the main protagonist assaults the various characters with a hammer and is eventually turned into a 'goonie' by the Good Fairy. The story followed a traditional tale structure with three events happening before the conclusion.

Lyndsey then explained that the children would be writing their own version of the story with dialogue. They had to choose characters from other traditional tales which included a bad character like Little Rabbit Foo Foo, a good character like the Good Fairy and four other characters like the worms, mice, tigers and goblins that feature in the original. The children chose characters like the Big Bad Wolf, ogres, giants, goblins and evil witches for their bad characters and characters like the Fairy Godmother, wizards, leprechauns, genies and talking animals for their good characters. Finally, they chose four other traditional tale characters such as Cinderella, Little Red Riding Hood, princes, princesses and other animals for their characters who are picked on by their bad character.

Using storyboards, the children then planned their storyline drawing pictures and writing sentences in cartoonlike form, but were asked not to add dialogue yet.

Once the stories were completed, the class shared with each other in talk partners and orally told their stories.

Lyndsey then asked how Little Red Riding Hood's grandmother would react to being hit on the head by Little Rabbit Foo Foo. The children gave answers like, 'How dare you!' or 'Oh now, now. You shouldn't do that!'

Lyndsey asked how the woodcutter from Little Red Riding Hood would react and got answers like, 'Oi! Pack it in!' or 'I'll chop yer head off!'.

The class then discussed how other characters would react to their bad characters and what they would say. Lyndsey explained that the way we speak is different from the way we write, but when writing speech, we should write the way that people speak. She asked her class to add speech to their storyboard. She explained that this should be in the form of dialogue between the characters.

Finally, the children read their stories to each other with a view to acting them out as dramatic performances later in the week.

The stories the Year 4 children wrote contained different characters, but the structure was the same. If children use a set structure, as they were encouraged to do so in the case study above, then this is not greater depth writing. However, lessons such as this can teach children strategies and techniques in writing, such as showing shifts in formality through dialogue, that they can later apply in other, less structured lessons. Using scaffolded techniques are essential for adding to children's writing toolkit. The greater depth writers will then go on and use these tools when the opportunities arise.

ACTIVITY 3   *SHREK!*

Read the children William Steig's *Shrek!* and ask them the differences between the movie and the book. Show the children the scene from the first movie when Shrek and Princess Fiona fall in love and enjoy 'true love's true kiss'. Afterwards, she becomes an ogress. This does not feature in the book, but rather Shrek meets an ogress, falls in love and then they kiss. Ask the children which version they prefer, then read the children Michael Rosen's *Little Rabbit Foo Foo* and ask the children how this could be turned into a film.

- Where does Little Rabbit Foo Foo sleep? Does he have any other family? Can they feature in the film version?
- What will the other creatures who live in the forest be thinking? What would they do about the rabbit's actions? Who will they ask to help them before the Good Fairy appears?
- What other characters may be needed in the film version? Does the setting need to be changed? What modern references could be included?

FOCUS ON RESEARCH

TRADITIONAL TALES

Traditional tales are essential for children's development of language and understanding of narrative structure. However, according to Zipes (1983), 'Not only are the tales considered to be too sexist, racist and authoritarian, but the general contents are said to reflect the concerns of semi-feudal patriarchal societies' (p. 170).

Zipes argues that rather than helping children, traditional tales actively damage children by reinforcing sexist and stereotypical views. However, a lot of traditional tales from Eastern Europe contain strong, feminist characters and certainly challenge sexism. Characters such as Masha in Baba Yaga Bony-Legs show great determination in diversity and demonstrate that a clever mind always wins the day.

Also, reading alternate versions of traditional tales, such as Robert Munsch's *The Paper Bag Princess* and Babette Cole's *Princess Smartypants*, break certain stereotypical ideas that may sometimes feature in the traditional tale. Winston (1998, p. 34) advocates using these alternate versions too, stating:

They attack the oppressive moralizing of the fairy tale and the outmoded values they embody, advocating new, more radical tales to restore the original role of the fairy tale, one whose moral force lies in its drive towards social and cultural liberation.

Conclusion

The beginning of this chapter stated that greater depth writers manipulate grammar and vocabulary for effect and do so with assured and conscious control. However, in order for children to be able to do this, we must first empower them by teaching strategies in writing. By encouraging children to read books written by a range of different authors, we are encouraging them to draw on the style of the authors they read. We want them to do this independently and we do not want them to rely on a particular technique all of the time, but rather to use a whole range of different techniques for a wide range of audiences and for a wide range of purposes. So, the more we encourage reading and the more we encourage writing in the classroom, the more we are helping children to become greater depth writers. When we model writing and scaffold writing, we are not discouraging greater depth writing, but rather giving children the tools necessary for them to go on to use these tools independently. It is when children begin to use what we have taught them, and what authors have taught them in books they have read, and what they have learnt from all of the other stimuli, both at home and school, that independent greater depth writing begins to emerge.

Special thanks

Lisa Payne, Leah Curry, Laura Smith, Jessica Todd and all of the staff at Ox Close Primary School. Ella Horner and Ted Fisher from Ox Close Primary School.

Recommended websites

Who is Harris Burdick? – www.houghtonmifflinbooks.com/features/harrisburdick/snicket_quote_popup.html (accessed 1 April 2019).

The Literacy Shed: The Images Shed – www.literacyshed.com/the-images-shed.html (accessed 1 April 2019).

Once Upon A Picture – www.onceuponapicture.co.uk/ (accessed 1 April 2019).

References

Bettelheim, B. (1975) *The Uses of Enchantment: The Meaning and Importance of Fairy Tales.* London: Vintage Books, Random House.

Bushnell, A., Smith, R. and Waugh, D. (2019) *Modelling Exciting Writing.* London: Sage.

Cole, B. (1996) *Princess Smartypants.* London: Puffin.

Carter, A. (1995) *The Bloody Chamber and Other Stories.* London: Vintage Classics.

Department for Education (DfE) (2018) *Key Stage 2 Teacher Assessment Exemplification Materials. English Writing: Working at Greater Depth within the Expected Standard: Frankie.* Available online at: https://assets.publishing.service.gov.uk/government/uploads/system/uploads/attachment_data/file/655619/2018_exemplification_materials_KS2-GDS__Frankie_.pdf (accessed 1 April 2019).

Gyöngyösi-Wiersum, E. (2012) Teaching and learning mathematics through games and activities. *Acta Electrotechnica et Informatica*, 12(3): 23–6.

Munsch, R. (2018) *The Paper Bag Princess.* London: Annick Press.

Roach, T (2018) *What Counts as Greater Depth Writing?* Available online at: www.teachwire.net/news/what-counts-as-greater-depth-writing UK Teach Wire (accessed 1 April 2019).

Rosen, M. (2003) *Little Rabbit Foo Foo.* London: Walker Books.

Standards Testing Agency (STA) (2018) *2018 Teacher Assessment Guidance: Key Stage 2.* Gov.UK: Crown copyright.

Steig, W. (1990) *Shrek!* London: Puffin.

Van Allsburg, C. (2011) *The Mysteries of Harris Burdick.* London: Anderson Press.

Van Allsburg, C. (2018) *The Chronicles of Harris Burdick.* London: Anderson Press.

Winston, J. (1998) *Drama, Narrative and Moral Education.* London: Falmer Press.

Zipes, J. (1983) *Fairy Tales and the Art of Subversion.* London: Heinemann.

2

DEVELOPING DEEPER WRITING IN EYFS AND KS1 THROUGH A PLAY-BASED APPROACH

Angela Gill

TEACHERS' STANDARDS

This chapter will help you with the following Teachers' Standards:

2d. demonstrate knowledge and understanding of how pupils learn and how this impacts on teaching;

3a. have a secure knowledge of the relevant subject(s) and curriculum areas, foster and maintain pupils' interest in the subject, and address misunderstandings;

3b. demonstrate a critical understanding of developments in the subject and curriculum areas, and promote the value of scholarship;

3c. demonstrate an understanding of and take responsibility for promoting high standards of literacy, articulacy and the correct use of standard English, whatever the teacher's specialist subject.

KEY QUESTIONS

- How do I motivate children to begin to write through free-play in designated areas of the classroom, such as role play, construction and art spaces?
- How do I support children through focused play, including model building, to stimulate, promote and plan for writing?
- How do I use outdoor play, including Forest School, to encourage and motivate writing?

Introduction

In this chapter, we will explore how early and emergent writing, as a precursor for writing in depth, can be developed in classrooms and educational settings where the focus is on play and the free choice of a range of play-based activities. Case studies from nursery, EYFS and KS1 settings will illustrate high-quality examples of indoor free-play opportunities, including role-play, construction, small word, and art and design areas, where early writing can be encouraged and developed through a range of media and medium. We will consider how the successful development of gross and fine motor skills are essential for young writers. Focused play, such as model-building using LEGO® or other construction materials, will be explored as a stimulus to initiate writing and as a support mechanism during the writing process. We will demonstrate how outdoor opportunities, such as Forest School, can be used to stimulate and motivate children in their writing.

The focus of the chapter will be on how experiences can be used to scaffold young children's learning in order to develop their early writing skills, with a view to enabling them to demonstrate depth in writing. The benefits of play will be explored when used to develop young children's confidence and independence in early writing. The chapter aims to inspire practitioners to confidently offer play-based activities, in a planned and structured way, to provide enhanced and deep writing experiences for all children in nursery, EYFS and KS1. Reflections from professionals, including a qualified LEGO® SERIOUS PLAY® facilitator, an ITE student and a primary school teacher trained in Forest School techniques, will illustrate how high-quality play opportunities can make an impact on the quality of writing outcomes.

Indoor play

Designing the classroom to promote free play and writing opportunities

Classrooms and other indoor educational settings can be designed to offer writing opportunities through free play. Art and design and messy areas can provide a range of materials that can help to develop fine motor skills, which can ultimately lead to successful pencil grip, control and letter formation. Gloop, sand, paint and glue can be used to explore mixing, pouring and spreading.

Role-play areas can be designed to include resources for mark-making and writing, offering a wide range of materials and the opportunity for children to choose their writing tools. Writing opportunities can be tailored to suit the theme of the role-play areas; a doctor's surgery might have appointment cards and prescriptions, and a garden centre might have plant labels and seed packets. Role-play areas might also have books, images, labels, signs and reading materials to engage and support children in their creative thinking, language development and writing.

A dedicated writing area can allow children to choose to engage with purposeful writing. Using themes, perhaps linked to events such as birthdays and Christmas, can lead to writing party invitations, addressing envelopes and gift tags, writing wish lists and thank you cards. These themes might also use the children's interests as a platform, or might be linked to the topic that is the current planning and teaching focus.

Other free-play spaces in the classroom can be designed to include writing aids – for example, clipboards might be provided in the construction areas to design plans and make labels for models and puppets might be made available in the small world area to encourage story telling.

ACTIVITY 1   PLANNING FOR WRITING OPPORTUNITIES FROM A RANGE OF ROLE-PLAY AREAS

Choose a role-play area – perhaps a café, hospital, estate agent's or ice-cream shop. Plan for a range of writing opportunities related to your chosen theme and consider how you would facilitate writing through free play in this area. Decide on the resources you would need and how the area might be designed. Draw a plan and make a list.

CASE STUDY

HOW FREE PLAY IS USED TO DEVELOP EARLY WRITING IN THE NURSERY SETTING

Busy Bears Children's Day Nursery, Durham, plan for indoor play-based activities, through which early writing skills are taught as an integrated element of the curriculum. In line with one of the three characteristics of effective teaching and learning in the EYFS Framework (DfE, 2017), the nursery practitioners plan their curriculum to encourage and support playing and exploring, where the children are encouraged to investigate, experience and 'have a go' at writing. The focus for those children in the nursery who are 40 to 60 months is on developing the physical skills necessary for writing, including holding a pencil and other writing medium, and on fostering the imagination, inspiration and creativity needed to talk about and create stories and other writing outcomes.

An example of a child's writing in the nursery, at 53 months, might look like the writing shown in figure 2.1.

The child already has a preferred dominant hand, a firm pencil grip and can produce recognisable writing that he can talk about and elaborate on.

In order to achieve this, a variety of activities are planned for by the nursery practitioners, through free play and adult-led group time. Gross motor skills are developed through physical activities such as lifting heavy blocks for strength, sorting large objects, or mixing,

Figure 2.1 An example of a child's writing at 53 months, Busy Bears Children's Day Nursery, Durham

scooping and filling in the messy area. Fine motor skills are developed through 'funky fingers' activities such as threading beads and pasta, weaving cards and joining large paper clips to make a chain. Games such as using tweezers to pick up small objects and making patterns with pegs and boards help children to develop a firm and accurate pencil grip. Imagination, inspiration and creativity are continually developed through discussion and chat, singing, retelling stories, predicting, explaining and pretending.

Using focused play to develop and support writing

Focused play activities, often led by an adult, can be designed to develop the attributes needed for writing. Using play dough, which the children can help to make, develops fine motor skills and allows children to refine manipulation and grip. Many children enjoy a 'dough disco', where they mould, shape and squeeze the dough in time to upbeat music. This may lead to similar activities, such as 'squiggle while you wiggle', which allows the children to use mark-making and writing materials in time to music. Completing jigsaws, playing musical instruments and building construction sets can all contribute to refining manipulation and control.

The skills needed to be able to write well can also be addressed through focused play. Providing a range of resources on which to write, such as whiteboards, sand boxes, illuminated glowboards and large rolls of paper, helps to deliver a multisensory approach to writing. This is reinforced by encouraging children to write in different positions, such as upside-down under tables and vertically inside large boxes.

Purposeful writing can be stimulated and enhanced by focused play. Making the giant from Jack and the Beanstalk a sandwich can lead to writing shopping lists and recipes. Listening to fairy tales, re-enacting the story and looking at story maps can prompt the writing of instructions to help Little Red Riding Hood get to grandma's house. Making a model of a dinosaur from construction materials can lead to writing an adventure story.

Using model-building as a stimulus for deeper writing

Ben Mizen, director of Ideas Alchemy Consultancy, is a qualified teacher and trained LEGO® SERIOUS PLAY® facilitator. He has worked alongside ITE tutors and students to develop a series of simple activities, described below, that focus on developing stories and narratives for deeper writing, where pupils, through model-building, will be

> *exchanging ideas and opinions, considering and evaluating each other's ideas, building up shared knowledge and understanding.*

> (Grugeon and Hubbard, cited in Cremin and Burnett, 2018, p. 244)

Each of the activities has been developed using the 'core process' and 'etiquette' of LEGO® SERIOUS PLAY® (LSP) by building upon open-source guidelines made available by the LEGO® Group under a Creative Commons licence. LSP, originally designed for business development, uses play as a driver and is based on

> *research which shows that . . . hands-on, minds-on learning produces a deeper, more meaningful understanding of the world and its possibilities.*

> (www.lego.com/en-us/seriousplay)

Figure 2.2   ITE student engaging in LEGO® SERIOUS PLAY®, Durham University

In all of the following examples, LEGO® bricks are utilised, as seen in Figure 2.2, where a BA Primary Education student is exploring how models might provide a creative starting point for story writing. However, other play materials can be used.

In each activity, the teacher poses a building challenge, sets the time for building and sharing. This process is underpinned with a set of simple rules that will need to be explained to the pupils (see table below). Deeper writing will then flow from the discoveries that pupils have made during this time of focused creative play.

The LSP Core Process and Etiquette

The LEGO® SERIOUS PLAY® Core Process		**LEGO® SERIOUS PLAY® Etiquette**
Phase 1	The teacher poses the building challenge to the pupils.	The LEGO model is the answer to the building challenge.
Phase 2	The pupils then build a LEGO model representing their reflections and thoughts on the challenge.	There are no wrong answers: what the model looks like is not the most important thing. If the pupil says that a model represents something specific, then that is what it is.
Phase 3	The pupils share the meaning and tell the story that they have assigned to their own models.	'Think with your hands': if you don't know what you want to build, it is often a good idea just to start building.
		What counts is your meaning of the model and only the person who built the model knows what it means. The focus must be on the model and the story around the model, not on the pupil describing the model.
		'Listen with your eyes': look at the model that is being shared – use your visual sense to grasp and understand even more of what the other participants are describing.
		Everybody participates during the full process.

(Adapted from The LEGO Group (2010). Open-source/<Introduction to LEGO® SERIOUS PLAY®, pages 14 and 18)

EXAMPLE ACTIVITY 1   DEVELOPING A FANTASY CHARACTER

Challenge: Make a model that tells a story about a new imaginary superhero or fantasy character.

- Think about the all elements that make up your character.
- What powers do they have?
- Do they have a sidekick or friends?

(Continued)

(Continued)

- Who is their nemesis?
- What's their back story?

Build time: You have 5 minutes to make your model.

Sharing: In pairs, describe your model and tell your story. Try not to leave out any details. You have 5 minutes.

Teacher guide: When the pupils have told their stories, encourage them to ask questions about the heroes they have heard about. You might need to provide some examples here to encourage the pupils – e.g. 'Why does your hero only have one leg? Tell me more.'

Deeper writing: After sharing, ask the pupils to make notes about the characters using all the details they have built into the model and described to their partner. From these notes, pupils can now write a detailed character profile.

The image below shows an example of a superhero, built by a BA Primary Education student, following the method above:

Figure 2.3   LEGO® SERIOUS PLAY® model, built by ITE student, Durham University

EXAMPLE ACTIVITY 2   A MYSTERIOUS JOURNEY

Challenge: Build a model that tells a story of 'the mysterious thing that happened on way your home'.

- Where have you come from? What were you doing?
- Think about the route you might take.
- Think who or what you might encounter.
- How did you get home eventually?
- Try to create a story that has a beginning, a middle and an end.

Build time: You have 5 minutes to make your model.

Sharing: In pairs, tell your mysterious story to each other. You have 5 minutes.

Teacher guide: Encourage the pupils to use descriptive words (adverbs and adjectives) that add to the sense of mystery.

Deeper writing: After sharing, ask the pupils to break down their stories into sections consisting of a beginning or introduction, a middle or dilemma, and an end or resolution. Get them to jot down the important things that happen in each section and the key descriptive words. Draw a story map showing the route. Use these resources as a plan and word bank for an adventure story.

EXAMPLE ACTIVITY 3   THE PERFECT DAY

Challenge: Build a model that tells a story of what makes the perfect day out for you.

- What are the things you enjoy doing most?
- Where might you be?
- Who might be with you? You could be all alone.
- It doesn't have to be what people might expect.
- It could be more than one thing, but it has to be perfect.

Build time: 10 minutes.

Sharing: In pairs, describe your model and tell your story. Try not to leave out any details. You have 5 minutes.

(Continued)

(Continued)

Teacher guide: During the sharing, ask the listener to jot down some notes of their partner's perfect day. Encourage them to capture what they think are the most important details.

Deeper writing: Now ask the pupils to write a 'Perfect Day' plan as a surprise gift for their partners – not their own. They must keep it secret and include a wonderfully detailed description of how they want the day to happen. At the right time, share these plans.

Acknowledgement: LEGO®, LEGO® SERIOUS PLAY®, the Minifigure and the Brick and Knob configurations are trademarks of the LEGO Group, which does not sponsor, authorise or endorse this work.

ACTIVITY USING LEGO® SERIOUS PLAY®

1. **Design your own session** Following the core process and etiquette of the three examples, create a fourth play/storytelling stimulus for deeper writing. Include a challenge, some build time and sharing to inspire deeper writing.

2. **Hands-on bricks** A quick story-making experience: find some LEGO® bricks and build a model of a cat using only six bricks. Now make up a story about why your cat is the most amazing cat in the world. After you've told your story, remove two bricks from the model and tell the story of why your cat is still the most amazing cat. Think about what's changed and add to the cat's amazing tale.

FOCUS ON RESEARCH

LEGO® SERIOUS PLAY® AND EDUCATIONAL THEORY

Two key educational theories that underpin the whole 'play' experience in LEGO® SERIOUS PLAY® are constructivism and constructionism.

In 1962, Jean Piaget is famously quoted as saying that 'play is the work of childhood'. Intentionally using play as a driver for learning experiences and knowledge sharing lies at heart of the LEGO® SERIOUS PLAY® method, whether used by children or adults. Is it possible that play could be the beginning of deeper writing and story telling that releases creative minds? Piaget's constructivism theory (1951) explains how knowledge is constructed when new information meets existing knowledge gained through the learner's experiences. Its emphasis is on the way that knowledge is created for learners to adapt to the world around them. Thus, learners who are in the process of playing by creating and sharing stories actually begin to generate new possibilities. This is what makes guided play experiences in the classroom an effective precursor to deeper writing work.

Constructionist learning theory takes this further by observing that learners construct mental models to understand the world around them. Discovery learning, collaborative work, hands-on activities and project-based tasks are a number of teaching and learning applications that root themselves in this theory. Seymour Papert, the author of constructionism, asserts that learning takes place when people are actively engaged in making a product, something external to themselves like a machine, a book, a sandcastle or even a story with LEGO® bricks. Thus, when pupils make stories or design characters out of LEGO® they are simultaneously constructing stories and knowledge in their minds. In the words of Papert (1990): 'Better learning will not come from finding better ways for the teacher to instruct, but from giving the learner better opportunities to construct.'

Outdoor play

In line with, and to enhance, the requirements of the EYFS Framework (DfE, 2017) and the National Curriculum (DfE, 2014), many nurseries and primary schools are offering opportunities for outdoor play as part of a rich and varied curriculum. Alongside dedicated outdoor space for children in nursery and EYFS, structured opportunities, such as Forest School, are being offered as a regular, timetabled activity. The value of outdoor play in the development of language, as a support for early writing and as a stimulus for writing in depth is being increasingly recognised.

CASE STUDY

USING FOREST SCHOOL TO GENERATE IDEAS FOR WRITING IN THE NURSERY SETTING

Busy Bears Children's Day Nursery, Durham, use Forest School as part of their outdoor learning provision. The overarching aim is that children will explore, investigate and experience for a number of aims, including developing early writing skills. Activities are sometimes child-led; the children's interest will help to guide the session and the children can choose how they want to mark-make and write, and decide what the writing outcome might be.

The trained facilitators within the nursery know that climbing, balancing, moving logs and erecting dens are all good ways of refining the children's gross motor skills.

(Continued)

(Continued)

Activities such as weaving, wrapping, binding and berry threading are used to develop fine motor skills. The inspiration for creative story development comes from talking about things they can see and hear, such as trees moving in the wind, birds chirping in the bushes and cones collected on the forest floor. It also comes from discussing the things they imagine, such as a troll crouching under a bridge and a fox hiding in its den. The image below shows a nursery child searching for fairy houses and toadstools:

Figure 2.4   A child searching for fairy houses and toadstools, Busy Bears Children's Day Nursery, Durham.

Inspiration can also come from listening to high-quality picture books while in the forest, such as *Stick Man* by Julia Donaldson and *We're Going on a Bear Hunt* by Michael Rosen. For more ideas about using picture books, see Chapter 3.

The nursery practitioners take writing resources to the forest, including pencils and notepads, so that the children can record the things they see, wax crayons for rubbings and sticky tape to collect interesting objects on journey sticks and memory cards. The children also use natural materials that they find while exploring; sticks for etching into the mud, and juicy berries and rough stones for writing names.

The nursery practitioners might end a Forest School session with circle time, where children sing and talk about the things that they have explored. They might also make a floor book, where children are invited to add their writing and mark-making to record their experiences. These plenary activities might take place in the forest or back in the nursery setting.

FOCUS ON RESEARCH

FOREST SCHOOL

Based on the Danish model, the Forest School approach was introduced to Britain in 1993 (Maynard, 2007). Concern about the growing decline in children's outdoor play at the time, in both the nursery and school setting, may have been a factor in the growing interest in Forest School. It has been defined by Murray and O'Brien (2005) as an inspirational process that allows children to achieve through hands-on learning experiences in a woodland environment. O'Brien (2009, p. 46) has observed that:

> Forest School embraces a broad concept: it takes place in school hours, on a regular basis, and it is not only focused on learning about nature but is linked to the national curriculum and foundation stage objectives such as English.

Using a constructivist approach, where children are learning by doing and are actively developing their understanding through interaction (Kahn, 1999), it is suggested that the experience of learning outdoors can have an effect on what is learnt (Dillon et al., 2005). The emphasis on practical activity appears to be linked to kinaesthetic learning and, without outdoor play, often young children are offered few opportunities to learn kinaesthetically (Rodd, 2002, cited in Maynard, 2007).

When engaging in Forest School activities with primary school pupils, Reynolds (2018) noticed a clear connection between pupil enjoyment and engagement, resulting in significant developments in understanding and learning, thus concluding that the regular provision of outdoor and experiential learning opportunities should be facilitated.

CASE STUDY

WRITING LINKED TO FOREST SCHOOL IN KS1

This case study demonstrates how pupil enjoyment and engagement of outdoor learning results in significant developments in the quality of writing. Hannah Williamson, Deputy Headteacher at Rainbird Primary, Excelsior Academy, Newcastle, is an experienced primary teacher and trained Forest School facilitator. Hannah writes:

> Forest School is an inspirational process that offers all learners regular opportunities to achieve and developing confidence and self-esteem through hands-on learning

(Continued)

(Continued)

experiences in a woodland or natural environment with trees. It is a specialised learning approach that sits within and complements the wider context of outdoor and woodland education.

At Rainbird Primary, Excelsior Academy, we use Forest School as a vehicle to develop language and writing for students across the school. All classes have the opportunity to experience Forest School during each academic year. These sessions are usually across a half-term period for each year group. During a typical half-term we will spend approximately six full days in the forest.

The format of our sessions includes opportunities for free play, opportunities for exploration and adult-led sessions. Over the past five years we have found that these sessions provide the perfect base on which to build pupil writing. We have high proportions of SEN and EAL students in our school, which often means that they have limited vocabulary. Having the opportunity to take part in these real-life experiences has a really positive impact on their acquisition of new vocabulary.

Some of the best outcomes have been as a result of the Forest School experiences our children have had. A Year 2 class were visiting the forest during their topic on survival. In the third session in the forest, a small group of girls and boys were exploring the forest looking for mini beasts, but on the journey, they discovered that a metal teapot had been left in the forest beside a tree.

Figure 2.5   A metal teapot found during forest school, Rainbird Primary, Excelsior Academy

They then began developing stories around how the teapot had got there, who owned the teapot and much more. On the return to school, the class teacher used the photos of the teapot as a writing prompt for a fantasy story. One of the outcomes from this experience is shown here:

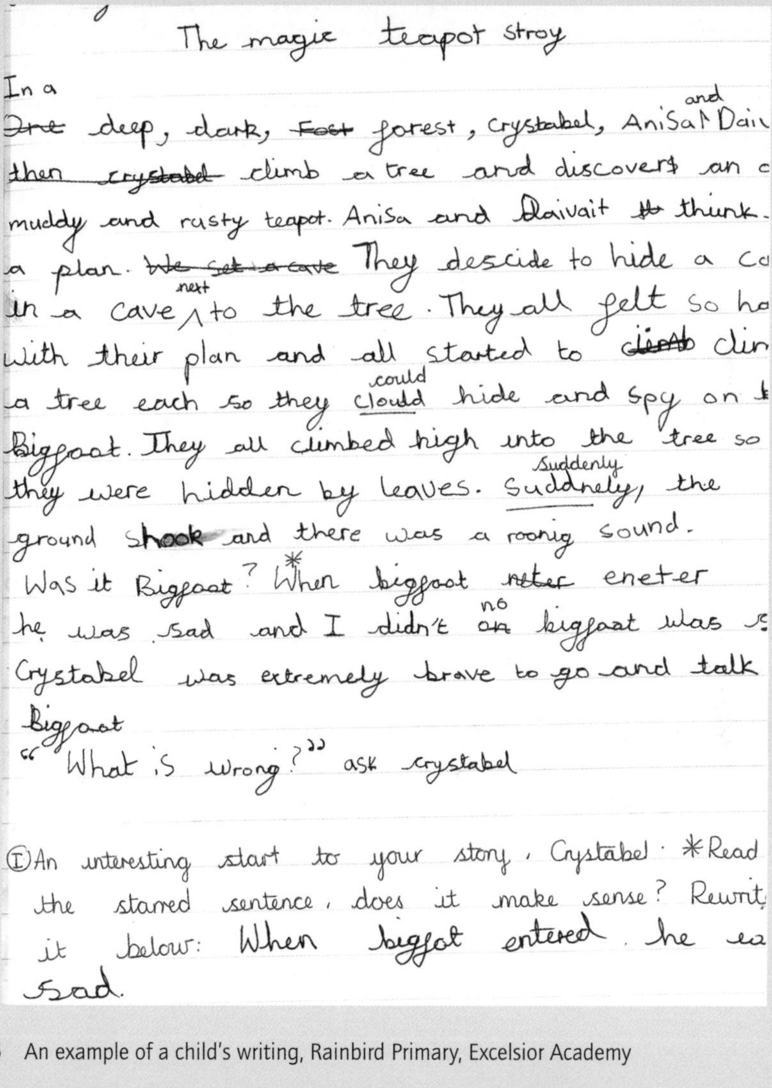

The magic teapot stroy

In a ~~One~~ deep, dark, ~~Fost~~ forest, crystabel, AniSa and Dai[...]
~~then crystabel~~ climb a tree and discovers an [...]
muddy and rusty teapot. AniSa and Daivait ~~th~~ think[...]
a plan. ~~We set a cave~~ They descide to hide a c[...]
in a cave next to the tree. They all felt so ha[...]
with their plan and all started to ~~climb~~ clim[...]
a tree each so they could hide and spy on [...]
Biggfoot. They all climbed high into the tree so
they were hidden by leaves. Suddenly, the
ground shook and there was a rooring sound.
Was it Biggfoot? * When biggfoot ~~neter~~ eneter
he was sad and I didn't no biggfoot was [...]
Crystabel was extremely brave to go and talk
Biggfoot
"What is wrong?" ask crystabel

(1) An interesting start to your story, Crystabel. * Read the stared sentence, does it make sense? Rewrite it below: When biggfot entered he wa[...] sad.

Figure 2.6 An example of a child's writing, Rainbird Primary, Excelsior Academy

Forest School gives our students real-life experiences which they can draw upon when they write. This provides them with new and additional vocabulary, an ability to make links within their writing and add further detail to the ideas that they have.

(Continued)

(Continued)

Another class had been working in the forest over a range of weeks. They particularly enjoyed when we made a fire and cooked sausage rolls and chocolate orange cake on it. One child used this experience to enhance her writing, a 'message in a bottle' written from the view of someone trapped on an island. Her Forest School experience made her writing come to life and sound more authentic.

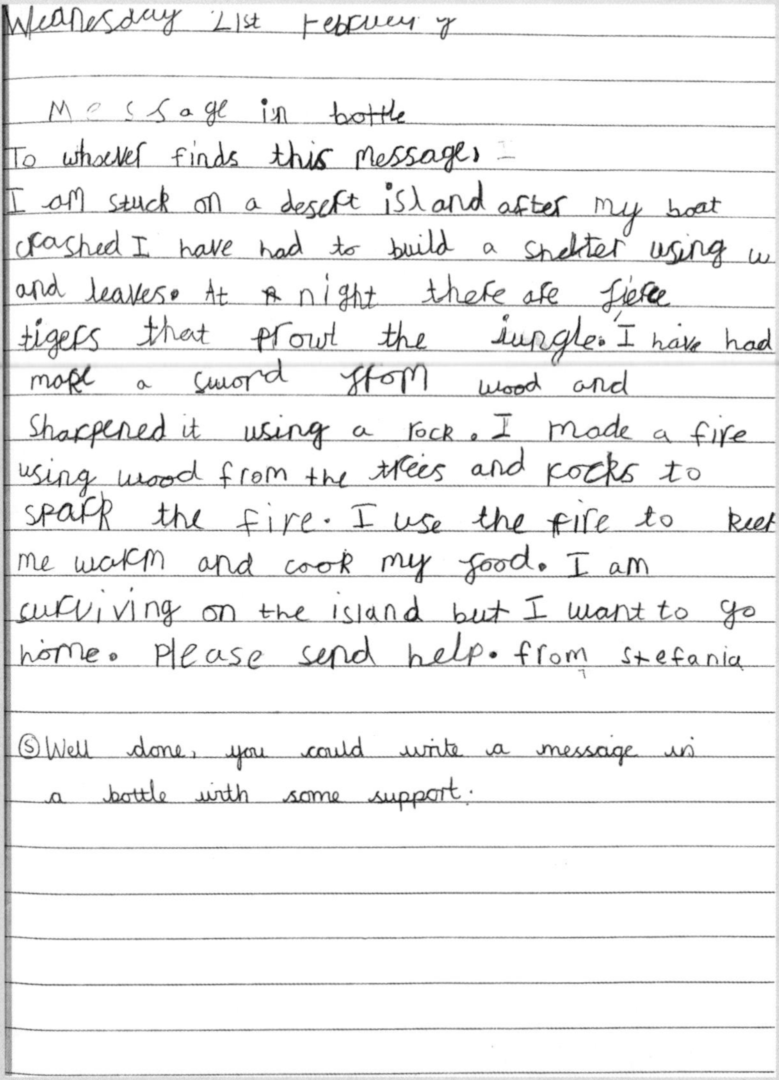

> Wednesday 21st February
>
> Message in bottle
> To whoever finds this message,
> I am stuck on a desert island after my boat crashed I have had to build a shelter using w and leaves. At a night there are fierce tigers that prowl the jungle. I have had made a sword from wood and sharpened it using a rock. I made a fire using wood from the trees and rocks to spark the fire. I use the fire to keep me warm and cook my food. I am surviving on the island but I want to go home. Please send help. from Stefania
>
> ⑤ Well done, you could write a message in a bottle with some support.

Figure 2.7   Another example of a child's writing, Rainbird Primary, Excelsior Academy

Another positive outcome that we have discovered from using Forest School to enhance writing is that many boys in our school are much more engaged when they are writing about or using their Forest School experience. This has been particularly evident within KS1. Forest School is an integral part of the education which our students receive and there are significant benefits to this on both academic and personal development.

ACTIVITY 2   PLAN FOR WRITING THROUGH FOREST SCHOOL ACTIVITIES

Design a writing opportunity based on a Forest School activity. It might be fiction or non-fiction, it could be collaborative or individual, and it might happen in the forest or back in the classroom. Decide on the writing outcome, list the resources needed, consider the health and safety implications, and plan how and where the children will write.

Exploring Forest School and writing in ITE

Many ITE providers see the value in outdoor learning and Forest School techniques and, as a result, offer their trainees experience of outdoor learning to support them in meeting the Teachers' Standards (DfE, 2011), in gaining QTS and in preparation for teaching. Philip Sprigg, a third-year BA Education trainee at Durham University, reflected on his experience of Forest School as part of his English Specialism module, and how this might impact on his teaching:

As a trainee, I would argue I have a heightened motivation in developing a deep and broad understanding of how best I can deliver a creative, inclusive and progressive curriculum. In light of this, whether it be English, maths, music or any other aspect of the curriculum, I am continually surprised at outdoor learning's ability to weave its way into the effective teaching and learning of even the most specific aspects of the curriculum. So much so, it would appear there is a multitude of untapped potential in outdoor learning that is not yet being fully utilised, including when providing opportunities to write, in supporting early writing and developing writing in depth. Having had experience in EYFS, KS1 and KS2 settings across my three years of teacher training, encouraging deeper writing, particularly in boys, is something I have noticed to, on occasion, be challenging. Therefore, I was keen to participate, along with my peers, in a Forest School workshop. It was led by a fully qualified outdoor learning practitioner and we were encouraged, through a range of hands-on activities and collaborative discussion, to consider the benefit of outdoor learning in developing writing.

The first activity required participants to stand in a circle. Only one stick was required – something easily obtained in most school environments. The stick was passed around the circle and we each, acting as the children in this scenario, had to use our imagination to transform the stick into some-thing else which looks similar. For example, some people said: 'I have a stick in my hand, but it isn't a stick. It's actually a telegraph pole/teaspoon/gear stick.'

These were just some of the many suggestions. We not only had to think of something, but remember everyone else's suggestions too! This activity – although simple – holds many opportunities for the promotion of deeper writing. Children have to really engage with this activity for two reasons: first, they have to manipulate their range of vocabulary to see what word is most suitable; and some children later on in the circle may have to change their idea based on what people have already said. This pushes children to make links between their previously developed vocabulary and the physical object in front of them. As the teacher, you can use this opportunity to expose children to new vocabulary: something whacky that they might not have heard of will automatically generate interest and progress children's vocabulary. Second, children have to engage their memory and listen closely to other responses. Developing memory is pivotal in learner's ability to recall informa-tion at the right times throughout the writing process.

As the teacher, it is our role to ensure that the activity is differentiated in ways where all can suc-ceed. Children at the start of the circle concern themselves only with thinking of a relevant noun, whereas children later in the circle had many responses to remember and think of their own word. By knowing your children, you can differentiate the activity by putting children who may strug-gle in thinking of a word – e.g. children with EAL and SEN – at the start and children with a wider vocabulary knowledge towards the end. You could also put the children in smaller groups of around four or five so they do not have to remember vast amounts of answers – again, allowing for all children to succeed. All of this culminates to allow all children to develop memorable vocabu-lary which they can incorporate within their deeper writing.

The second activity involved the use of flint, steel and cotton wool to make a fire. Under instruction, the flint was rubbed against the steel to create a spark which saw the cotton wool flame. Often, due to the constraints of health and safety, lack of time and resources, experiences such as these are limited to video or verbal description to act as a stimulus to children's writing. Although this can generate good written pieces, the value of outdoor learning is in that it allows children to engage with the experience first-hand. During the workshop, we used this experience as a stimulus to create poetry.

Flint and steel poems

> *As cold as an icicle,*
> *Until appearing like a magician . . . the flame!*
> *As hot as the sun,*
> *Red like the poppies in November,*
> *Flint and Steel together like they are one.*

And:

> *From tools as cold as ice*
> *Comes a glow that's warm and nice*
> *Only big enough for mice*
> *But giving off smells that entice!*

Due to the fact that the experience was authentic and not fabricated, the poems created consisted of much more descriptive content and were arguably of far greater quality than could have been expected. This ability to draw on the senses more easily is a key skill in developing children's deeper level of writing, and once again, a reason for the use of outdoor learning in a progressive curriculum. When outdoor learning is planned effectively with close consideration of how all pupils can be supported through differentiation, children can generate a deeper level of writing through authentic, first-hand experience which will elicit quality writing.

Exploring outdoor play for a range of opportunities and writing outcomes

Of course, Forest School is not the only approach to outdoor play that can be used. Other incarnations, such as beach school, are becoming increasingly popular. Visits to parks, farms and other open-air locations can be used as opportunities for stimulating language and writing. However, some of the most useful and readily available resources are the local area around a school, and for many, dedicated outdoor spaces and the school grounds themselves.

When considering how to support early writing, and the development of deeper writing, research by O'Brien (2009) suggested that Forest School (and other outdoor learning opportunities) improves motivation and encourages concentration, characterised by a keenness to participate in exploratory learning for extended periods. Gross motor skills can be developed through the exploration of tyres and large construction sets, steering bikes and scooters, parachute games, connecting tubes and pipes and engaging in chasing games. Opportunities to develop fine motor skills might come from using chalk for mark-making on walls and floors, using paintbrushes and rollers of different sizes to paint doors and windows, and exploring mixing, pouring and filling in mud kitchens.

In addition, it was noted that outdoor learning contributes to the development of language and communication skills; visual and sensory experiences prompt more sophisticated use of oral and written language (Murray and O'Brien, 2005). Discussing what is happening over the fence, or who might be on the passing bus, speculating about where the overhead plane is going and who the passengers might be, and selling imaginary ice-creams from the outside hut, are all inclusive activities that develop language, allow children to make connections and foster imagination, provide inspiration and creativity for story-telling and other writing opportunities. Dyson and Gallannaugh (2007), as cited by Reynolds (2018, p. 24), observed that

primary school children benefited hugely from experiential learning activities that significantly widened their life experience, enabling them to then be able to discuss their understanding and thereby develop their writing skills from a much more solid position of conceptual understanding.

It is interesting to note that Reynolds (2018) suggests that outdoor learning is most successful when it is supported by focused classroom learning, and so opportunities for writing in depth in the classroom, as a result of learning outdoors, should be sought. An example of this might be to use the 'take one book' principle. This method involves using a high-quality book as a stimulus and the anchor point for several weeks of planned learning. Jolliffe and Waugh (2018) emphasise the need for a holistic approach, so that speaking and listening, reading, writing and drama, together with skills such as spelling and punctuation, are integrated, in authentic and meaningful contexts. High-quality talk and writing opportunities, based on picture books related to the outdoors, such as *Stick Man* by Julia Donaldson and the *Leaf Man* by Lois Elhert, can be planned over a series of lessons or weeks. Alongside reading the texts, children might use the school grounds to find leaves, sticks and other natural objects, and return to the classroom to:

- develop their language around description or enquiry using the natural objects as a stimulus;
- create characters such as *Leaf Man* and *Stick Man* using the objects collected;
- transfer knowledge and skills to formulate ideas and speculate about their characters;
- engage in writing opportunities, based on their characters, such as name tags or other labels, lost and found posters, interview questions and collaborative stories.

For more information about 'take one book', and for further ideas for using picture books to develop writing in depth, see Chapter 3.

Conclusion

Experiences through play can be used to scaffold young children's learning in order to develop their early writing skills, with a view to enabling them to demonstrate depth in writing. By offering a broad range of diverse play-based activities, in a planned and structured way, a myriad of associated writing experiences can be provided for all children in nursery, EYFS and KS1.

Indoors or outdoors, free or focused, play is used widely to support writing and to develop writing skills. From the refinement of gross and fine motor skills to creative engagement, play allows children to develop the necessary physical attributes and to be stimulated and motivated to write for purpose and in depth.

Further reading

Blair, S. and Rillo M. (2016) *Serious Work: How to Facilitate Meetings and Workshops Using the LEGO® SERIOUS PLAY®* Method, Pro Meet.

Bushnell, A. and Waugh, D. (2017) *Inviting Writing: Teaching and Learning Writing Across the Primary Curriculum.* London: Sage.

Bushnell, A., Smith, R. and Waugh, D. (2018) *Modelling Exciting Writing: A Guide for Primary Teaching.* London: Sage.

James, A. (2014) Learning in three dimensions: using Lego SERIOUS PLAY for creative and critical reflection across time and space, in Layne, P.C. and Lake, P. (eds) *Global Innovation of Teaching and Learning in Higher Education: Transgressing Boundaries. Professional Learning and Development in Schools and Higher Education*, Vol. 11. Cham: Springer, pp. 275–94. Available online at: https://doi.org/10.1007/978-3-319-10482-9_17

James, A. (2015) Innovative pedagogies series: Innovating in the creative arts with LEGO. York: Higher Education Academy. Available online at: www.heacademy.ac.uk/system/files/alison_james_final.pdf (accessed 23 January 2019).

James, A. (2016) Play and 3D enquiry for stimulating creative learning, in Watts, L. and Blessinger, P. (eds) *Creative Learning: International Perspectives and Approaches in Higher Education*. New York: Routledge.

James, A. and Brookfield, S. (2014) *Engaging Imagination: Helping Students Become Creative and Reflective Thinkers*. San Francisco, CA: Jossey Bass.

James, A. and Brookfield, S. (2016) The serious use of play and metaphor, in Wang, V. (ed.), *Adult Education in the Digital Age*. Hershey: IGI Global, pp. 118–33.

Knight, S. (2013) *Forest School and Outdoor Learning in the Early Years* (2nd edn). London: Sage.

Kristiansen, P. and Rasmussen, R. (2014), *Building a Better Business Using the LEGO® SERIOUS PLAY® Method*. Hoboken, NJ: Wiley.

The LEGO Group (2010). Open-source/<Introduction to LEGO® SERIOUS PLAY® Available online at: http://seriousplaypro.com/about/open-source/ (accessed 23 January 2019).

McCusker, S. (2014) LEGO SERIOUS PLAY: Thinking about teaching and learning. *International Journal of Knowledge, Innovation and Entrepreneurship*, 2(1): 27–37.

Recommended websites

LEGO® BuildToExpress®: BuildToExpress was a teaching process that combined a facilitative teaching method with hands-on learning. LEGO Education discontinued this product, however, teaching ideas and processes similar to LSP are still available – https://education.lego.com/en-us/support/buildto-express/faqs

LEGO® SERIOUS PLAY® – www.lego.com/en-us/seriousplay

SeriousPlayPro: an open community of individuals who are interested in creative strategising and problem-solving – http://seriousplaypro.com

References

Cremin, T. and Burnett, C. (2018) *Learning to Teach in the Primary School* (4th edn). London: Routledge.

Department for Education (DfE) (2011) *Teachers' Standards in England from September 2012*. London: DfE.

Department for Education (DfE) (2014) *National Curriculum: Programmes of Study for English*. London: DfE.

Department for Education (DfE) (2017) *Statutory Framework for the Early Years Foundation Stage*. London: DfE.

Dillon, J., Morris M., O'Donnell, L., Reid, A., Rickinson, M. and Scott, W. (2005) *Engaging and Learning with the Outdoors – the Final Report of the Outdoor Classroom in a Rural Context Action Research Project*. Berkshire: National Foundation for Educational Research.

Jolliffe, W. and Waugh, D. (2018) *Mastering Primary English*. London: Bloomsbury.

Kahn, P. (1999) *The Human Relationship with Nature: Psychological, Sociocultural and Evolutionary Investigations*. Cambridge, MA: MIT Press.

The LEGO Group (2010) Open-source/<Introduction to LEGO® SERIOUS PLAY®, Available online at: http://seriousplaypro.com/about/open-source/ (accessed 25 February 2019).

Maynard, T. (2007) Forest Schools in Britain: an initial exploration. *Contemporary Issues in Childhood Education*, 8(4): 320–31.

Murray, R. and O'Brien, E. (2005) *Such Enthusiasm – a Joy to See: An Evaluation of Forest School in England*. Farnham: Forest Research.

O'Brien, L. (2009) Learning outdoors: the Forest School approach. *Education 3–13*, 37(1): 45–60.

Papert, S. (1990) Introduction, in *Constructionist Learning*. Cambridge, MA: A Media Laboratory Publication.

Piaget, J. (1951) *The Child's Conception of the World*. London: Routledge.

Piaget, J. (1962) (trans. C. Gattegno and F.N. Hodgson) *Play, Dreams, and Imitation in Childhood*. New York: W.W. Norton & Company.

Reynolds, O. (2018) A critical analysis of outdoor learning experiences and the impact on pupil development and conceptual understanding. *The STeP Journal*, 5(1): 22–9.

3

DEVELOPING DEEPER WRITING IN KS1 THROUGH THE USE OF HIGH-QUALITY PICTURE BOOKS

Megan Stephenson

KEY QUESTIONS

- How do I use high-quality texts to motivate and sustain motivation over extended sequences of learning?

(Continued)

(Continued)

- How do I scaffold learning so that children can demonstrate depth in writing over time?
- How do I foster independence to enable children to develop ownership and find direction and meaning in their writing?
- How do I embed the teaching of SPaG?

Introduction

Much has been written about the need to raise pupils' standards in writing over the last few years. Changes in English teaching as a result of the introduction of the revised National Curriculum, 2014 witnessed 'a heavy emphasis on the teaching of vocabulary, spelling, grammar and punctuation' (Jolliffe and Waugh, 2018, p. 19). In many cases, this meant an increase in the teaching of such topics through more discrete grammar sessions in the primary classroom.

In this chapter we will explore how the high demands of a curriculum-heavy content can be met through the creative planning, teaching and delivery of engaging material.

We will consider the use of high-quality books that engage children and develop the love of reading into writing. A range of 'hook' stimuli that introduce and engage children in quality books will be introduced. The focus will be on how experiences can be used to scaffold young children's learning in order to enable them to demonstrate depth in writing. This style of working involves planning from the same quality text over several weeks to establish complete immersion in the stimulus, so children feel part of the narrative.

There are also examples of formative assessment, where the teacher has developed the learning through addressing misconceptions at the point of writing or reviewing a pupil's work from a previous day using pupil peer review to adapt ideas. Such excellent practice aims to develop pupils' evaluative skills and encourages them to reflect on the relative success of certain vocabulary or punctuation choices. Over an extended sequence of learning, the children develop a *sense of ownership* and experience *writing for a range of purposes and audiences*. The outcomes of each period of learning follow National Curriculum guidelines and provide a clear purpose for writing, giving added motivation for children's learning. Emphasis is placed on how to *examine spelling, punctuation and grammar objectives for Key Stage 1 and also how these can be embedded* in purposeful and meaningful contexts, linked to the high-quality texts and multisensory experiences used as stimuli. From this early age, pupils demonstrate a pride and develop confidence when evidencing the programmes of study in the National Curriculum and revisiting these in different contexts.

Finally, this chapter aims to inspire and give confidence to trainee teachers and practitioners to engage with high-quality texts to provide enhanced and deep writing experiences for all children in Key Stage 1 and beyond. Examples of pupils' work and case studies are used throughout.

Getting it right from the start for our Key Stage 1 Learners

Choosing the most relevant text to introduce to the children means a teacher being familiar with and developing an interest in children's books and current authors themselves. They must be confident in the knowledge that their choices will motivate pupils while developing a depth of learning. The attitude of the teacher towards books and reading is crucial when developing the young pupil's motivation. Studies identifying the most effective literacy teachers show that those who identified themselves as 'Reading Teachers' were more successful in introducing children to new writers and genres, and selecting the most relevant of texts to support extended study (Medwell et al., 1998; Hall, 2013).

Many authors have also identified the value of and need for teachers to show themselves to be writers or authors in view of their pupils. This can take many forms, including presenting 'What A Good One Looks Like' or WAGOLL (an example material written by the teacher) for the pupils to review; and shared, modelled and guided writing sessions that provide children with a range of opportunities to discuss an author's choice of language and improve upon it themselves. Roth and Guinee (2011) looked at how teachers worked with children using interactive writing methods to demonstrate the value of their own ideas and that of their pupils. Moreover, in using such a method, the staff developed an empathy for the challenges faced by their pupils when writing regularly.

Practical approaches encouraging pupils to view their teachers as writers come from the demonstration of best practice and sharing ideas with pupils. In order to become competent and confident writers, pupils need scaffolded support throughout their primary years and the following principal approaches are widely viewed as techniques that schools should adopt to support children's learning:

1. Modelled writing – Children observe a model of good writing, produced by their teacher or previous published material.
2. Shared writing – Pupils and teacher take part in writing together.
3. Supported composition – Pupils and teacher experiment with writing together.
4. Guided writing – Teacher supports pupils in their own writing, offering support and guidance.

(Jolliffe and Waugh, 2018, p. 108)

All of the above promote the ultimate aim of pupils writing independently, using the skills, knowledge and confidence gained from accessing a range of teaching strategies.

An example WAGOLL

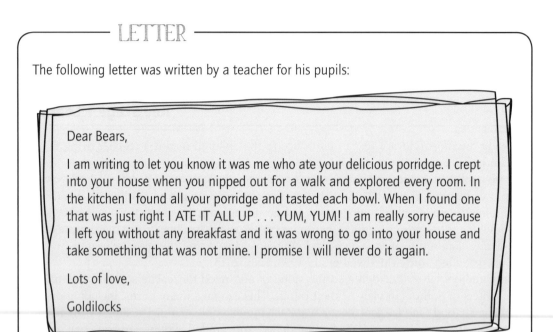

LETTER

The following letter was written by a teacher for his pupils:

Dear Bears,

I am writing to let you know it was me who ate your delicious porridge. I crept into your house when you nipped out for a walk and explored every room. In the kitchen I found all your porridge and tasted each bowl. When I found one that was just right I ATE IT ALL UP . . . YUM, YUM! I am really sorry because I left you without any breakfast and it was wrong to go into your house and take something that was not mine. I promise I will never do it again.

Lots of love,

Goldilocks

The letter was then used as a prompt for the pupils to work in pairs and identify the language Goldilocks had used to 'explain' what she had done and also a discussion of how it is important to admit when you have done something wrong.

Take One Book

Using a 'Take One Book' approach has been adopted recently by many forward-thinking schools. This method involves using the high-quality book as a stimulus and the anchor point for several weeks of planned learning. The aim is for pupils to develop a sustained, shared thinking about all aspects of the text and encourages them to fully engage with the materials in depth. In addition, it provides a wealth of opportunity to use cross-curricular links offering breath and balance.

FOCUS ON RESEARCH

Jolliffe and Waugh (2018, p. 22) explore the implementation of this practice in schools. They emphasise the need for such an approach to be whole-school led, through an holistic approach, *so that speaking and listening, reading, writing and drama together with skills such as spelling and punctuation are integrated, in authentic and meaningful contexts.* It is important that using such texts involve the pupils reading or having read to them the whole text over several days or weeks. This allows pupils and staff to analyse the use of language and explore its meaning and purpose.

A suggested planning format using a high-quality text

Stage	Example activities	Purpose and outcomes
Introducing	Introducing the book using a hook stimulus.	Provides an engaging and motivational introduction to an unknown or unfamiliar text.
Exploring and familiarising	Pre-reading activities, including word and sentence level tasks that investigate and reinforce comprehension.	Encourages reasoning about language choices used in the book. Boosts the speed of processing of the language and embeds comprehension of the text.
	Predicting outcome from the story using images or key phrases from the text.	Provides opportunities to ask and answer open-ended questions.
	Exploring new language used in the text and adopting the use of such in short writing tasks.	Allows an understanding through writing response in the text.
	Experimenting with the use of key vocabulary choices.	Promotes experimenting with a range of writing experiences with specific purposes and audiences in mind.
	Read and respond to the text.	Begin to use the language in the text in own writing.
Embedding	Reread the text and sequence the content.	Demonstrates a depth of understanding.
	Use a range of writing opportunities and repeat some of these after work is marked and feedback provided (edit and redraft).	Demonstrates ability to respond to feedback and improve use of language/edit punctuation or sentence choices. Improves both composition and transcription skills.
Securing and deepening knowledge	Review own learning by revisiting earlier writing activities and comparing progress.	Demonstrates independence.
	Write extended pieces often for publication.	Demonstrates a depth of learning in composition and transcription skills.

The process of developing such a sequence of learning needs the carefully planned implementation of a range of key teaching strategies. These are outlined in the table in Activity 1 and were identified by Jolliffe and Waugh (2018, p. 112). In turn, they provide opportunities for pupils to incorporate ideas and language from the texts into their own written pieces.

ACTIVITY 1

1. Read the seven strategies listed below.

2. Note down opportunities for using each one in the classroom in the third column below and choose two Key Teaching Strategies for Writing.

Key teaching strategies for writing

Writing strategy	Definition	E.G. of perfect writing opportunity . . .
Planning	Generating ideas and recording in arrange of formats.	
Drafting	Getting ideas into order and using a familiar format.	
Sharing	Peer and teacher feedback provides opportunities to adapt or confirm initial ideas work.	
Evaluating	Cross-reference ideas against the set success criteria.	
Revising	Changing content in light of feedback (this would still be draft form).	
Editing ·	Making additional edits that include a focus on composition (SPaG checks necessary at this stage).	
Publishing	Rewriting, with additions to improve both compositional and transcription for a specific purpose and audience.	

(Adapted from Jolliffe and Waugh, 2018, p. 112)

Such a way of working provides parallels with the Talk for Writing programme devised by Pie Corbett (www.talk4writing.co.uk/resources). However, this approach adds a greater 'depth' as the children are not expected to 'learn by heart', 'replicate' or 'amend' the content of the given features of a text. The Take One Book approach allows children to *respond* to different aspects of the content and at times adapt features of the language and vocabulary choices while demonstrating a true sense of ownership in the process.

Countenancing such an in-depth exploration into one book provides a wealth of learning opportunities, but also crucially provides the children with the time to:

- discover new and exciting texts they have not been introduced to before;
- predict the outcomes;
- become familiar with them;

- immerse themselves in the characters and storyline;
- study the language and structure in the text to build on their own vocabulary;
- use writing to convey meaning through a range of genres;
- edit and review writing in order to improve upon it;
- create several pieces of writing that demonstrate a depth of learning and often empathy;
- publish completed writing and present through a range of mediums.

FOCUS ON RESEARCH

Jolliffe and Waugh (2018) cite that in innovative schools where such working practice has been implemented, the success rates are high for pupils' engagement and attainment. They note several key features necessary for success:

1. Linking topics using high-quality texts.

2. Planning longer sequences of work that provide opportunities to explore language.

3. Children have time to think and plan their ideas before they write.

4. Grammar is taught explicitly and within the context of the book.

5. Modelling by the teacher demonstrates how to proofread and check that writing is accurate and appropriate vocabulary used.

(p. 29)

ACTIVITY 2

A selection of high-quality books that have been recommended and 'tried and tested' as KS1 texts in schools is listed below.

- *The Bog Baby* – Jeanne Willis
- *Leaf Man* – Lois Elhert
- *Lost and Found* – Oliver Jeffers
- *Oliver's Vegetables* – Vivian French
- *Stick Man* – Julia Donaldson
- *The Kiss That Missed* – David Melling
- *The Lighthouse Keeper's Lunch* – Ronda and David Armitage

Make a list of five more books you have seen in the primary classroom that would lend themselves to working in this way.

How to use a 'hook' stimulus to engage our young writers

Cremin et al. (2015) examined inventive strategies that teachers have demonstrated to increase motivation and engagement in young children. The texts were chosen to plan from enhanced pupils' experiences, and provided opportunities to read and respond to a range of materials in depth. Encountering a wide range of texts provided pupils with opportunities to express differing own opinions and make decisions about what they have read.

They suggest that:

> *Creative teachers seek out fiction texts that require children to actively participate in making meaning, texts that trigger multiple questions and deep engagement and that build bridges of understanding.*

Once texts are chosen, how they are introduced is crucial to secure that initial level of excitement and anticipation from children. Providing a level of intrigue, excitement and mystery prior to commencing a topic has become a valued way of introducing a new high-quality book.

The authors continue:

> *In exploring such texts, creative teachers employ a wide range of open ended strategies that foster children's curiosity and develop their personal and creative responses.*

(Cremin et al., 2015, p. 116)

CASE STUDY

INTRODUCING A HIGH-QUALITY TEXT USING A HOOK STIMULUS

Introducing *Leaf Man* by Lois Elhert to Year 1 pupils in the second half of autumn term. The overall topic for the term is called, 'Where Do All The Leaves Go?'

Cathy, an experienced KS1 teacher, had been asked to pilot a new way of working in her school to help raise engagement among the Year 1 pupils. She had planned to incorporate some outside learning into the topic. She always worked closely in school with her teaching assistant and the parallel Year 1 colleague. All three members of staff planned and reviewed lessons together. On the Monday morning before the children arrived, she prepared the classroom, arranging a huge pile of autumnal coloured leaves into a builder's spot in the centre of the carpet area. She wrote a note and rolled the script up (carefully hiding it among the leaves) along with a pre-prepared map of the outside grounds of the school attached. She created added mystery by meeting the children in silence that morning and allowing them to enter the class-room before her – providing a perfect balance of surprise and excitement. Simultaneously, the classroom assistant went outside and left clues in the form of arrows and laminated leaves that matched those that Cathy had identified on her map in preparation for the pupils going on a journey. The children were organised into a circle and one child was chosen to find and read the note in and among the leaves. The note read:

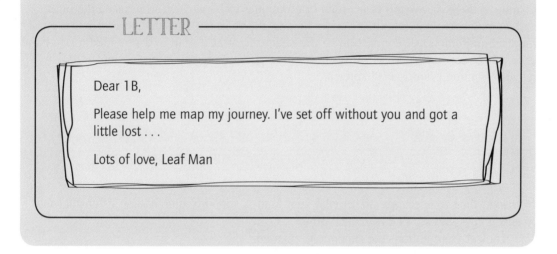

LETTER

Dear 1B,

Please help me map my journey. I've set off without you and got a little lost . . .

Lots of love, Leaf Man

Before setting off on their journey around the school, children were asked to work in pairs and formulate their ideas and speculate about Leaf Man. Cathy encouraged the pupils to use 'question words' to gather a list of questions they wanted to answer about the book. Question words had been a main feature of their previous sequence of learning, and she wanted them to adapt and transfer the skills and knowledge into this context. Cathy recorded the responses on the whiteboard next to a large illustration of the front cover of the book.

The children then embarked on a journey around school using their maps of the outside of school and completed an orienteering exercise that mirrored the journey of Leaf Man in the story. They talked about what they could see and some took photos on iPads as they reached each new vantage point. Right at the end of their travels, they discovered a laminated leaf on top of the book itself. This time the note had been torn and they were unable to read anything other than the words 'Thank you'.

The children returned to class and created their own Leaf Men using the leaves stockpiled and discovered earlier. After a break, the children were allowed to hold their own Leaf Men creations as they listened to the book being read by its author on YouTube (https://youtu.be/4g97WMh73eM) with the illustrations being projected alongside on the smartboard.

The children listened pensively as they compared their journey through school with that of Leaf Man. A spontaneous discussion then began initiated by the children as to why the word 'man' in the character's name should have a capital letter. The children had previously studied a selection of the *Mr. Men* series of books by Roger Hargreaves, and Cathy had used these titles as a means of introducing children to proper nouns. The title used for the book was another good example of where a noun had been used as a name in a title and therefore became a proper noun.

Using a range of techniques, including outdoor learning, the teacher has provided intrigue and mystery for the pupils. Mapping the journey through the school grounds develops a cross-curricular link through Geography and P.E. (National Curriculum, 2014). As noted in Chapter 2, there is a wealth of learning opportunities to be gleaned from using the outdoors, and in particular the school grounds. Taking the learning outside increased the pupils' physical and emotional connection to the character of Leaf Man and provided a first-hand experience. For further ideas on how to develop outdoor play and learning from a wider range of starting point, see Chapter 2.

ACTIVITY 3

Having time to speculate about who Leaf Man is supports the children's thinking and encourages them to talk with each other.
  Look at the questions the children formulated:

- Where has he come from?
- What does he look like?
- What has he seen?
- Who is he with?
- How will we know we have found him?

What might be an appropriate first task for the pupils to complete after listening to the text read aloud by the author?

The following planning displayed as a Thought Shower shows the learning opportunities that Cathy and colleagues recorded when planning the subsequent sequence of learning. It shows a range of Speaking and Listening, Reading and Writing opportunities to be explored.

Year 1

The Leaf Man – Lois Elhert
- Text type (Story)

Hook

Map the journey of The Leaf Man around our school grounds. Set clues for children to detect where he has travelled and how...

2. Capturing Ideas

Role play/re- enactment the story

Discuss the setting and compare to school grounds

Interview/Hot Seat the Leaf Man

Make posters in ICT using a large font asking for help to find The Leaf Man

Responding to the Text

- Use picture on Front of cover and respond to questions about what the Leaf Man might be like
- What type of house might they live in?

Writer talk – look at and discuss different fonts and bold or size of writing to provide emphasis in the story....

Different sentence layouts

Written Outcomes

1. Write the journey of the Leaf Man
2. Invite the Leaf Man in from the cold
3. Describe the Leaf Man's favourite tree
4. Write a response to a note from the Leaf Man

Sentence Games

- Play sentence/not sentence game based on the book.
- Count/clap the syllables in the sentences from the book
- Extend the sentence using a conjunction .../adjective

3. Grammar Ideas

Revisit proper nouns – Mr Men books

Writing capital letters for names and places in the story – (Recap work on Mr Men)

Use prepositions to describe plants/houses in the story – On – Under – behind – on top – over the hill

Compose and embed sentences before writing them – recite them together – use fingers to count words in sentence

Introduce idea of a time trial sentence (record after repeating)

Extend sentences using the conjunction 'and'

Repeat adding adjectives

Modelled writing – reply letter in response to plea for help

Shared writing – Description of what Leaf Man can see from his ariel view

Guided writing – Recount of their Leaf Man's 'typical' day. (Add additional sentence starters to show passage of time)

Independent writing – All of the above after edit and redraft in group or one to one with TA

Exploring the use of 'hooks' and writing in ITE

Many ITE providers demonstrate the value of using 'hooks' as stimuli when planning writing opportunities. These are used as ways of supporting their students in evidencing across the Teachers' Standards (DfE, 2011) in gaining QTS, and in preparation for excellent planning, teaching and learning. The following examples come from two final-year BA Primary Education trainees at Leeds Trinity University, reflecting on how such hooks had influenced their teaching after completing a Developing the Core Curriculum Module.

Vicky describes her experience of using hooks:

> I have learnt at university and in discussion with fellow students to build a bank of ideas. I've found that most props are good hooks and can be used in a variety of ways in different age ranges to promote effective and engaging writing. My focus on placement has been traditional tales and I found that using hooks greatly improved the pupils' writing capabilities. I used a range of hooks to engage and motivate children and these included:

- *wanted posters;*
- *props (including bowls of warm and cold porridge);*
- *images;*
- *role play.*

Vicky goes on to describe how combining the use of such hooks and props and indoor play within role play provides children with the ideas and materials necessary for writing. For further suggestions on how to develop 'indoor play' when planning for further deeper writing opportunities with young children writing, see Chapter 2.

Hannah, the second student, notes the value of using the children's imaginations to develop learning. She describes how she noticed that the children used their imagination to turn cardboard boxes into exciting things:

> the stimuli came from the children, they were already hooked – I just had to build on their interest. I asked a child what he would need to transform his cardboard box into a dinosaur, and he replied with a list of materials. I embraced the idea and planned the next writing focus around writing a list. The children were enthusiastic and committed to writing their list carefully and correctly because it was purposeful to them. If they didn't write it down, how else would Miss Page know what supplies to buy at the weekend . . . ?

Examples of successful 'hooks' using high-quality books

Stickman – Julia Donaldson	SOS message from Stickman's family asking for help in bringing him home safely to them. This message is written using sticks and is left out under a large tree in the school grounds – the tree where our stick family once lived.
Bog Baby – Jeanne Willis	Children find unidentifiable spots of 'gloop' leading to a mini pond (made inside a builder's spot). The book is next to the pond and the children listen to the story read by the teacher sitting around the pond.

Meerkat Mail – Emily Gravett	Children discover a suitcase in the classroom, items are revealed one by one related to where the character Sunny the meerkat will be visiting.
Oliver's Vegetables – Oliver Jeffers	Children find a basket of unusual fruit and vegetables, including beetroot and cabbage, tomatoes and rhubarb. They have a set of instructions to follow that guides them through using their sense of smell and taste to explore each one. A note from Oliver's grandad then asks them to share the story and compare their opinions with Oliver himself.
Funnybones – Janet and Allan Ahlberg	Invite a doctor of medicine into school who brings a life-sized skeleton and leaves this for the children to refer to over the course of studying the book/s.
The Lighthouse Keeper's Lunch – Ronda Armitage	Children are invited to a picnic in the school grounds. When they get to the picnic area, the book is waiting for them to enjoy listening to as they eat.

Modelling the use of vocabulary and supporting pupils' understanding of the language in high-quality texts

Exploring the use of new or unfamiliar vocabulary in a high-quality text is vital if the initial engagement from the hook is to be maintained during the reading process. Such work provides opportunity for discussion about meaning and also spelling conventions used. Moreover, defining and clarifying the meanings of such words gives pupils an understanding of a wider vocabulary and supports the fluency of reading such words in context.

This process was identified as a key teaching strategy within the Reading Recovery Programme and is sometimes known as 'taking the bugs out of the book' (Clay, 1993). Much has been written about using key vocabulary to provide opportunities for comprehension. Cremin et al. report on the importance of pupils being given time to make sense of the texts they read collectively or individually, and of the need to engage with such materials while bringing their own life experiences to the fore.

> *Each reader brings him/herself to the text, their life experience, prior knowledge of the issues encountered, as well as cultural perspectives and insights. Meaning is thus created in the interaction between the author, the text and the reader.*

(Cremin et al., 2015, pp. 105–6)

Example of introducing new vocabulary to children

The dialogue below demonstrates how a Year 1 teacher is introducing the children to a new word while developing their knowledge about language they will meet in the book.

This activity was introduced as a starter or pre-learning task before the book *Meerkat Mail* by Emily Gravett was read in the first term of Year 1.

Teacher	Right, here is a word we are going to meet in the story quite a lot. Use your phoneme fingers to sound out the word.
Child A	P er f e c t – (sound talks and then blends the word correctly).
Teacher	Yes, well done – it says perfect. Do you know what perfect means?
Child B to child A	My mum says 'perfect' when I get my spellings right.
Teacher	Wow – does she?
Child B	Is it perfect if you get one wrong?
Child A	No, I don't think so. They have to be all right to be exactly right.
Teacher	Excellent. Perfect might mean everything is just right. Can you think of another example of perfect?
Child C	My room is perfect when it is all tidy.
Teacher	Yes, brilliant example. When is your room not perfect?
Child A	When it's messy and the toys are out?
Teacher	Well done. Let's put our ideas about what perfect means to us into our thought showers?

This exemplifies the following teaching sequence:

• Teacher guides the pupils through the definition by using their own experience and understanding of the word and placing this into a familiar context.
• The children then record their ideas independently.

The following sample of work shows how Child A recorded his thoughts.

Figure 3.1 Child A has written 'Perfect means just right'

The class then listened to the teacher read the first part of the story. When the word 'perfect' was read aloud for the first time, a discussion followed. This time the discussion around the word related to the context of the story but needed no further explanation.

ACTIVITY 4

Think about how each element of the example relates to the National Curriculum for Year 1 in English listed below.
  Children should be taught to:

- link what they read or hear to their own experiences;
- discuss word meanings, linking new meanings to those already know;
- understand books by drawing on what they already know or on background information and vocabulary provided by the teacher;
- participate in discussion about what is read to them, taking turns and listening to what others say.

Creating and embedding depth using the same high-quality text

The final section of this chapter provides an extended case study and samples of work from the same child as they were taught a sequence of learning from a high-quality text.

Becky, an experienced Year 2 primary teacher, has excellent subject knowledge and the insight to know what motivates and inspires the children in her particular class. She has worked in the school for a number of years and has excellent professional relationships with her colleagues and members of the community. This was her fourth consecutive year in Year 2 and she wanted to embed the teaching of SPaG teaching while providing the children with a truly memorable half-term of learning. She was also tasked with accelerating pupil progress in writing. The pupils were used to working in pairs, small mixed-ability groups and independently. They were familiar with her different approaches and techniques and would often be encouraged to work outside, in the hall, exploring the corridors, and also on field trips to the local village. The text chosen was *The Light House Keeper's Lunch* by Ronda Armitage.

Predicting story content

Becky chose an interesting and intriguing teaching strategy when first introducing the children to the text, revealing only sections of the front cover and encouraging the pupils to 'predict' what they thought the story might be about. Lots of discussion took place, as well as intrigue and valuable open-ended discussion being created. The children looked at the images first and then discussed with a partner what they thought the story might be about. They then recorded their thoughts independently.

ACTIVITY 5

1. Look at the sample of writing this Year 2 child produced after looking at 'sections' of the front cover for the story. What 'literal' predictions has the child made based on the images?
2. How has 'inference' been used?
3. What spelling target do you think the teacher has identified after marking the work?
4. How might this fit into the next learning sequence planned?

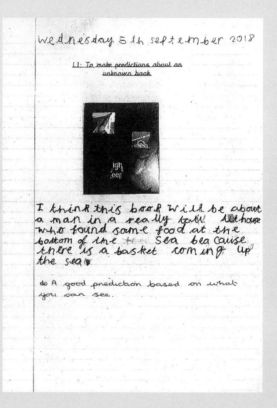

Figure 3.2   Child predicts what might happen in the story after viewing the front cover

Using the vocabulary in the text to expand word choices in the pupils' own writing, Higgins (2015) explored ideas that empowered pupils to make their own language choices in their writing. Through self-evaluation and reflection, he studied how pupils could be supported in developing capabilities of improving their work through the revision process. In previous teaching sequences, Becky had noticed that when the pupils were encouraged to explore the language they were reading, they became more engaged and in turn would begin to experiment with the use of such in their own writing to make it more powerful and pro-vide meaning.

An effective way to do this was found to be through:

- reading the book in short sections together;
- highlighting and identifying the key vocabulary;
- classifying this vocabulary into word types (e.g. nouns and adjectives);
- expanding these nouns and building noun phrases;
- using these noun phrases to write a short piece.

Through the use of verbal feedback, Becky has supported the child in developing the phrases into sentences. The child explores and expands the use of the language and vocabulary in the text in their independent writing.

The three pieces of work produced by the child show how this learning unfolded.

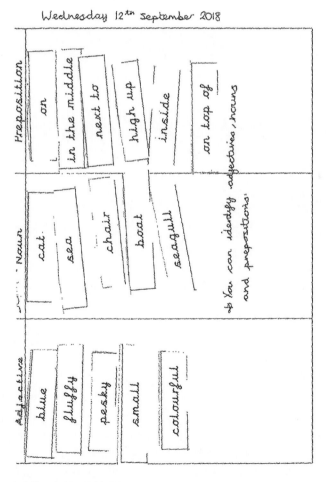

Figure 3.3 Sorting vocabulary into word types

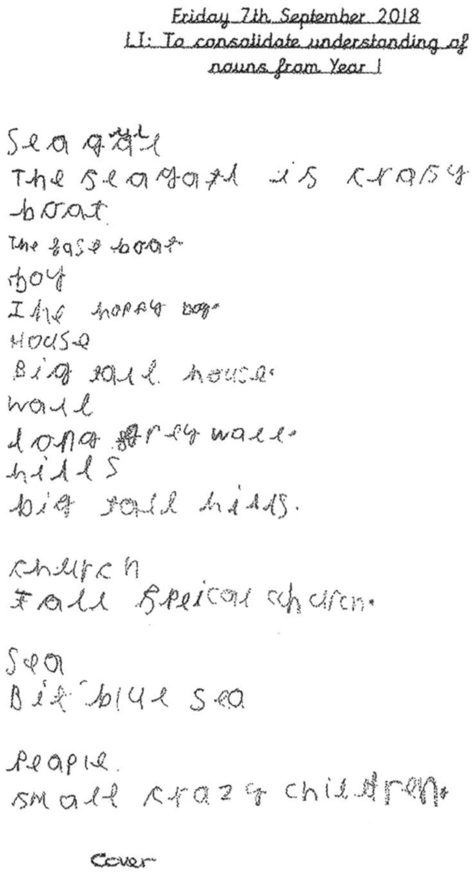

Friday 7th September 2018
LI: To consolidate understanding of
nouns from Year 1

sea gull
The seagull is crazy.
boat
The fast boat
boy
I he happy boy
House
Big tall house.
wall
long grey wall.
hills
big tall hills.

church
Tall special church.

sea
Big blue sea

people.
small crazy children.

Cover

Figure 3.4   Expanding noun phrases

ACTIVITY 6

Follow the sequence in Figure 3.3 by choosing a noun and an adjective from the list and develop your own expanded noun phrase (including a preposition) using the vocabulary choices available.

FOCUS ON RESEARCH

writing should be incorporated into a task that is necessary and relevant for life.

(Vygotsky, 1978, p. 118)

It is crucial for children to see the relevance and purpose of what they are being asked to write about so that they can identify with and 'buy into' the context. Children who see themselves as authors and who have a specific purpose will be motivated to achieve their best results. Writing with a true purpose and in many cases to receive acknowledgement from the intended reader provides a key motivator to the author. Therefore, the subject matter and stimulus material are crucial if pupils are to demonstrate a depth of understanding. Combining composition and transcription skills is also crucial; Cremin writes about both these areas of the National Curriculum working hand in hand when supporting pupils' creative imagination (Cremin, 2015). The compositional elements provide the most significant evidence when promoting pupil voice, but when those elements are supported by explicit teaching of the transcription skills (with reference to handwriting and spelling in particular) true depth of understanding can be achieved.

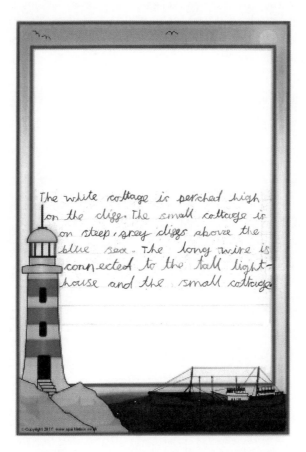

Figure 3.5   Child extends noun phrases using expressive vocabulary to develop a descriptive writing piece

CASE STUDY

As the children continued to study the story and completed a range of reading and writing tasks responding to the book, Becky gradually introduced them to the main 'problem' facing Mr Grinling (the lighthouse keeper), which was how to protect his lunch from the main protagonists of the book, the *seagulls*! Lots of discussion and debate followed about how such a problem could be solved. The merits of dialogic teaching and learning through a depth of discourse are well documented. Alexander (2008) comments and recommends weaving discussion into question formulation and lively debate. All these methods were a daily occurrence at the start of each English lesson, for recapping purposes but also to move the issues on during this teaching sequence.

Inventive and intricate planning meant that the children embarked on a day visit to the seaside town of Filey where they met a local resident. This person had invented 'seagull-proof bags' in her spare time to help reduce a very similar issue in her hometown. On their return to school, the children received a letter from Mr Grinling asking for their help in solving his problem. The class then embarked on a series of lessons that provided them with a depth of understanding of letter writing, but always keeping in mind the 'issue' of the pesky seagulls and finding a real solution to the 'problem' of the seagulls interfering with Mr Grinling's lunch.

The pupils completed the tasks below over the coming weeks:

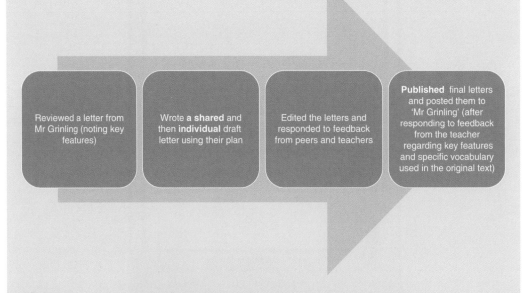

Figure 3.6   The sequence of learning that pupils complete to support deeper writing in KS1

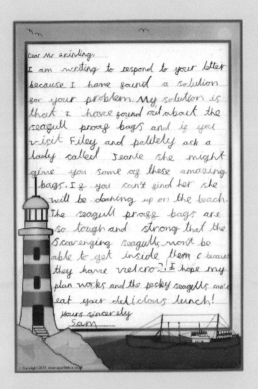

Figure 3.7 This is an example of the final letter

The school had identified the following criteria for pupils working at greater depth in Year 2.

Working at greater depth, the pupil can:

- write effectively and coherently for different purposes, drawing on their reading to inform the vocabulary and grammar of their writing;

- make simple additions, revisions and proofreading corrections to their own writing;

- use punctuation taught at Key Stage 1 mostly correctly;

- spell most common exception words;

- write effectively and coherently for different purposes, drawing on their reading to inform the vocabulary and grammar of their writing;

- make simple additions, revisions and proofreading corrections to their own writing;

- add suffixes to spell most words correctly;

- use diagonal and horizontal strokes to join some letters.

From child's letter illustrated in Figure 3.7, the depth of their understanding of the issue in hand is obvious. The 'solution' provides evidence for this feeling 'real to them' and using their first-hand experience to explain their thinking. The above example also provides us with evidence to support Reynolds's work on outdoor learning, which is most successful when it is planned alongside classroom-focused task (Reynolds, 2018). The ingenuity of combining a visit to Filey with meeting the lady, combined with subsequently providing a range of reading and writing opportunities meant that the children had a clear purpose for their final written piece. The child is mastering the writing process both through carefully orchestrated composition and also in the care he takes in the transcription; both support him getting 'their message across' – it's a winning combination.

Conclusion

In order for children to evidence a depth in writing, they require the correct stimuli, learning environment, scaffolding and support. Using a high-quality book to provide opportunities to explore, debate the meaning of and experiment with new language, in short and extended writing tasks, provides a platform for children to become engaged with and immersed in the content, and a context for the learning. The planning and teaching by staff, who have excellent subject knowledge, is key to this, enabling pupils to accelerate and evidence their progress in both compositional and transcriptional skills over an extended sequence of learning.

Children who have opportunities to verbalise their ideas and share new discoveries with their peers learn to adapt and take on board others' contributions, weaving them into their own work and consciousness. Teachers who model and use a range of teaching strategies nurture individuals as writers, using the building blocks of the curriculum, expertly integrating the subject matter and material at all times. Creating such a positive learning environment and providing a purpose for writing motivates and engages pupils, giving them the opportunity to demonstrate a depth in writing.

Further reading

Bushnell, A. and Waugh, D. (2017) *Inviting Writing: Teaching and Learning Writing Across the Primary Curriculum*. London: Sage.
Bushnell, A., Smith, R. and Waugh, D. (2018) *Modelling Exciting Writing: A Guide for Primary Teaching*. London: Sage.

Recommended websites

Stefan Kucharczyk – Articulate – www.articulateeducation.co.uk
Literacy shed – www.literacyshed.com/
Reading Recovery Lessons – www.literacylearning.net

References

Alexander, R. (2008) *Towards Dialogic Teaching: Rethinking Classroom Talk*. Cambridge: Dialogos.

Clay, M. (1993) *Reading Recovery: A Guidebook for Teachers in Training*. Ginn Heinemann Professional Development.

Cremin, T., Reedy, R., Bearn, E. and Dombey, H. (2015) *Teaching English Creatively*. Abingdon: Routledge.

Department for Education (DfE) (2011) *Teachers' Standards in England from September 2012*. London:DfE.

Department for Education (DfE) (2014) *The national curriculum in England Framework document December 2014*. Available online at: https://assets.publishing.service.gov.uk/government/uploads/system/uploads/attachment_data/file/381344/Master_final_national_curriculum_28_Nov.pdf

Hall, K. (2013) Effective literacy teaching in the early years of school: a review of the evidence, in Larson, J. and Marsh, J. *The Sage Handbook of Early Childhood Literacy* (2nd edn). London: Sage, pp. 33–40.

Higgins, S. (2015) Research-based approaches to teaching writing, in Waugh, D., Bushnell, A. and Neaum, S. (eds), *Beyond Early Writing*. Northwich: Critical Publishing.

Jolliffe, W. and Waugh, D. (2018) *Mastering Primary English*. London: Bloomsbury.

Medwell, J., Wray, D., Poulson, L. and Fox, R. (1998) *Effective Teachers of Literacy: A Report of Research Project Commissioned by the Teacher Training Agency*. Exeter: University of Exeter.

Reynolds, O. (2018) A critical analysis of outdoor learning experiences and the impact on pupil development and conceptual understanding. *The STeP Journal*, 5(1): 22–9.

Roth, K. and Guinee, K. (2011) Ten minutes a day: the impact of interactive instruction on first graders' independent writing. *Journal of Early Childhood Literacy*, 11(3): 331–61.

Vygotsky, L. (1978) *Mind in Society: The Development of Higher Psychological Processes*. Cambridge, MA: Harvard University, p. 118.

4

DEEPER WRITING AT KS2

Adam Bushnell

TEACHERS' STANDARDS

This chapter will help you with the following Teachers' Standards:

2d. demonstrate knowledge and understanding of how pupils learn and how this impacts on teaching;

3a. have a secure knowledge of the relevant subject(s) and curriculum areas, foster and maintain pupils' interest in the subject, and address misunderstandings;

3b. demonstrate a critical understanding of developments in the subject and curriculum areas, and promote the value of scholarship;

3c. demonstrate an understanding of and take responsibility for promoting high standards of literacy, articulacy and the correct use of standard English, whatever the teacher's specialist subject.

KEY QUESTIONS

- What does greater depth writing at KS2 look like?
- How can writing at greater depth be achieved?
- Which genres of writing lend themselves to developing deeper writing?
- How can we extend more able to pupils in their writing?
- How does modelling writing aid children in becoming greater depth writers?

Introduction

In order to teach children how to write at greater depth effectively, we must encourage independence in writing. Scaffolding is essential to give children the tools necessary to become a writer, but to find an individual written voice, this has to come from the child. When we scaffold writing techniques such as using figurative language, correct use of punctuation, varied sentence openers and all of the other strategies that lead towards effective writing, we are empowering children in their writing. Scaffolding is something that all teachers must model effectively in order to lead children towards independence.

This chapter will explore how modelling writing and scaffolding techniques lead the way towards independence. We will examine effective lessons that have led to writing towards greater depth and achieved greater depth writing. Through the use of books, websites, film and a lot of discussion, we will look at what works best to achieve the best writing possible. We will also examine which genre of writing is the most effective. The DfE (2018) showcases these genres in writing: Short Story, Description, Explanation, Newspaper Report, Diary and Letter writing. They give samples of a range of Year 6 pupils' writing, including one who is named 'Frankie'. The document states that these examples of Frankie's writing have been selected as they draw upon a wide range of this pupil's writing. It goes on to state the following.

Working at greater depth

The pupil can:

- write effectively for a range of purposes and audiences, selecting the appropriate form and drawing independently on what they have read as models for their own writing (e.g. literary language, characterisation, structure);
- distinguish between the language of speech and writing and choose the appropriate register;
- exercise an assured and conscious control over levels of formality, particularly through manipulating grammar and vocabulary to achieve this;
- use the range of punctuation taught at Key Stage 2 correctly (e.g. semi-colons, dashes, colons, hyphens) and, when necessary, use such punctuation precisely to enhance meaning and avoid ambiguity.

(DfE, 2018)

Frankie's writing is annotated throughout the document and it is made clear that a range of writing has been used to show evidence of greater depth writing. Greater depth cannot be ascertained through individual pieces of writing as a selection of writing is needed. However, in this chapter, we will look at individual lessons that can be replicated or adapted in the classroom that lead to a range of greater depth writing in KS2. The writing can be examined against the criteria needed to achieve working at greater depth, as is demonstrated with Frankie's work.

Frankie: evidence check

The following tables show how Frankie's work has met the 'pupil can' statements across the collection for 'working at greater depth within the expected standard'.

There is no expectation for teachers to produce such tables, or anything similar. These simply help to illustrate where Frankie's work has demonstrated the 'pupil can' statements in these six examples. As stated in the framework guidance, individual pieces of work should not be assessed against the framework.

Frankie: evidence check

The following tables show how Frankie's work has met the 'pupil can' statements across the collection for 'working at greater depth within the expected standard'.

There is no expectation for teachers to produce such tables, or anything similar. These simply help to illustrate where Frankie's work has demonstrated the 'pupil can' statements in these 6 examples.

As stated in the framework guidance, individual pieces of work should not be assessed against the framework.

End-of-Key stage 2 statutory assessment – working at greater depth within the expected standard							
Name: Frankie	A	B	C	D	E	F	Collection
The pupil can:	Narrative	Description	Explanation	Newspaper report	Diary	Letter	
• write effectively for a range of purposes and audiences, selecting the appropriate form and drawing independently on what they have read as models for their own writing (e.g. literary language, characterisation, structure)	✓	✓	✓	✓	✓	✓	✓
• distinguish between the language of speech and writing and choose the appropriate register	✓	n/a	n/a	✓	✓	✓	✓
• exercise an assured and conscious control over levels of formality, particularly through manipulating grammar and vocabulary to achieve this	✓	✓	✓	✓	✓	✓	✓
• use the range of punctuation taught at key stage 2 accurately (e.g. semi-colons, dashes, colons and hyphens) and, when necessary, use such punctuation precisely to enhance meaning and avoid ambiguity.	✓	✓	✓	✓	✓	✓	✓
(No additional statements for spelling or handwriting)							

Figure 4.1   DfE's end of Key Stage 2 statuary assessment grid
Source: DfE (2018)

Writing at greater depth in KS2 needs to meet the criteria above, but must also meet the criteria necessary for working towards and within the expected standard. The lessons and the writing within this chapter explore how this can achieved in a realistic way, but also with activities that make the whole process enjoyable. When children are interested in what they are writing about, this can aid the writing process significantly.

Descriptions using 'show but don't tell'

Anton Chekhov is quoted on many websites to have said, 'Don't tell me the moon is shining; show me the glint of light on broken glass.' However, this is an interpretation and abbreviation of the real quotation that comes from a letter that Chekhov wrote to his brother Alexander in May 1886 when he offered advice on how to become a successful writer:

In descriptions of Nature one must seize on small details, grouping them so that when the reader closes his eyes he gets a picture. For instance, you'll have a moonlit night if you write that on the mill dam a piece of glass from a broken bottle glittered like a bright little star, and that the black shadow of a dog or a wolf rolled past like a ball.

(Chekhov, 1959, p. 14)

When using figurative language such as similes, as in the letter from Chekhov, it is important that children do not overuse them. Two similes are used to describe both light and darkness, creating an oxymoron. The feeling of the light that glitters is in stark contrast to the black shadow that sinisterly rolls past. Often children overuse descriptive techniques when they first discover them. However, when writing at greater depth, it is important that children learn to use more subtle approaches. Children need to be given examples of overuse in order to understand when they are using too much description or when they are relying too heavily upon a particular form of description.

Telling when describing is something that children do when they are becoming independent writers. They might describe a character as feeling scared or happy. As they develop their writing, instead of telling how the characters are feeling, they use descriptions where the character may have goose-bumps and be staring breathlessly with wide eyes, thus showing fear, or that the character's heart skipped a beat as the smile constantly widened, thus showing happiness.

If children are describing a blood-soaked battlefield, instead of telling the reader that there was the taste of blood in the air, they could show that there was blood by describing a metal tang taste. The suggestion of blood is there without being explicitly described. This is what greater depth children will do without being asked. They instinctively insert those descriptions.

The case study below shows a group of children writing descriptions of a forest. The teacher wanted the children to use figurative language techniques previously learnt, but also wanted the children not to overuse them. He discussed the term 'show but don't tell' and encouraged the children to do this in their writing.

CASE STUDY

YEAR 3 CLASS WRITING FOREST DESCRIPTIONS

Charlie, a Year 3 teacher, was reviewing the figurative language his class had been learning about throughout the term. The children had covered similes, personification, metaphor and alliteration. He brought up a Fantasy Name Generator website that also generates vast and varied descriptions from flags to personalities to weapons and also forests. The website's first forest description was:

The forest was humble, bright, and budding. Its canopy was competed for by cedar, larch, and birch, sufficient twinkling lights burst through their crowns for a medley of shrubs to rule the thick layer of leaves below.

(Continued)

(Continued)

Coiling branches clung to most trees, and a medley of flowers, which claimed quiet corners, adorned the otherwise brown backdrop.

A variety of wild noises, most belonged to bird songs, filled the air, and almost completely muffled the occasional splashes of frogs jumping in the nearby lake.

He then selected 'Get a Description' and a second appeared:

The forest was far-reaching, spacious, and ancient. Its canopy was claimed by hickory, cottonwood, and chestnut, and ample openings let enough dancing beams of light through for a motley of plants to cultivate the rich grounds below.

Bundled climbing plants clung to a couple of trees, and a hodgepodge of flowers, which were common to this area only, added colourful variety to the otherwise green view.

A discord of sounds, belonging mostly to birds and vermin, echoed in the air, and were in harmony with the sounds of a fight over dominance between larger animals.

Every time Charlie clicked on 'Get a Description' a new three-paragraph description appeared. Each description followed a pattern of three adjectives in the first sentence, then light from the canopy in the second sentence, then the branches, which mostly used personification in the third, and finally sounds from animals in the fourth.

Charlie explained that the class were going to follow this same pattern of writing, but that he wanted them to include other figurative language descriptions and not just personification. He wrote on the board: 'The groaning trees were withered white witches that whispered in the wind.' Then Charlie asked the class what type of figurative language he had used. Most said alliteration, but one or two children noticed the metaphor and personification at the beginning of the sentence where the trees were witches.

Charlie asked the class if this was a good description and the class nodded as one. He then highlighted the words that began with 'w' and asked the question again. One child pointed out that there were five 'w' words. Charlie asked how many times were they allowed to use alliteration and class chorused 'three'. He reminded the children that using figurative language such as similes, personification, metaphor and alliteration was *showing* the reader what the forest was like and not just *telling* the reader. He gave examples of these, such as descriptions like 'the branches flung fireworks into the sky bursting with colour' instead of 'Autumn leaves were on the branches' or 'the falling leaves were fragile creatures that crumbled onto the forest floor' instead of 'the leaves were dry and crunchy'.

Charlie wrote on the board:

The forest was _____, _____ and _____ .

Its canopy was _____ .

The sounds of _____ were _____ .

He asked his lower ability children to use the sentence starters on the board, his middle ability children to also use them but to include any figurative language descriptions that they could think of.

While the rest of the class were busy writing, Charlie worked with a group of four children identified as working towards greater depth. He showed these greater depth children some writing that Year 6 had produced who also described forests. Tia, a Year 6 pupil, had written: 'I can blow you off your path. The trees dance to my soft blow as you try to walk past. You approach me so angrily and with power I push you, pull you and drag you through the mud. Whoosh! I am in control because I am the wind!'

Charlie asked the children if they guessed that it was the wind that was talking during the description and they had not until the end. He read it again and the four children discussed what they like and didn't like about it. Charlie then read a description which Luke, a Year 6 pupil, had written:

'I am an assassin. I will kill in this old, bushy forest. My heart is racing just like a super car. Everything just keeps going faster and faster. Suddenly, the car stops. Air is muted, everything still. Not a peep is heard. My sweat is my fear, just dripping down my spine. I tense all of my muscles, take aim on my target; he doesn't know what will hit him. I don't use a gun, just my fearful claws. I pounce on my prey. He is dead. I munch on his insides, so tasty he is. He was a lion and I am a dragon.'

The teacher asked the four children if they knew what the assassin was before it was revealed at the end. They animatedly talked to each other about the techniques used in both descriptions.

Charlie then asked them to write a forest description in any way they wanted to. Three children wrote from different perspectives and one wrote a straightforward forest description. The three children who used their own perspectives took Tia and Luke's ideas as stimulus, but added their own ideas too. One child wrote as if they were a leaf that had fallen to the forest floor, another child wrote as if they were a tree and the third child wrote from the perspective of a spider.

Throughout their writing activity, Charlie reminded the whole class to show him the forest through their words and not just tell him what was there. The class worked in mixed ability talk partners at the end of the lesson and shared their writing with each other.

The teacher in the case study above used advanced and technical vocabulary throughout the lesson for a Year 3 class, but the children were used to the terminology as they had been learning about figurative language and 'show and don't tell' methods for describing throughout the term as an ongoing learning objective. The Fantasy Name Generator can also be used for further writing opportunities, as in the activity below.

ACTIVITY 1   DESCRIPTION GENERATORS ON THE FANTASY NAME GENERATOR WEBSITE

Go to the bottom of the Home Page on www.fantasynamegenerators.com.
   Use the Description Generator to select what you want the children to describe and click on the title. Consider:

- What pattern does each description follow? What sentence starters are always used? Which of your five senses will the children include in their descriptions?
- How can you enhance these descriptions to include figurative language? What types of figurative language do you want the children to include?

Above the Description Generator is Other Generators, which include a Haiku Creator, Riddle Generator and Slogan Generator.

- What generator will you use to help your class describe something? How will you use it?
- How will you use the structure offered? How can the descriptions be improved?

FOCUS ON RESEARCH

Scaffolding and modelling writing is something that we as teachers will inevitably do. Encouraging children to become greater depth writers does not mean that we can no longer do this.
   According to the DfE (2018, p. 13) in the KS2 teacher assessment guidance:

A piece of writing may provide evidence of a pupil demonstrating some 'pupil can' statements independently, but not others. For example, a pupil may produce an independent piece of writing which meets many of the statements relating to composition and the use of grammar, but they did not demonstrate independent spelling where the teacher has provided the pupil with domain specific words or corrected their spelling. This does not mean that the entire piece is not independent.

As long as the children have used their own ideas and developed what we have modelled, then this is still independent writing and can still be described as greater depth writing, as long as the writing meets the criteria necessary and the criteria is consistent throughout the whole piece of work.

Writing food descriptions

From squiggly spaghetti in *The Twits* to doughnuts and goose livers in *Fantastic Mr Fox*, food features in all of Roald Dahl's children's books. The author's widow, Felicity Dahl, wrote a selection of tales and recipes called titled *Memories With Food at Gipsy House*. This book has since been renamed *Roald Dahl's Cookbook*. She also completed his unfinished recipe book, *Roald Dahl's Revolting Recipes*. In the Introduction, she explains that food was important to the author. His books also appear to carry lessons that we can learn through food. For example, in *Charlie and the Chocolate Factory*, we are warned of the dangers of excessive eating through the character Augustus Gloop. In *George's Marvellous Medicine*, George seeks to fix his grandma's horrid ways by making her a potion that is intended to make her good. In *The BFG*, the giant declares that snozzcumbers are *one extremely icky-poo veggitible*, before concluding that *veggitibles are very good for you!* He goes on to tell Sophie all of the reasons why she needs to eat vegetables. Food seemed to be an inspiration to Dahl and we can use it to be an inspiration for writing in the classroom.

A model we can use for food descriptions can be taken from Marks & Spencer's advertisements. In 2005, Marks & Spencer released an advert for their chocolate pudding narrated by Dervla Kirwan. It included the line, *This is not just a chocolate pudding, this is a Marks & Spencer chocolate pudding*, and sales of the pudding went up by 3,500 per cent. The company then continued to use the same format in its advertising, riding on the success of the chocolate pudding. In 2014, Marks & Spencer's executive director of marketing, Patrick Bousquet-Chavanne, said their advertising showcased *the sensual and surprising aspects of food – like its textures and movement – in a modern, stylish and precision format.* It seems to be how the food is described that makes the adverts and subsequent sales so successful.

In the case study below, the teacher uses two Marks & Spencer adverts with descriptions like *hand prepared turkey with apple and sage stuffing wrapped in maple cured bacon* and *melt in the middle Belgian chocolate pudding served with extra thick Channel Island cream.* The children first improve these descriptions with adjectives, verbs and adverbs, then write their own descriptions of their favourite food.

CASE STUDY

YEAR 5 CLASS WRITING FOOD DESCRIPTIONS

Tom, a Year 5 teacher, downloaded the *Letters from the Lighthouse Scheme of Work* (2017) from the TES website. The resources were created by a user known as boothy380. The class had only read up to Chapter 1 of the book and Tom reread an extract from the first page:

> *'It's like brains,' Cliff, my eight year old brother said, lifting the pan lid to show us. It was probably only minced meat and potatoes, but you never knew with Mum's dinners, especially the ones you had to reheat when she was working late.*

Tom asked the children to describe the food that was like brains. He scribed their answers on the board. He then read another extract on the second page:

> *But we had to eat the horrid supper, of course. No one checked food away with a war on, not even stuff that resembled brains.*

Tom then asked the children to write their own descriptions of the 'horrid supper' on whiteboards. The class watched an extract from the movie *Hook* where the Lost Boys in Neverland enjoy an imaginary feast. Robin Williams looks on amazed as the empty bowls, plates and pots are scooped up and devoured. He uses his imagination and a sumptuous feast appears of all of his favourite food.

Tom then asked the class what their favourite food was. An animated discussion took place describing pizzas, burgers and a whole range of desserts. The class were given circle planners, and first nouns and adjectives, then verbs and adverbs. They were asked to add three metaphors and choose three of their five senses. Once this was completed, the children were encouraged to magpie ideas from each other by moving around the class and reading other children's circle planners. They could only magpie three things.

Liam, a Year 5 pupil working towards greater depth writing, produced a particularly detailed circle planner.

Liam then went on to copy the quote from the first page of *Letters from the Lighthouse* into his book and continued the narrative in a different way from the book. He imagined a feast and described the food using his circle planner. Tom explained to the class that they did not have to include all their planning and could add anything new they wanted to.

The children shared their work in pairs and discussed what they like about each other's writing. Tom then asked his class to imagine that they were Olive from *Letters From The Lighthouse* and write a tweet about their imaginary food experience in no more than 140 characters including spaces and punctuation (in the style of Twitter when it was first launched).

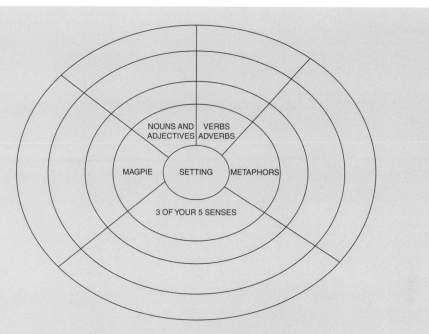

Figure 4.2   Circle planner sheet

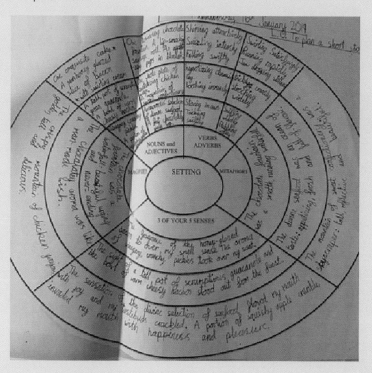

Figure 4.3   Y5 pupil's completed circle planner sheet

(Continued)

(Continued)

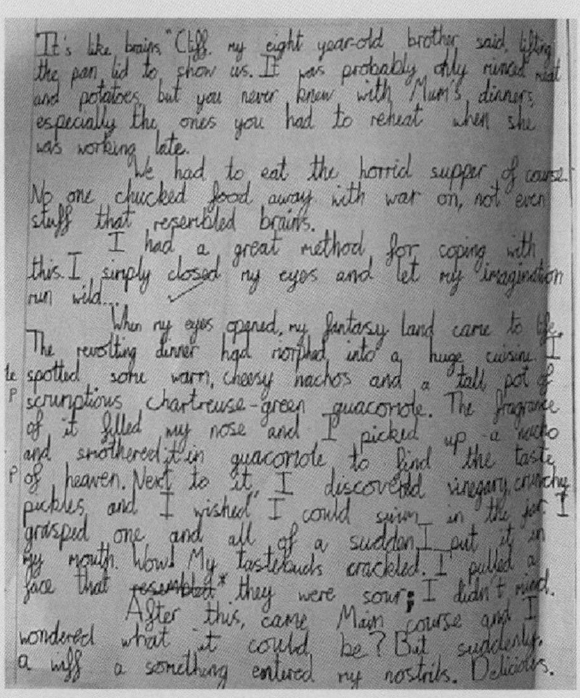

"It's like brains." Cliff, my eight year-old brother said, lifting the pan lid to show us. It was probably only minced meat and potatoes but you never knew with Mum's dinners, especially the ones you had to reheat when she was working late.

We had to eat the horrid supper of course. No one chucked food away with war on, not even stuff that resembled brains.

I had a great method for coping with this. I simply closed my eyes and let my imagination run wild...

When my eyes opened, my fantasy land came to life. The revolting dinner had morphed into a huge cuisine. I spotted some warm, cheesy nachos and a tall pot of scrumptious chartreuse-green guacamole. The fragrance of it filled my nose and I picked up a nacho and smothered it in guacamole to find the taste of heaven. Next to it, I discovered vinegary, crunchy pickles and I wished I could swim in the jar. I grasped one and all of a sudden I put it in my mouth. Wow! My tastebuds crackled. I pulled a face that ~~resembled~~* they were sour; I didn't mind.

After this, came Main course and I wondered what it could be? But suddenly, a whiff a something entered my nostrils. Delicious.

Figure 4.4 Y5 pupil's completed work

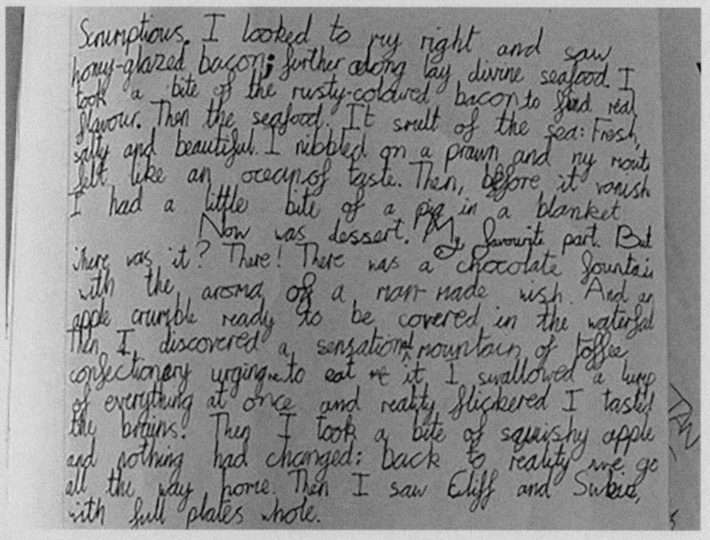

Scrumptious. I looked to my right and saw honey-glazed bacon; further along lay divine seafood. I took a bite of the rusty-coloured bacon to find real flavour. Then the seafood. It smelt of the sea: Fresh, salty and beautiful. I nibbled on a prawn and my mouth felt like an ocean of taste. Then, before it vanish I had a little bite of a pig in a blanket.

Now was dessert. My favourite part. But where was it? There! There was a chocolate fountain with the aroma of a man-made wish. And an apple crumble ready to be covered in the waterfall. Then I discovered a sensational mountain of toffee confectionery urging to eat it. I swallowed a lump of everything at once and reality flickered I tasted the brains! Then I took a bite of squishy apple and nothing had changed: back to reality we go all the way home. Then I saw Cliff and Sukie, with full plates whole.

Figure 4.5 Y5 pupil's completed work continued

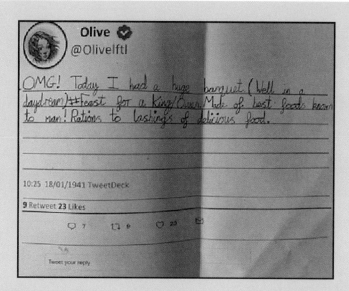

Figure 4.6   Y5 pupil's 'tweet'

Liam was not working at greater depth at this time, but he was working towards great depth. In order to help Liam become a greater depth writer, Tom encouraged his pupil to write in the style of his favourite authors; to edit, adapt and improve his own writing, particularly focusing on structure, characterisation, and using a range of punctuation, but also to read as often as possible a wide range of books. He also discussed how best to show shifts in formality within Liam's writing and how his pupil could keep a sustained level of formality when appropriate to the genre.

ACTIVITY 2   WRITING TV ADVERTS

Show the children the Marks & Spencer advert for their 'Best Ever Burger' from 2018: www.youtube.com/watch?v=qwpxM3mE7is

- What would go into their 'best ever burger'? Would it be chicken, beef or meat-free? What else would go into the burger? What bread would they use?
- Can the children create an advert of their own for a new product? What product will they design and advertise? What language will be used?
- What other TV adverts can be used in this same way? What other recipes could be written? Other than persuasive writing, explanations and instructions linked to recipes, what other writing opportunities are there inspired by this advert?

FOCUS ON RESEARCH

The KS2 teacher assessment guidance from 2018 makes it explicitly clear that writing must be created independently, but that the planning stages can be guided by teachers and peers. It states:

Pupils' writing upon which teachers base their judgements must be produced independently. The national curriculum is clear that writing should also be produced through discussion with the teacher and peers.

(DfE, 2018, p. 13)

The assessment guidance goes on to show:

Writing is likely to be independent if it:

- emerges from a text, topic, visit, or curriculum experience in which pupils have had opportunities to discuss and rehearse what is to be written about
- enables pupils to use their own ideas and provides them with an element of choice, for example writing from the perspective of a character they have chosen themselves
- has been edited, if required, by the pupil without the support of the teacher, although this may be in response to self, peer, or group evaluation
- is produced by pupils who have, if required, sought out classroom resources, such as dictionaries or thesauruses, without prompting to do so by the teacher

Writing is not independent if it has been:

- modelled or heavily scaffolded
- copied or paraphrased
- edited as a result of direct intervention by a teacher or other adult, for example when the pupil has been directed to change specific words for greater impact, where incorrect or omitted punctuation has been indicated, or when incorrectly spelt words have been identified by an adult for the pupil to correct
- produced with the support of electronic aids that automatically provide correct spelling, synonyms, punctuation, or predictive text
- supported by detailed success criteria that specifically direct pupils as to what to include, or where to include it, in their writing, such as directing them to include specific vocabulary, grammatical features, or punctuation

(DfE, 2018, p. 14)

Therefore, as long as the editing to improve a piece of writing has been done independently by the child, this can still be more evidence of writing at greater depth.

Dialogue within short narrative stories

Story-writing is perhaps among one of the best ways to achieve examples of writing at a greater depth, as pupils can consciously control the narrative themselves and make many varied vocabulary and grammar choices throughout. Shifts in formality can be clear and strong when reflected through dialogue. Characterisation changes and shifts in plot can also be revealed using devices such as dialogue, but not in an excessive way. A greater depth writer uses this technique in a controlled manner, mindful of the reader audience, but this has to be done independently. Scaffolded writing is essential to model the tools necessary for independent writing, but when it comes to greater depth writing, it is the child that selects their own form and content.

By revealing character through dialogue, children can show what others think of a particular character, reveal past events and show personality in subtle ways that show the reader only what the author wants them to know at that time. Greater depth writers make this consistent throughout the story. The more children read this technique in books, the more this empowers them to mimic it themselves, but in their own style.

The DfE (2018, p. 6) states in the teacher assessment exemplification:

> Greater depth pupils can write effectively for a range of purposes selecting the appropriate form and drawing independently on what they have read as models for their own writing.

So, by reading more, children's writing improves and moves them towards being greater depth writers. It is important that children read a range of books, however, so that they do not just mimic their favourite authors alone, but rather practise a variety of techniques.

Herts for Learning English team (Hodgson, 2018) recommend that when writing at greater depth, it is important to ADD LO(v)E:

Audience and purpose

Derived from reading and

Developed through spoken language

Levels of formality

Organisation

Vocabulary

Variation of sentence structures to suit purpose

Editing for accuracy and enhancement

This seems a good model to follow when assessing children who are working towards greater depth. In the case study below, a Year 6 teacher encourages independent ideas and writing based around their Second World War topic that leads to examples of greater depth writing.

CASE STUDY

YEAR 6 CLASS WRITING INDEPENDENTLY

Debra is one of three Year 6 teachers at a mainstream primary school. The children are not streamed and work in mixed-ability classes. Their autumn term topic was the Second World War and they had been studying this as a cross-curricular subject. In English, the children had written non-chronological reports, descriptions of London during the Blitz, and narrative stories around evacuees.

Debra introduced the Holocaust to the children by sharing the picture books *Rose Blanche* by Ian McEwan and *Erika's Story* by Ruth Vander Zee. Both books are illustrated by Roberto Innocenti. *Rose Blanche* is about a girl called Rose and her observations of all the changes going on around her as her home town is occupied by Nazi soldiers and *Erika's Story* is set in Nazi-occupied Europe where a Jewish couple realise their fate is sealed and make a heart-rending decision so that their infant daughter might live.

Debra went on to discuss concentration camps and showed the children the BBC drone video exploring the camp as it is today. She then showed them a PowerPoint presentation online that described what led to such genocide. This led to a lengthy discussion about how hate can escalate to murder.

Images of Auschwitz were then shared and Debra answered the children's questions. Fact files were then written by the children about Auschwitz.

In the following lesson, Debra asked the children what they would do if they were in a Nazi-occupied country during the Second World War. She showed the children the propaganda film made by the Nazis to persuade Jewish people to voluntarily leave the ghettos they had been forced to live in and take the trains to the camps. In the film, it shows the camp of Terezin in the Czech Republic. The Nazis had sent thousands of inmates from Terezin to Auschwitz so that the camp looked less crowded. The living quarters were made to look comfortable and the bunks were two-tiered rather than the reality of three-tiered bunks. The women in the film looked well fed and happy, unlike the horror of what the conditions were really like. Debra explained that the Nazis used films like this to persuade people to voluntarily take the trains to the camps.

Debra then asked the children if they would have taken the train. She asked them if they would have believed the Nazis. She then posed the questions, 'What if you were Jewish? Or a traveller? Or gay? What would you do?'. She explained that the Nazis persecuted all of these people and more.

This sparked animated discussions. The class concluded that the people would have had four options, which Debra wrote on the board. These were:

1.   Take the train.
2.   Fight against the Nazis.
3.   Try to leave the country.
4.   Go into hiding.

She asked the children to decide which option they would have chosen. None put their hands up for taking the train; a lot of boys put their hands up for fighting; most of the rest of the class selected that they would want to leave the country, and a few chose to go into hiding.

Debra explained that most people chose to take the trains as they hoped life would be better at the camps than life in the ghettos. She also explained that some, however, did choose to fight and these were known as Partisans. She told the children that to leave the country you might have needed to be rich in order to bribe your way out. She then asked the children if they knew of anyone that lived in a Nazi-occupied country that had tried to hide. Some children nodded and answered that they had heard of a book about Anne Frank. This introduced the new class text of *The Diary of a Young Girl* by Anne Frank, which they would look at the following day.

The children went on to write explanation texts about what they would choose to do if they were forced to leave the ghetto in a Nazi-occupied country during the Second World War. The next day, after sharing the opening chapter to Anne Frank's diary, Debra asked the class to write a first-person narrative that recounted the life of someone who lived through the Holocaust. They could write this in any way they wished. She modelled an opening paragraph about a person describing their journey to the train station as they left the ghetto. She included descriptive sentences about how this person was feeling. This writing was edited and improved over several further lessons. The writing was then shared in talk partners at the end of each lesson.

Most of the class chose to write the same thing that their teacher had modelled. However, three children chose to write in a different way. One child wrote about a real person named Michael Pawlak after doing some research on Holocaust survivors on the BBC website and reading about him the night before. Another child wrote a diary entry in the style of Anne Frank, but instead of writing to her diary 'Kitty', as she does in her book, the child wrote to an undertaker with the instruction 'only to be read at my funeral'. The third child wrote a case file for a missing person. All three of these children chose put their own interpretation on the activity they were given. It is this individuality in writing that is what leads to greater depth writing.

ACTIVITY 3   *ONCE* BY MORRIS GLEITZMAN

Read the children the opening chapter to *Once*, which describes Felix's life in an orphanage during the Nazi occupation of Poland. The text is written in the first person and is written in the way a child would speak.

- How can this text inspire first-person narratives? What techniques does the author employ to describe the horror of the time? In what way is humour used? Why does the narrator ask the reader questions?

(Continued)

(Continued)

- Can the children mimic the style written? What other settings could be described? The ghetto? Auschwitz?
- How is Mother Minka described? What characters can be included in first-person narratives of this style?

FOCUS ON RESEARCH

WHAT DOES THE DFE SUGGEST?

If children have a particular weakness that affects the overall quality of their work, this can be considered by the teacher when making a judgement on greater depth writing. Children should meet all of the required 'pupil can' statements, but the 2018 teacher assessment guidance does say that teachers can use *a more flexible approach – teachers can now use their discretion to ensure that, on occasion, a particular weakness does not prevent an accurate judgement of a pupil's overall attainment being made* (DfE, 2018, p. 5).

The guidance goes on to say:

A particular weakness may well relate to a specific learning difficulty, but it is not limited to this. In addition, a specific learning difficulty does not automatically constitute a particular weakness which would prevent an accurate judgement. The same overall standard must be applied equally to all pupils.

(DfE, 2018, p. 13)

So children with dyslexia, for example, who find spelling an area of difficulty still need to meet the spelling and handwriting criteria. However, if there are occasional mistakes in certain pieces of work, this can be taken into consideration.

Conclusion

Independent, individual writing with unique ideas is what greater depth looks like in Key Stage 2. When children show a shift in formality and this is done effortlessly, they are showing clear signs of working at greater depth. As we stated in Chapter 1, greater depth writers manipulate grammar and vocabulary for effect and do so with assured and conscious control. These children draw on the style of the authors they read. They do this independently, but do not rely on a particular technique all of the time, but rather use a whole range of different techniques for a wide range of audiences and for a wide range of purposes. Children select their own form and use it with flair.

According to Ros Ferrara (2017):

> *The children who are judged to be writing at greater depth are children who stand out as writers. They are the children who take our breath away when we read their texts. There will not be many of these children and the number will vary from cohort to cohort. Whilst we cannot "teach" children to be greater depth writers, we can most certainly offer them opportunities, choices and ensure that any technical aspects of writing are secure and their use understood.*

(Ferrara, 2017, p. 1)

In order to achieve this, however, we as teachers still need to model and scaffold writing, as by doing this we are giving children guidance to help them to grow into the writers that we know they have the potential to become. A range of genres need to be explored, since no one genre works better than another. All genres could potentially show that a writer is working at greater depth. It is the individual choice of the child. Our role is to help these children to find their own unique written voice.

Special thanks

Tia Orton and Luke Wilson from Year 6 in Thornley Primary School.
Liam Taylor from Year 5 in St Thomas More RCVA Primary School.
Tom Hunt from St Thomas More RCVA Primary School.
Debra Ridley from New Silksworth Academy.

Recommended websites

BBC drone video of Auschwitz – www.youtube.com/watch?v=449ZOWbUkf0 (accessed 15 February 2019).
Holocaust PowerPoint – https://slideplayer.com/slide/7850900/ (accessed 25 February 2019).
Hook 'Use Your Imagination' – www.youtube.com/watch?v=uPCzjHPS--U (accessed 27 January 2019).
Letter from the Lighthouse resources – www.tes.com/teaching-resource/letters-from-the-lighthouse-scheme-of-work-11663723 (accessed 15 February 2019).
Marks & Spencer's 'Best Ever Burger' – www.youtube.com/watch?v=qwpxM3mE7is (accessed 27 January 2019).
Michael Pawlak's story – www.bbc.co.uk/history/ww2peopleswar/stories/69/a4823769.shtml (accessed15 February 2019).
Terezin propaganda film
www.youtube.com/watch?v=TmIPNktUeoI (accessed15 February 2019).

References

Carroll, E. (2017) *Letters from the Lighthouse*. London: Faber & Faber.
Chekhov, A. (1959) *The Unknown Chekhov: Stories and Other Writings Hitherto Untranslated by Anton Chekhov*. Translated with an Introduction by Avrahm Yarmolinsky. New York: Noonday Press.

Dahl, R. (2016) *The Twits*. London: Puffin.

Dahl, R. (2016) *Fantastic Mr Fox*. London: Puffin.

Dahl, R. (2016) *Charlie and the Chocolate Factory*. London: Puffin.

Dahl, R. (2016) *George's Marvellous Medicine*. London: Puffin.

Dahl, R. (2016) *BFG*. London: Puffin.

Dahl, R. and Dahl, F. (1996) *Roald Dahl's Cookbook*. London: Penguin.

Dahl, R. (1996) *Revolting Recipes*. London: Red Fox.

Department for Education (DfE) (2018) *Key Stage 2 Teacher Assessment Exemplification Materials. English Writing: Working at Greater Depth Within the Expected Standard: Frankie*. Available online at: https://assets.publishing.service.gov.uk/government/uploads/system/uploads/attachment_data/file/655619/2018_exemplification_materials_KS2-GDS__Frankie_.pdf (accessed 26 January 2019).

Ferrara, R. (2017) *Writing at Greater Depth: Providing a Pathway for Able Writers*. Saddleworth: Focus Education.

Frank, A. (2007) *The Diary of a Young Girl: Definitive Edition*. London: Penguin.

Glietzman, M. (2006) *Once*. London: Puffin.

Hodgson, C. (2018) *10 key updates for 2018 KS2 writing assessment*. Herts for Learning: Hertfordshire. Available online at: www.hertsforlearning.co.uk/blog/10-key-updates-2018-ks2-writing-assessment (accessed 27 January 2019).

McEwan, I. (2004) *Rose Blanche*. London: Red Fox.

Ridley, L. (2014) *Marks And Spencer Is Bringing Back Its Food Porn Adverts. Huffington Post*. Available online at: www.huffingtonpost.co.uk/2014/09/02/marks-and-spencer-food-pudding-advert-this-is-not-just-any_n_5751628.html?guccounter=1&guce_referrer_us=aHR0cHM6Ly93d3cuZ29vZ2xlLmNvLn VrLw&guce_referrer_cs=WOGp30_XrRv9amSMYe8yGA (accessed 27 January 2019).

Zee, R. (2013) *Erika's Story*. London: Creative Paperbacks.

5
DEVELOPING UNDERSTANDING OF LANGUAGE AND DEEPER WRITING

David Waugh

KEY QUESTIONS

- How can we help children to gain a deeper understanding of language to enable them to vary their language and make use of a range of literary devices to enhance their writing?
- How can we develop children's vocabularies to enable them to produce deeper and more varied writing?

Introduction

Brien (2012, p. 152) has argued that 'a school should be a place where a love of language oozes out of the woodwork'. This chapter will emphasise the importance of engaging children with language and will focus on some of the prerequisites for developing deeper writing, including vocabulary, both within children's writing and for discussing writing. The *Oxford Language Report: Why Closing the Word Gap Matters* (2018) illustrates the problem of children having narrow vocabularies and asserts that 'Over half the teachers surveyed reported that at least 40% of their pupils lacked the vocabulary to access their learning' (p. 2). The chapter will discuss the challenges involved in expanding vocabulary in order to enable children to write at a deeper level, and will consider strategies for developing children's vocabularies. It will also examine the place of spelling, handwriting and grammatical knowledge in developing children's writing.

As you saw in Chapter 1, Roach (2018) identifies three key indicators of greater depth writing: concision (which involves planning and self-editing), punctuation for effect, and evidence that high-quality literature has influenced the writing styles. This chapter, therefore, will explore ways of developing knowledge and understanding about language, and will explore strategies for developing vocabulary through examples of good practice in the classroom.

Developing knowledge about language

There has long been a debate about the most effective way of developing children's knowledge about language and whether it is necessary for them to have an explicit understanding of grammatical features if they are to write well.

FOCUS ON RESEARCH

IS THERE VALUE IN DIRECT TEACHING OF GRAMMAR?

Bunting (2003) asserted:

> In terms of pedagogy, writing is controversial because of debates about what children need to know about language: the question is whether children need to know about the forms of the English language in order to be able to write, or whether knowledge about forms emerges through writing.
>
> (p. 17)

The value of discrete and decontextualised grammar lessons has long been questioned, most notably by Myhill, one of the authors of the SPaG element of the National Curriculum (see Myhill et al., 2011; Myhill et al., 2012). It is interesting, therefore, to note that Safford found that this had increased since the introduction of the SPaG test, but that teachers actually found that pupils enjoyed learning grammar.

As Myhill (2012, p. 22) points out, 'A writing curriculum that draws attention to the grammar of writing in an embedded and purposeful way at relevant points in the learning is a . . . positive way forward.' However, this may present a significant challenge for some teachers who had little experience of grammar teaching when they were pupils. In England, the introduction of a test on spelling, punctuation and grammar has added a further challenge for teachers and pupils.

Safford (2016) conducted 16 teacher interviews and an online survey of 170 teaching staff to

> *discuss their knowledge, understanding and enjoyment of grammar at their own level, and their skills for teaching pupils; they also discuss their observations of how pupils have responded to explicit grammar teaching and the grammar test*
>
> (p. 1)

Safford's conclusions are interesting. She found that:

1. since the introduction of the statutory SPaG test in primary schools, time spent teaching decontextualised and contextualised grammar has increased significantly;
2. grammar is now taught explicitly and formally as a classroom literacy routine;
3. the test format influences grammar teaching content and approaches;
4. teachers observe that pupils enjoy learning grammar and taking the test;
5. teachers disagree about the extent to which explicit grammar teaching and testing have a positive impact on pupils' language and literacy skills;
6. teachers feel more confident about teaching grammar.

Teachers' growing confidence about teaching grammar is reassuring, but there remains a controversy about the strategies that might be deployed. Gough and Tunmer (1986) and later Rose (2006) promoted a simple view of reading (SVOR), which would enable teachers to assess children's literacy needs. The SVOR's four quadrants represented progress in language comprehension and word recognition. A similar model for writing skills focuses on compositional skills and their transcriptional skills (Berninger et al., 2002). As with the SVOR, the model shows that some children will be good at both elements, while others may have accurate writing (good transcription) that might be unimaginative or not very engaging for readers (weaker compositional skills). Other children may produce interesting writing with inaccurate spelling, grammar and punctuation (good composition, weaker transcription), while yet others may be weak in both areas.

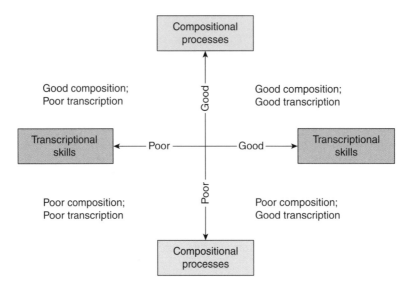

Figure 5.1   A simple view of writing

Source: Bevilacqua and Fenton (2009) PowerPoint presentation.

This model, as its name indicates, is simple and enables us to consider the key components of writing. It also prompts the question: 'How can we address children's weaknesses in writing so that we can help them to become good at both composition and transcription?'

FOCUS ON RESEARCH

ACHIEVING A BALANCE

Daffern et al. (2017, p. 10) maintained:

> One of the key challenges is to ensure instruction in spelling, grammar and punctuation are carefully balanced with other important aspects of written text creation, such as text structure, vocabulary usage and handwriting.

Daffern et al. looked at data from 819 Australian primary school pupils and found that spelling, grammar and punctuation jointly predict written composition achievement, with spelling as the main predictor.

Medwell and Wray (2007) emphasised the importance of developing legible and speedy handwriting and 'in particular the automaticity of letter production as this frees up working memory to deal with the complex tasks of planning, organizing, revising and regulating the production of text' (2007, pp. 11–12).

The importance of a balanced and integrated approach is emphasised in the National Curriculum:

> 6.1   *Teachers should develop pupils' spoken language, reading, writing and vocabulary as integral aspects of the teaching of every subject. English is both a subject in its own right and the medium for teaching; for pupils, understanding the language provides access to the whole curriculum. Fluency in the English language is an essential foundation for success in all subjects.*
>
> (DfE, 2013, p. 10)

Given the pressures they are under to help their pupils achieve good marks in the SPaG test, it is understandable that many resort to giving instructions such as 'include at least three fronted adverbials, two subordinate clauses and three semi colons in your writing'. This can produce rather artificial texts that are written to gain marks rather than to communicate in a meaningful way. The writing below followed lessons emphasising the importance of including fronted adverbials for SATs:

> *Recently, I went to summer camp! Cautiously, I stayed there for one week. Stupidly, I got expelled! Angrily, my dad would be mad. Would he ground me? Reluctantly, I tried sleep, but sadly, I couldn't!*

However, there is a value in children understanding ways of varying their writing to make it more interesting and there are clear benefits to them having a vocabulary with which to discuss language. Just as when discussing mathematical concepts we use a range of technical terms such as 'scalene', 'isosceles' and 'equilateral triangles' to enable us to communicate clearly what kind of geometrical shape we are referring to, it is also valuable to be able to use terms like 'adverbial', 'subordinate' and 'semi-colon'. While we may sometimes do this through discrete grammar lessons, often there are opportunities within other activities to develop children's knowledge about language in meaningful ways. The strategies described below illustrate some of these.

Simple strategies to develop knowledge about language and transcription skills

Read to children

This is perhaps the most valuable activity we can engage in if we want to broaden children's understanding of language and literacy. Many children start school having had extensive experience of having stories and poems told and read to them. They know how books work: they understand what the cover is, and that we start at the front and follow the story page by page. They are familiar with stories and story language, even if they are unable to read the words on the page. Sadly, some children do not have such fortunate experiences and their early experiences of reading at school can be challenging. As teachers, we need to ensure that all children are exposed to a broad and rich range of texts that they can enjoy and discuss. If we make stories engaging and exciting, we whet children's appetites for independent reading. We also provide a model for reading and can show how using expression and varying our voice can bring text to life. Children who struggle to read independently can discover what a book can 'sound' like and this can influence their own reading. Reading to children also provides lots of opportunities to talk about language and to discuss new words and phrases.

Reading dialogue

Children can be engaged in texts through taking part in reading them. By selecting passages of dialogue in which children can be assigned the roles of characters in a story, they can learn how to use punctuation to help them to read the actual words characters say (without the addition of 'said Jo', etc.) and how they might be spoken, for example, as exclamations or questions. As a shared reading activity, the whole class might read the text together, but pause when there is direct speech so that the characters can say their lines. This draws attention to speech marks and other punctuation as well as promoting discussion about vocabulary, including alternatives to 'said', helping prepare children to write their own dialogue.

Hot-seating

Inviting children to answer questions from classmates in the role of a character from a story promotes discussion and comprehension skills. It is also a good preparation for deeper writing, since it allows children to think more deeply about character traits and possible motivations for actions when writing their own stories. Hot-seating is most productive when children are given time to discuss and prepare questions before asking them. Richer written character descriptions can follow as children draw upon vocabulary and ideas from the question-and-answer session.

Conscience alley

This drama technique involves the class forming two lines between which a child in role walks slowly. One line of children promotes one course of action for the character, while the other line presents an alternative. Everyone can say whatever they like, and the character has to listen and then discuss what they would decide to do and why. Again, this probing of motivations promotes deeper writing when children go on to write stories.

Predictions

The power of leaving stories at exciting moments is well known to TV and film companies, as exemplified by thriller serials such as *Line of Duty* or *Killing Eve*, and all soap operas. This leads viewers to speculate about possible future events and to want to watch subsequent episodes. By leaving stories at cliff-hanging moments, teachers can invite children to predict what might happen next and, perhaps, to write their own version of events. Their engage-ment with a story and subsequent discussion can provide stimulation for deeper and more interesting writing (see, for example, the case study on Erin's writing later in this chapter).

Practise handwriting and keyboard skills

As Medwell and Wray (2007) have shown, automaticity in writing is important if children are to be able to get their ideas down quickly without worrying about the physical process of writ-ing. It is important, therefore, that we help children to develop a swift and legible style of handwriting and that they practise using it so that it flows. It is equally important that we teach keyboard skills. All schools have computers and many provide a tablet or laptop for every child, but often children's effective use of these devices is hampered by their weak keyboard skills.

Shared writing

By acting as a scribe and modelling the writing process for children, we can help them to understand how writers think and work. We can garner their ideas and turn these into coher-ent texts, all the time articulating our thoughts aloud: 'Oh, I need a capital letter here because that's his name. I'd like to use a more interesting word than "nice" – does anyone have any suggestions? That's three times I've used the verb "said" – can anyone suggest a synonym I might use?' The National Curriculum states that in Year 6 children should learn: 'The differ-ence between vocabulary typical of informal speech and vocabulary appropriate for formal speech and writing (e.g. said versus reported, alleged, or claimed in formal speech or writ-ing)' (DfE, 2013). Not only can we show how we write, but we can also make incidental and relevant use of terminology in a meaningful way. We can also show the strategies we use when we are unsure about spellings or phrasing.

ACTIVITY 1

Consider how you could use some of the techniques described above to create opportuni-ties to develop children's knowledge and understanding of language.

Developing vocabulary

This section will show what is required by the National Curriculum for vocabulary develop-ment and will exemplify, through examples of research, suggested teaching and learning strategies and case studies, how this can be achieved in the classroom. The National Curriculum emphasises the importance of developing children's vocabulary:

6.4   Pupils' acquisition and command of vocabulary are key to their learning and progress across the whole curriculum. Teachers should therefore develop vocabulary actively, building systematically on pupils' current knowledge. They should increase pupils' store of words in general; simultaneously, they should also make links between known and new vocabulary and discuss the shades of meaning in similar words. In this way, pupils expand the vocabulary choices that are available to them when they write. In addition, it is vital for pupils' comprehension that they understand the meanings of words they meet in their reading across all subjects, and older pupils should be taught the meaning of instruction verbs that they may meet in examination questions. It is particularly important to induct pupils into the language which defines each subject in its own right, such as accurate mathematical and scientific language.

(DfE, 2013, p. 11)

As you read the rest of this section, keep in mind the requirements above and two key elements which are highlighted in the National Curriculum:

- *Pupils' acquisition and command of vocabulary are key to their learning and progress across the whole curriculum. Teachers should therefore develop vocabulary actively, building systematically on pupils' current knowledge.*

- *They should increase pupils' store of words in general; simultaneously, they should also make links between known and new vocabulary and discuss the shades of meaning in similar words. In this way, pupils expand the vocabulary choices that are available to them when they write.*

(DfE, 2013)

In 2008, the Department for Children, Schools and Families (DCSF) produced guidance based upon research to help teachers address the needs of children who start school with limited vocabulary. The report cites key research, including the following:

Duke and Moses (2003) concluded that 'reading to children and getting children to read' themselves are the basis of vocabulary growth, together with engaging children in 'rich oral language' and *'encouraging reading and talk at home'*.

Duke and Moses (2003) also pointed to the effectiveness of *raising word consciousness* by playing with words through games, songs and humour, and encouraging children to recognise when they have encountered new words and notice special characteristics of words.

FOCUS ON RESEARCH

DEVELOPING VOCABULARY

In the USA, the National Reading Panel's review (2000) identified five basic approaches to vocabulary instruction that should be used together:

- *explicit instruction* (particularly of difficult words and words that are not part of pupils' everyday experience);

- *indirect instruction* (i.e. exposure to a wide range of reading materials);
- *multimedia methods* (going beyond the text to include other media such as visual stimulus, the use of the computer or sign language);
- *capacity methods* (focusing on making reading an automatic activity);
- *association methods* (encouraging learners to draw connections between what they do know and unfamiliar words).

Evidence from Apthorp (2006) supports and extends the National Reading panel's conclusions. She concluded that there was a solid evidence base supporting three key elements of vocabulary instruction:

- *defining and explaining* word meanings;
- arranging *frequent encounters* with new words (at least six exposures to a new word); and
- encouraging pupils' *deep and active processing* of words and meanings in a range of contexts.

Vocabulary in action

In Chapter 12, which focuses on classic texts, you will see how vocabulary can be developed and enhanced when context is provided, and when texts are discussed and read aloud. In both the preceding and the following research focuses, the value of hearing text is emphasised. You may recall studying a Shakespeare play at school and finding it difficult to understand when reading it, but you may also have been taken to a theatre or shown a film version and have been able to follow the plot and understand the language much more easily – we tend to understand when plays are performed better than when we read them independently. Vocabulary that is unfamiliar becomes comprehensible because someone else is reading or saying it, and is using expression and perhaps actions. Children access stories and language beyond their reading levels when they are read to and when they see performances. Dialogue makes more sense when we act it out, and when context and visual aids are provided.

FOCUS ON RESEARCH

THE IMPORTANCE OF READING IN VOCABULARY DEVELOPMENT

A study in the USA by Duff et al. (2015) found that a child's initial reading level would be positively related to his or her rate of growth in a reading skill. In other words, those who already had broad vocabularies developed their vocabularies at a faster rate than

(Continued)

(Continued)

those who did not. They discovered that 'fourth-grade reading-word skill was related to the rate of change in vocabulary growth between the fourth and 10th grades'.

Duff et al. concluded that their study provides:

strong support for the existence of a Matthew effect* between word-reading skill and vocabulary. It is significant that the magnitude of the effect on absolute vocabulary levels was found to be large. The effect seems to be driven by strong readers, rather than weak readers, an encouraging finding for those concerned about outcomes for weak readers. More broadly, these findings point to the importance of reading to the process of vocabulary acquisition in older children and adolescents.

(p. 10)

* often placed in situations where they gain more, and those who do not have advantages typically struggle to achieve more.

The problems faced by children with underdeveloped vocabularies are further highlighted by Tunmer and Chapman (2012, p. 457), who note:

Children with poorly developed vocabulary knowledge will have trouble identifying and assigning meanings to unknown printed words (especially partially decoded words, irregularly spelled words, or words containing polyphonic or orthographically complex spelling patterns), if the corresponding spoken words are not in their listening vocabulary.

Below, you will find examples of simple activities that you might use to engage children with vocabulary, all of which should support their understanding of language and help prepare them to write in greater depth.

Simple strategies for developing vocabulary

Provide word cards when reading

Prepare for reading aloud to children by making a set of vocabulary cards. These can include names of characters, as well as interesting nouns, verbs, adverbs and adjectives. Give at least one to each child and read from your list to see who has which word and to ensure everyone knows how to say his or her word. Explain that you will pause at different points in the story to ask whose word has come up. When you do this, ask children to talk about their word and its significance to the story: 'What kind of character? Who does the adjective describe?' etc. This activity not only focuses on vocabulary, but also leads to discussion about reading comprehension. A further development is to involve the children who have cards with the names of characters in reading or even acting out dialogue.

Collect synonyms

When reading a story, give children sheets of paper with pictures and/or names of characters on them, and ask them to write quick descriptions of the characters' moods and feeling at different points in the story. As a whole class activity, collect examples and write them on the board. Look for opportunities to link words together and to seek synonyms. For example, if a character is described as 'sad' and 'unhappy', ask if anyone can think of any other words with similar meanings. If none are forthcoming, tell the children you will start to sound a word you have thought of and that they can call out as soon as they think they know what it might be – for example, 'm . . . i . . . s . . . miserable'.

Add morphemes

When studying lists of words to spell – for example, those in the National Curriculum for Years 3–4 and Years 5–6, challenge children to modify the words by adding prefixes and/or suffixes. Almost all of the words in the lists can be modified. For example, the word 'develop', which appears in the Years 5–6 list could become: 'develops', 'developing', 'developed', 'developer', 'undeveloped', 'underdeveloped', 'redeveloped', and so on.

Discuss the words the children create and ask them to check in dictionaries to confirm that they exist. Talk about the meanings of different morphemes and how they are used. Not only does this activity support learning the spellings, but it also enables children to learn about how words work and how they can be modified to create new words.

Word windows

This activity can be used alongside other morpheme activities. You might create examples using a computer, but in its simplest form this activity involves stapling two pieces of card together, the top one of which will have three flaps numbered 1, 2 and 3. Cards with words with three morphemes (e.g. exported (ex-port-ed)) can be slotted between the stapled cards and teams take turns to choose a flap to open to reveal part of the hidden word. They then have to suggest as many words as they can which the word could possibly be. For example, if 'port' was revealed, they might suggest 'reported', 'deported', 'supported', 'reporting', etc. They then ask to reveal another morpheme by choosing another of the numbered flaps and make further suggestions as to what the word might be.

Magpie words

When children are writing independently, give them opportunities to pause and share what they have written with writing partners. Partners can give praise, make suggestions for improve-ments, and ask if they can 'magpie' some words or phrases to use in their own writing.

Word of the day

Have a 'word of the day' displayed, together with its definition and examples of its use in sentences and longer texts. Discuss the word and encourage children to use it orally and in writing. Once the idea is established, create a rota so that children take turns to provide the daily word.

ACTIVITY 2

Consider a text you are sharing with children. How could you use some of the techniques described above to create opportunities to develop children's oral and writing vocabularies?

Strategies in action

This section will draw on case studies to demonstrate how a deeper understanding of language can help to foster deeper writing.

CASE STUDY

DEVELOPING A NOVEL WITH YEAR 5 AND YEAR 6 CHILDREN

David was invited to work with a group of 12 Years 5–6 pupils in a school in the north-east of England over two terms, to help develop greater depth in their writing. The children had previously worked with David on activities related to his children's novels. To stimulate the children's writing, David wrote an opening chapter for a story called *Twins?* in which two boys see their reflections in a security mirror in a crowded shop and realise that they are identical.

Discussion about how the story might continue was followed by note-making and sharing of ideas and vocabulary. Most children wrote independently, but two wrote together and another two worked alongside each other to create parallel stories from the different perspectives of the two boys.

Throughout the seven afternoons when the group worked with David and the school's literacy coordinator, work was read aloud and discussed. There was a focus on use of language, on use of punctuation for effect, and on vocabulary. David took work away and provided written feedback and highlighted areas where writing might be developed, and children looked through this and responded.

At the end of the project, David drew upon some of the children's ideas to complete his own version of the story, and a book was created and published, which included both his and the children's stories. The school caretaker, an amateur artist, produced the book's cover and the book was 'launched' at a social event for children and their families.

The excerpt below was written by Erin and imagines the scene after one of the boys has made a significant discovery. Note the range of vocabulary, the varied length of Erin's sentences and the use of short powerful sentences that convey tension and the pace of events happening.

I walked downstairs and sat on the grey and black fabric sofa. My mum looked scared so I asked her what was wrong. She began to cry. I couldn't understand what would be so upsetting. Then she told me the deep terrifying truth. She told me how she stole me when I was just born. I was shaking. I was upset and felt a rollercoaster of emotions run through me. I felt sick. The woman I thought might have been dangerous was not the dangerous one. The woman I had been living with for the past ten years was the one who was dangerous. I quickly ran to my room and dialed 999. Quivering with fear, I had a conversation with the 999 operator, "I need the police; my mum has just told me some terrifying news. She kidnapped me as a baby: help!" I ended the phone call, as I could hear her bounding footsteps coming up the stairs towards my bedroom door. Then I heard a sound like music to my ears – the police sirens in the distance. Her footsteps retreated down the stairs. I took a sigh of relief: she was going to do the right thing and face up to her crimes.

I felt conflicted; on one hand she was my capturer, but on the other she was the only mother I'd known and loved. I kind of regret calling the police, but I feel like it was the right thing to do.

ACTIVITY 3

Analyse Erin's writing in terms of DfE (2016, p. 6) indicators of deeper writing:
    The pupil can:

- write effectively for a range of purposes and audiences, selecting the appropriate form and drawing independently on what they have read as models for their own writing (e.g. literary language, characterisation, structure);
- distinguish between the language of speech and writing, and choose the appropriate register;

(Continued)

(Continued)

- exercise an assured and conscious control over levels of formality, particularly through manipulating grammar and vocabulary to achieve this;
- use the range of punctuation taught at Key Stage 2 correctly (e.g. semi-colons, dashes, colons, hyphens) and, when necessary, use such punctuation precisely to enhance meaning and avoid ambiguity.

(DfE, 2018)

Now keep the indicators in mind as you read the case study of Bella's writing.

CASE STUDY

BELLA'S WRITING

As part of their PGCE course, trainee teachers at Durham University have some lectures in schools, followed immediately by working with children to put theory into practice. They focus on children's reading and writing, and evaluate these and go on to support children in writing about topics that interest the children. In the example below, Lorna, a mature trainee, worked with Bella, a Year 6 pupil who was on the autism spectrum.

Preparation for the writing began the previous week when Lorna and Bella discussed the purpose for the writing and a possible audience. Bella said that she wanted to write a poem, so the two of them made notes on topic, genre and vocabulary which might be used, and created a basic outline for a story/poem. They looked out of the window at blossom-covered trees in the school grounds and Bella talked about how it reminded her of a tree in her grandfather's garden.

Lorna brought pictures and bags containing grass, plants, moss, wood and soil which Bella could see and smell to stimulate her writing. Lorna also typed a range of vocabulary, some of it from Bella and additional words that Lorna felt might be useful. These were divided into four senses: smell, sight, touch and hearing. After further planning, Bella began to write, often pausing to stand up, look out of the window and put herself into the position of her heroine. Bella's occasional frustration at her lack of fluency in her writing was overcome when Lorna occasionally acted as scribe. There was constant reading and rereading as the work was drafted, edited and revised. At the end of the session Lorna took away Bella's writing and typed it and presented it attractively with a border of pink blossom.

In discussions with her tutor, Lorna described what she had learnt:

When working with children it is important to encourage them to consider all their senses and to try to put themselves in the place of either their audience or their character. If we can start from the premise of what a child can do rather than what they can't, their abilities not their disabilities, then we can often achieve more and develop an enthusiasm and passion for learning/writing.

When Lorna's tutor delivered the children's work to the school, Bella was thrilled to see her writing and immediately read it aloud to the headteacher and her teaching assistant.

As I peer out the window I can see the wild and I am jealous of other children who play out with their friends, while I have none. My dad is a millionaire. I don't like it. He always demands me to stay inside, no matter how many times I tell him I want to go out. He won't look at me or listen to me. I feel so lonely and isolated from my own father, who only cares about money and himself.

The breath-taking sunrise began to come up, I have to sneak out! I was curious to see what beauty looks like outside while my dad hides me from it. As I got out I saw everything I'd dreamed of. I could smell the scent of cherry blossoms and pine trees. I crossed the enchanting bridge that leads out to a beautiful bright meadow.

I skipped along the way happily. I could smell the damp grass mixed with flowers and woodland. As I came out of the leafy bushes, I could see what I've never seen before, a strawberry blossom tree. I could smell the scent. It was magnificent. I was joyful and thrilled by the wilderness my dad had hidden from me. I thought why would he do that? Life is beyond more than money. I felt peace once and for all.

(By Bella Anna Winter, age 11)

Conclusion

The case studies above show that, given the right stimuli and support, children can produce writing that demonstrates a deeper knowledge of language and a broader use of vocabulary than they might achieve independently. By making discussion about language an integral part of reading and writing, we can open up a range of possibilities for deeper writing.

ACTIVITY 4

Audit a classroom in which you work; does a love for language 'ooze out of the woodwork' Brien (2012, p. 152)? Is the classroom a rich literature environment?

• Are books and digital media accessible?
• Are there displays that provide synonyms for a range of common adjectives?

(Continued)

(Continued)

- Is new vocabulary displayed and explored?
- Are there opportunities for children to use the vocabulary investigated in texts?
- Are children involved in selecting the book that is chosen as the 'read aloud' text – perhaps through hearing snippets of different books before expressing preferences?
- Is poetry visible in the classroom (a really rich source of language used for different effects on the reader)?
- Are jokes, puns and 'words of the day' activities available?

(Adapted from Carter, 2017, p. 48)

Further reading

For research on whether we need a vocabulary for discussing writing, see:

Watson, A. (2015) The problem of grammar teaching: a case study of the relationship between a teacher's beliefs and pedagogical practice. *Language and Education*, 29(4): 332–46. DOI: 10.1080/09500782.2015.1016955. Available online at: https://educationendowmentfoundation.org.uk/projects-and-evaluation/projects/ipeell-using-self-regulation-to-improve-writing/

References

Apthorp, H. (2006) Effects of a supplemental vocabulary programme in third grade reading/language arts. *Journal of Educational Research*, 100(2):67–79.

Berninger, V.W., Vaughan, K., Abbott, R.D., Begay, K., Coleman, K.B., Curtin, G. and Graham, S. (2002) Teaching spelling and composition alone and together: Implications for the simple view of writing. *Journal of Educational Psychology*, 94(2): 291–304.

Bevilacqua, P. and Fenton, S. (2009) Communication, language and literacy: PowerPoint presentation for National Strategies.

Brien, J. (2012) *Teaching Primary English*. London: Sage.

Bunting, R. in Graham, J. and Kelly, A. (2003) *Writing Under Control*. London: David Fulton.

Carter, J. (2017) Vocabulary development, in Waugh, D., Jolliffe, W. and Allott, K. *Primary English for Trainee Teachers*. London: Sage.

Daffern, T., Mackenzie, N. and Hemmings, B. (2017) Predictors of writing success: how important are spelling, grammar and punctuation? *Australian Journal of Education*, 61(1): 75–87.

DCSF (2008) *Vocabulary: What Can Teachers Do to Increase the Vocabulary of Children who Start Education with a Limited Vocabulary?* Nottingham: DCSF.

DfE (2018) *Key Stage 2 Teacher Assessment Exemplification Materials English Writing: Working at Greater Depth within the Expected Standard: Frankie.* Available online at: https://assets.publishing.service.gov.uk/government/uploads/system/uploads/attachment_data/file/655619/2018_exemplification_materials_KS2-GDS__Frankie_.pdf (accessed 1 April 2019).

Duff, D., Tomblin, J.B. and Catts, H. (2015) The influence of reading on vocabulary growth: a case for a Matthew effect. *Journal of Speech, Language, and Hearing Research*. 58: 853–64.

Duke, N. and Moses, A. (2003) *10 Research Tested Ways to Build Children's Vocabulary*. New York: Scholastic. Available online at: http://teacher.scholastic.com/products/readingline/pdfs/ProfessionalPaper.pdf (accessed 7 May 2019).

Gough, P.B. and Tunmer, W.E. (1986) Decoding, reading and reading disability. *Remedial and Special Education*, 7: 6–10.

Medwell, J. and Wray, D. (2007) Handwriting: What do we know and what do we need to know? *Literacy*, 41(1): 10–15.

Myhill, D., Lines, H. and Watson, A. (2011) *Making Meaning with Grammar: A Repertoire of Possibilities*. Exeter: University of Exeter.

Myhill, D.A., Jones, S.M., Lines, H. and Watson, A. (2012) Re-thinking grammar: the impact of embedded grammar teaching on students' writing and students' metalinguistic understanding. *Research Papers in Education*, 27(2): 139–66.

Myhill, D.A. (2012) The role for grammar in the curriculum, in *Meeting High Expectations: Looking for the Heart of English*. Available online at: https://heartofenglishblog.wordpress.com/meeting-high-expectations/the-role-for-grammar-in-the-curriculum-debra-myhill/ (accessed 7 May 2019).

National Reading Panel (2000) *Teaching Children to Read: An evidence-based Assessment of the Scientific Research Literature on Reading and its Implications for Reading Instruction. Reports of Subgroups*. NICHD.

Oxford Language Report (2018) *Why Closing the Word Gap Matters*. Available online at: www.headteacher-update.com/best-practice-article/reading-writing-and-the-importance-of-vocabulary/82451/

Roach, T. (2018) *What Counts as Greater Depth Writing?* Available online at: www.teachwire.net/news/what-counts-as-greater-depth-writing

Rose, J. (2006) *Independent Review of the Teaching of Early Reading: Final Report*. Nottingham: DfES.

Safford, K. (2016) Teaching grammar and testing grammar in the English primary school: the impact on teachers and their teaching of the grammar element of the statutory test in Spelling, Punctuation and Grammar (SPaG). *Changing English*, 23(1): 3–21. DOI: 10.1080/1358684X.2015.1133766

Tunmer, W.E. and Chapman, J.W. (2012) The simple view of reading redux: vocabulary knowledge and the independent components hypothesis. *Journal of Learning Disabilities*, 45(5): 453–66.

6
NON-FICTION WRITING

Kate Allott

KEY QUESTIONS

- How do I recognise the particular challenges non-fiction writing provides for children?
- How do I understand the key factors that lead to successful non-fiction writing?
- How do I develop a range of strategies that support different phases of the non-fiction writing process?

Introduction

The National Curriculum programme of study states that children in Year 2 should be able to write 'narratives about personal experiences' (2013, p. 31), and Rebecca does this successfully here, without adult support. She has a sense of her audience, as her explanation of the Watch organisation shows, and she includes a great deal of interesting information in a relatively short piece. She ends with a humorous touch, which again shows some awareness of audience. Over the next few years, she and her classmates will learn to 'plan their writing by identifying the audience for and purpose of the writing, selecting the appropriate form and using other similar writing as models for their own' (DfE, 2013, p. 47). These are complex skills, which need to be taught systematically and effectively.

Andrews et al. (2009) suggest that over many years there has been a tendency to give insufficient emphasis to non-fiction writing, both in the curriculum and in practice in schools. While the balance of fiction to non-fiction will vary from classroom to classroom and from school to school, it is certainly important to reflect on what that balance is and should be. The balance needs to be considered both in terms of how much time children spend on non-fiction writing (bearing in mind that much of this will be in subject areas other than English), and also how much of the teaching time given to writing focuses on the specific demands and skills associated with non-fiction. It may be that while children do spend a significant amount of time engaged in non-fiction writing, teaching tends to focus more on fiction writing skills.

This chapter will consider how deeper writing of non-fiction texts depends on secure knowledge of the topic being written about and critical reading skills. Non-fiction writing is often strongest when a cross-curricular approach to planning is adopted, so that topics being studied in foundation subjects are linked to appropriate text types being taught in English. Children's writing is then grounded in a genuine interest in and sound knowledge of the topic. Critical reading skills are also important, and in their own writing children should learn to present information which has been checked where necessary and which is used in a fair and impartial way. They also need to understand the structure, features and language of information texts in order to be able to write with confidence and skill.

ACTIVITY 1   CROSS-CURRICULAR OPPORTUNITIES FOR WRITING

Non-fiction writing often works best when it is linked to what children are learning in areas of the curriculum other than English. For each of the following Key Stage 2 units, plan writing opportunities for a range of types of text, considering for each what the audience and purpose for the writing might be. The first example has been completed for you.

Unit of study	Possible writing tasks	Purpose	Audience
Geography Key Stage 2: earthquakes.	Explanations of why earthquakes occur; recounts of recent earthquakes; instructions for what to do in the event of an earthquake.	To inform via a display.	Visitors to the school, other classes.
Science Year 5/6: the circulatory system – identify and name the main parts, and explain the functions of the heart, blood vessels and blood.			
Art and design Key Stage 2: Sir Christopher Wren.			
Design and technology Key Stage 2: designing and making a carrier bag.			

Reading into writing: gathering information

Not all information writing begins with reading; instructions or explanations may draw on a demonstration of what to do or how something works, while a recount may retell a first-hand experience. In these cases, good observational skills and memory are the essential skills.

However, for many topics, first-hand experience is not possible or appropriate, and other sources of information need to be used. Deeper writing goes hand in hand with deeper reading.

FOCUS ON RESEARCH

THE EXEL PROJECT

Wray and Lewis (1997) reported an influential project investigating children's non-fiction literacy skills and developing more effective approaches to teaching these. The project team developed a model, known as the EXIT model (EXtending Interactions with Texts), which moved from pre-reading, where readers began with their existing knowledge of a topic and clarified their purposes for reading, into reading, where they located and interrogated sources of information, recording what they learned, and finally communicated the information through writing. Alongside this model of the reading and writing process, Wray and Lewis advocated a teaching model for non-fiction reading and writing based on teacher modelling, shared activity in which the teacher and class together engage with a reading or writing task, supported activity – for example, through the use of writing frames – and finally independent activity. The approach was taken up by the National Literacy Strategy (1998) in its introductory training materials for all schools.

Information gathering, as Wray and Lewis proposed, should begin with a review of what is already known of the topic to be studied. We rarely start from a position of complete ignorance, and if we pool our information we may have a useful starting point. It is important not to dismiss any misconceptions or inaccuracies at this point, as the research should do this, and that helps children to understand why fact checking is so important.

Research is more effective and focused if a purpose has already been decided on – not simply 'finding out about' but answering specific questions that have arisen from the first discussion. Using a number of sources leads to interesting comparisons: 'Why do different sources select different information to include? What do we do if they contradict each other? Do different sources encourage us to see the topic in different ways – for example, having more sympathy for one viewpoint than for another?' Regular consideration of such questions, in whole-class and group reading discussions, will not only support children's non-fiction writing, but will also help them to adopt a more critical approach to texts they encounter in the wider world and in adult life.

While some children seem able to remember quantities of information quite effortlessly, others do not, and learning skills of recording information which they may then use in their writing becomes important. Note-making can include identifying key points, summarising texts, writing in a concise way, using abbreviations and omitting non-essential words, using symbols such as arrows, and so on. At the same time, the reader can look ahead to the writing stage, and it may be useful for children to write each note on a separate piece of paper so that they can be moved around in the planning and organising stage.

ACTIVITY 2   THE TEXT BOX

A collection of 'real' non-fiction texts is an invaluable resource for teaching non-fiction writing. Gather a range of texts that you will be able to make available for children to browse, as well as for planned teaching activities. Consider the level of difficulty of each text, and whether it might be suitable only for older readers.
   Among the hundreds of possibilities are:

- advertisements
- biographies (brief)
- blurbs
- book and film reviews
- brochures
- certificates
- diary extracts
- encyclopaedia entries
- epitaphs
- greetings cards
- headlines
- invitations
- information leaflets
- instructions for games
- letters to local newspapers
- notices
- recipes
- photographs of epitaphs on gravestones
- signs
- wanted and for sale notices.

Critical reading

Critical reading skills are important. Children need to learn that content matters, and in order to make judgements about what they read and what they choose to include in their writing, they must evaluate the sources they use critically. This aspect of reading is of increasing concern, as shown by a recent report on 'fake news' and the teaching of critical literacy (National Literacy Trust, 2018). The report suggested that while it is easier than ever before to gather information, readers of all ages often find it very difficult to know whether material is accurate and unbiased. Of course, the presentation of information in a misleading way, or even of false information as fact, is nothing new. Darrell Huff's *How to Lie with Statistics* (1954) and Lance Packard's *The Persuaders* (1957) on advertising, were hugely influential in exposing such strategies when they were first published, but the battle to restrain the types of techniques they described, not only in the commercial world but also in politics, is more important than ever. A cavalier attitude to truth, and to the idea that facts are sacred, is not acceptable. Children need to learn that sometimes it is necessary to question what is presented to them as fact just as much as they question opinions.

To become critical readers, children need to learn to:

- Evaluate the reliability of the source: when was this written or said and by whom? What expertise does the author have? Is the author writing from a particular viewpoint? Could the author be biased in any way? Could the content be out of date?
- Check the accuracy of facts when appropriate.
- Distinguish between fact and opinion, and note how facts can be presented in ways that encourage a particular response through the language used.
- Make inferences to build a fuller understanding of the text.
- Consider what evidence is provided to support opinions.
- Evaluate the strength of arguments.
- Reflect on how language is used, perhaps to sensationalise a topic or encourage the reader to adopt a particular view.
- Evaluate the content – how relevant and interesting is it? Does it provide satisfactory answers to questions the reader has about the topic?
- Compare alternative sources, noting any discrepancies.

Children need systematic and regular teaching to develop such skills, yet the National Literacy Trust report (2018, p. 21) indicated that only 50 per cent of teachers questioned stated that they taught critical literacy, and of those only about 30 per cent said that they did so very often, with 32 per cent saying they did so sometimes, 24 per cent not often and 14 per cent rarely.

The content of information writing

Deciding what to include in information writing is a challenge. If children have researched a topic thoroughly, they should be able to move beyond the 'everything I know about . . . ' approach, to consider what is most important and interesting. This involves evaluating not only the information, but also the intended audience. Judging what readers might already know and what they might want to know is a sophisticated process. Even for a relatively simple form such as an account of an experience, these decisions need to be made carefully. The recount might include explanations – for example, of how a water mill works – and descriptions (of a castle or animals in a wildlife park), without overwhelming the reader with too much detail, as well as comments that personalise the account and bring it to life.

Persuasive and discursive writing provide additional challenge. Even in persuasive writing, there is no longer a case to be made for highly selective use of information, and for doubtful claims and exaggeration. While it might be claimed that this approach can be fun or can alert children to the dangers of such techniques, there is also the danger that they come to see them as acceptable. However, there is a clear code of conduct for advertisers (Committee of Advertising Practice, 2010, p. 11), which not only states that communications should be honest and truthful, but also says they should be 'prepared with a sense of responsibility to consumers and society' and should reflect the spirit of the code rather than simply the letter. Deeper writing of persuasive texts should encourage children to respect and work within the boundaries set for the outside world. In discursive writing, children need to be able to recognise opposing viewpoints, evaluate the strength of arguments and evidence, and understand the need for objectivity and an open mind. This does not mean they cannot make a strong and convincing case for a view they believe in, but that they should able to provide reasons for supporting that view.

Cognitive skills such as reasoning, which are applied in critical reading, are also significant in non-fiction writing. Again, this focus reflects concerns about the state of public debate, which often seems to be based on unsubstantiated claims and assertions, 'facts' that can easily be disproved but that continue to be circulated, and prejudices rather than reasoned argument. There are strong links here with the Department for Education's non-statutory programme for citizenship (2015), which states among other objectives that children should be taught:

- to research, discuss and debate topical issues, problems and events;
- to resolve differences by looking at alternatives, making decisions and explaining choices;
- to explore how the media present information.

Children need to learn that arguments must be supported by reasons, evidence and examples if they are to be considered seriously. They need to be able to evaluate claims and opinions critically, not simply decide which they agree with. They need to be able to challenge the thinking of others, but to do so in a non-confrontational and moderate way, recognising that this often leads to more productive debate.

CASE STUDY

THE ART OF PERSUASION

Session 1: Will, a recently qualified teacher, began a unit of work on persuasive writing by presenting his Year 6 class with a wide range of persuasive texts, including advertisements, leaflets, letters, signs, speeches and opinion columns from newspapers. He asked the children what all the texts had in common. After discussion in pairs and groups, they decided that the texts were trying to make the audience change its mind or adopt a particular course of action. He then asked the children, working in pairs, to choose two texts and decide which was most likely to work for them. Once they had agreed, they presented their two texts to another pair to see whether they were in agreement and to justify their own choice. The class then collectively collated a 'what works' list.

The children's responses showed that they did not like to feel they were being manipulated or deceived. They were critical of what they saw as inflated claims, exaggeration and hyperbolic language. They were less able to identify a lack of balance – for example, in the speeches and opinion columns, which appeared to support claims with evidence, and where it was not apparent what had been omitted from the discussion.

Session 2: Will made a speech to the class arguing that all zoos should be closed down. He gave the children opportunities to question and challenge his arguments, and then they voted on the issue. A significant majority supported the proposal. Will then distributed a leaflet he had prepared, arguing the case for zoos. Children were surprised to find that there were convincing arguments for the other side in the debate. Will asked whether it was right that in his speech he had ignored those arguments in order to make his case stronger.

In following sessions, the children selected an issue of importance to them, researched it thoroughly, and worked towards a piece of writing that expressed their own view while recognising counter-arguments and presenting evidence for both sides.

Skills of reasoning, which underpin many types of information writing, can be taught through approaches such as Philosophy for Children, which was first developed by Lipman (1980). Lipman argued that philosophy was the best way of teaching critical thinking, giving children experience in reasoning in 'communities of inquiry' – typically, the class and their teacher. The approach teaches considerate, rational debate, using specially written stories and materials as the starting points for the discovery of the rules of logic. Teachers need to have an open, questioning attitude and to be trained thoroughly if the approach is to be effective.

Preparation for writing: mentor texts

Rushing into writing once information has been collected can result in disappointing outcomes. Of course, if children are confident writers and familiar with the genre, little preparation may be needed, but even skilled writers need preparation when faced with an unfamiliar text type. The preparation involves analysis of model texts, oral rehearsal and planning of the writing. Dorfman and Cappelli (2009) describe texts used at this stage as *mentor texts* – carefully chosen, high-quality texts that are shared over and over with children until they have absorbed the characteristic features and language of that text. The Talk for Writing approach (Corbett and Strong, 2011), which also advocates repeated readings of key texts, suggests analysis through 'boxing up' the text – labelling sections to make the structure explicit – and may involve specially produced examples, though an evaluation of the approach by the Education Endowment Foundation (Dockrell et al., 2015) questioned whether such examples were always similar enough to real texts, and whether misconceptions might arise as a result. There was also a concern that the 'boxing up' strategy worked better for some text types than for others.

Oral rehearsal

As with much writing, oral classroom activities can provide a valuable way of rehearsing not only the content of the writing, but also the language, and developing a writing voice for non-fiction depends on speaking and listening activities such as presentations and debates. Less formal activities can also be very useful in giving children opportunities to communicate information, ideas and views clearly and effectively. These can include:

- snowballing, in which children share ideas with a partner, then each pair works with another pair, and so on until the whole class is involved;
- envoying, in which children discuss in groups and then send an envoy to present their ideas to another group;
- jigsawing, in which children work independently on different parts of the main task, share what they have learned with other 'experts', and report back to a mixed group who then have a shared understanding of the whole task;
- hot-seating, where the drawback that only one child has the opportunity to speak, and most of the class is relegated to a passive role, can be mitigated by pausing after each question to give time for paired talk, where children consider what the response might be.

In all of this, the teacher's role as expert practitioner is crucial.

FOCUS ON RESEARCH

WHAT WORKS IN THE TEACHING OF ARGUMENT WRITING?

A review of research by Andrews et al. (2009) suggested that evidence from a number of studies identified key features of effective teaching of what was described as argument writing, and which included persuasive and discursive writing. These features included:

- the teaching of cognitive reasoning skills;
- oral discussion to provide a basis for the writing of discussions;
- a clear understanding of the audience for the writing;

- a writing process that led from planning into drafting, revision and editing;
- collaborative writing, so that discussion between writers supports the written version;
- teacher modelling of the writing and explicit explanations of the learning processes involved.

It should be noted that all the studies reviewed were carried out in North America, although there seems no reason why the findings should not apply elsewhere. It is also worth noting that the findings could also be relevant to other forms of non-fiction writing, and indeed to fiction writing.

The writing process: planning

As Andrews et al. (2009) suggested, successful writing is likely to follow well-planned oral activities, and then to make use of the well-established model of the writing process in which planning leads into drafting, redrafting and editing. While younger or less skilled writers may base their writing very closely on a model, or make use of a writing frame that essentially structures the writing for them, more skilled writers are likely to begin their planning process by considering who their intended audience is and what the purpose of the writing is. They will be familiar with a range of non-fiction text types, taught earlier in their school careers, but will understand that many texts do not conform to a simple model, instead including features of more than one.

Most writing begins with an introduction to the subject being written about, and ends with a conclusion that draws together the threads of what has been considered, but the main body of the writing could be organised chronologically, which is relatively straightforward, or in some other way. The writer of an information text needs to decide how to organise the material, grouping it logically into sections, and then consider how to sequence the various sections. In discursive writing, the decisions will involve whether, for example, to group all the points supporting one point of view together, or whether to have more of a to-and-fro structure, where a point supporting one side is then countered or balanced by an opposing point. Writers who are operating at a deeper level show awareness of the need to make such decisions and are confident to do so. They also make decisions about how to record their planning, depending on their own preferences and what is most appropriate for the writing task.

The writing process: drafting

For the skilled writer, drafting is often a constant process of trying out words, phrases and sentences, and crafting them until they 'sound right' and create the desired effect. Children may consciously use techniques such as repetition or alliteration, but when they are writing at a deeper level, such techniques are used purposefully rather than simply to meet a set of predetermined criteria. They may also consider vocabulary choices carefully to ensure that the writing achieves what it is intended to. Some writers may constantly reread and redraft as they write; others prefer to produce a rough first draft then go back to it to polish it. Again, children working at this deeper level are likely to be able to articulate how they write and why. They are likely to pay little attention to spelling and handwriting at this stage, as they will have achieved a level of automaticity in their handwriting and will have a secure knowledge of the spelling of most or all of the words they use.

They may give more conscious consideration to sentence structure and punctuation, because they will be aware of the choices that they can make in how they punctuate their writing, and the impact that can have. They may, for example, use short sentences to give key points emphasis, while linking other information in efficient multi-clause sentences. Non-fiction writing probably lends itself to the collaborative writing which Andrews et al. (2009) refer to even more than fiction. After all, professional novelists and poets do not expect to write collaboratively, even if they value feedback from others and respond to it, but non-fiction texts may well be co-authored. Even when children are writing individually, they are likely to want to share their writing in order to gain feedback that can help them improve it. Children writing at this deeper level will be less reliant on checklists that they have been given to support their evaluation of their writing; they will have the confidence to be self-critical and to be able to reflect honestly on whether they have achieved the purpose for their work.

Spelling, punctuation and grammar in non-fiction writing

Non-fiction writing can pose particular problems for spelling, as it may include specialised vocabulary which the children have not encountered before beginning to learn about the topic. While they will see the words when they are reading about the topic, this may not be enough for them to internalise the spellings, so a focus on key words before they begin to write can be helpful: this can involve discussing any difficulties with the words, and practising using the look-say-cover-write-check technique. In terms of grammar and punctuation, non-fiction writing is likely to involve careful use of language devices that link parts of the writing together – clauses, sentences and sections of the writing. These cohesive devices may be used to indicate chronology or cause and effect. They include adverbials such as 'fortunately', 'admittedly', 'however', 'meanwhile', 'nevertheless', 'therefore', 'to conclude'.

These show the logical links between statements, so that an argument or explanation can be developed. In addition to varying sentence length, questions, exclamations and commands can be used to draw readers in or call them to action. Punctuation marks grammatical boundaries in order to clarify meaning, and non-fiction writing offers good opportunities to explore the use of colons, to introduce not only lists but also examples, and brackets, commas or dashes used to separate off additional pieces of information. In non-fiction writing, there are also options not open to fiction writers; the National Curriculum programme of study for Years 5 and 6 refers to children learning to 'Draft and write by using further organizational and presentational devices to structure text and to guide the reader (e.g. headings, bullet points, underlining)' (DfE, 2013, p. 47).

CASE STUDY

BRINGING IT ALL TOGETHER

Lorna, a Year 4/5 teacher, wanted her class to know more about the suburban area they lived in. She researched the area herself first, and identified and photographed a number of interesting features within half a mile of the school, which included:

- a plague stone;
- the site of the gallows where public hangings took place;
- a large pond where clay was once dug out to make bricks;
- a pinfold (a pound for stray animals);
- the old school, now a branch library;
- the site of the toll house on the main road, commemorated by a house name.

Session 1: Lorna began her local history unit by showing the children the photographs, and asking them to work in pairs to note any information they had about each feature, and anything they could infer about it. Some of the children had never noticed some features, or knew where they were but not what they were. Lorna suggested that this was probably the case for most local residents, and that an information leaflet about the area could be popular. She suggested that the children work in groups, each focusing on a different feature, researching it and then writing the section of the leaflet. This gave the class a clear audience and purpose for their writing.

Session 2: Lorna took the children on a walk around the area, visiting each of the features they planned to write about. They looked carefully at the features, noting their appearance and any information given about them at the site, and took additional photographs to capture the best images possible.

Session 3: Lorna had gathered a range of sources for the children to use for their research, including a booklet about the area written by a local historian, and online resources produced by a local history group. Before beginning their reading, the groups generated a list of questions about their feature. They shared the questions with the whole class, to check that they had not left out anything significant. The children worked in pairs on their sources, contributing any information they found to group notes for each question. They concluded the session by considering whether they had found sufficient information to answer each of their questions, and whether any of the information needed to be checked through further research.

Session 4: the children considered a mock-up of the leaflet, showing how the space might be used, and estimated what the word limit for each section would be. They discussed criteria for the text, thinking about who would be likely to read the leaflet and what the readers might find interesting. Lorna had gathered a number of leaflets from the

(Continued)

(Continued)

local tourist information centre, and the children used these to inform their discussion. They then worked in pairs to draft their own sections, and shared these with other members of their group. They soon realised how selective they needed to be in terms of the material they included, and how important it was to be concise and clear.

Session 5: the groups put together a final draft of their section, either using one version they considered worked best or using elements from different versions. Each group then presented their section to the rest of the class for comments and agreed any final changes. As a class, they decided what title to give the leaflet and what other introductory information they needed to include. They also selected the images they would use and the font.

Lorna produced the final version for the children to check. She then copied leaflets for each child to take home, for display in the school's reception area, in each classroom, and in the local library. A board of 'reviews' in the classroom included many positive comments from families, staff and other children.

Conclusion

It might be thought that children who are writing non-fiction texts at a deeper level do not need the support of a teacher; they are capable of selecting and researching topics independently, and of producing high-quality texts which they can evaluate and improve effectively. It is important that they are given some autonomy over their writing, and indeed children welcome and value being given choices rather than always being set tightly constrained tasks (Grainger et al., 2003). However, this does not mean that the teacher is redundant. Even professional writers do not operate in a context where there is no support and feedback during the writing process. Skilled writers in the primary classroom can provide useful support to their peers, but the teacher's guidance and support, often through discussion in guided writing sessions, is vital. Teacher modelling also continues to be important, though the modelling will demonstrate increasingly sophisticated techniques. Wray and Lewis (1997) suggest that modelling of the more formal language often appropriate in non-fiction writing, and also of how to ensure cohesion, is valuable for young writers.

Rereading writing, adding in where necessary, links between sentences and larger units, is a key strategy in producing high-quality writing, as such cohesive links not only make the writing flow better, but also show the logical connections between elements. Wray (2006) also emphasises the importance of modelling the process of checking that meaning is clear – in other words, considering the text from the audience's point of view. In addition to modelling, children need to see teachers responding as readers – in other words, judging non-fiction writing by its use, interest and ability to engage the reader, rather than by a set of somewhat arbitrary criteria. This works best in the context of guided writing groups, where teacher and children together can discuss children's developing and completed work. This review process is the important final stage of deeper writing.

Further reading

Bushnell, A. and Waugh, D. (2017) *Inviting Writing: Teaching and Learning Writing Across the Primary Curriculum*. London: Sage.

Bushnell, A., Smith, R. and Waugh, D. (2018) *Modelling Exciting Writing*. London: Sage.

References

Andrews, R., Torgerson, C., Low, G. and McGuinn, N. (2009) Teaching argument writing to 7- to 14-year-olds: an international review of the evidence of successful practice. *Cambridge Review of Education*, 39(3): 291–310.

Committee of Advertising Practice (2010) *The CAP Code: The U.K. Code of Non-broadcast Advertising and Direct and Promotional Marketing*. London: Committee of Advertising Practice.

Corbett, P. and Strong, J. (2011) *Talk for Writing Across the Curriculum: How to Teach Non-fiction Writing 5–12 Years*. Maidenhead: Open University Press.

Department for Education (DfE) (2013) *The 2014 Primary National Curriculum in England*. London: Department for Education.

Department for Education (DfE) (2015) *Citizenship Programmes of Study: Key Stages 1 and 2*. London: Department for Education.

Dockrell, J., Marshall, C. and Wyse, D. (2015) *Talk for Writing: Evaluation Report and Executive Summary*. London: Education Endowment Foundation.

Dorfman, L.R. and Cappelli, R. (2009) *Non-fiction Mentor Texts: Teaching Informational Writing Through Children's Literature, K-8*. Portland, ME: Stenhouse Publishers.

Grainger, T., Goouch, K. and Lambirth, A. (2003) 'Playing the game called writing': Children's views and voices. *English in Education*, 37(2): 4–16.

Huff, D. (1954) *How to Lie with Statistics*. London: W.W. Norton.

Lipman, M. (1980) *Philosophy in the Classroom*. Philadelphia, PA: Temple University.

National Literacy Strategy (1998) *Literacy Training Pack: Module 6 Reading and Writing for Information*. London: Department for Education and Employment.

National Literacy Trust (2018) Fake news and critical literacy: final report. London: National Literacy Trust.

Packard, V. (1957) *The Hidden Persuaders*. New York: D. McKay Co.

Wray, D. (2006) *Teaching Literacy Across the Curriculum*. Exeter: Learning Matters.

Wray, D. and Lewis, M. (1997) *Extending Literacy: Children Reading and Writing Non-Fiction*. London: Routledge.

7

DEEPER WRITING THROUGH WRITING FOR CHILDREN

Dan Hughes

TEACHERS' STANDARDS

This chapter will help you with the following Teachers' Standards:

2d. demonstrate knowledge and understanding of how pupils learn and how this impacts on teaching;

3a. have a secure knowledge of the relevant subject(s) and curriculum areas, foster and maintain pupils' interest in the subject, and address misunderstandings;

3b. demonstrate a critical understanding of developments in the subject and curriculum areas, and promote the value of scholarship;

3c. demonstrate an understanding of and take responsibility for promoting high standards of literacy, articulacy and the correct use of standard English, whatever the teacher's specialist subject.

KEY QUESTIONS

- How do I identify the benefits and challenges of being a writer–teacher?
- How do I understand the critical processes involved in writing for children?
- How can I develop a range of ideas to explore the writing process in greater depth?

Introduction

For skilled and experienced teachers, the question of whether or not they see themselves as a writer is a problematic one. Many responses suggest that writing is part of their professional lives every day – writing letters to parents, producing newsletters, writing in home-school liaison books among many other functional purposes. However, if asked if they write for themselves, or purposefully for the children they teach, the answer is much different. Teachers would say that they might write a shopping list, a to-do reminders list or, in the best-case scenario, a daily diary or journal. However, the answers rarely involve a poem, an adventure story or an information text on the local history of the village in which they live. Eyres (2017) states that most teachers do not profess to be writers. To create empowered, engaged and autonomous writers, developing knowledge and awareness of how to write at greater depth is essential. Therefore, writing for children regularly, and writing for yourself, may help to unlock some of the mysteries of teaching writing and supporting the progress of the children you teach.

Writing is a profoundly challenging and personal experience. Engaging pupils in this process can be difficult, time-consuming and requires an in-depth knowledge of the pupils that we teach. The aim is for pupils to see themselves as writers and value writing as both a creative and functional tool. Understanding what it means to be a writer and the positive impact it can have on pupils' self-esteem is a persistent and nagging goal that teachers strive for, yet can prove elusive. This chapter will argue that unless teachers allow themselves to openly and freely engage in the writing process, understanding how to teach children writing will remain a distant ideal.

The National Curriculum

The revised National Curriculum (DfE, 2014) emphasised two critical aspects of teaching writing: *transcription* and *composition*. Both elements can be argued to be essential to develop children as writers. The transcription element focuses on the skills needed to write, including spelling and handwriting. As a teacher, these may prove challenging. Identifying strategies to support both, such as being familiar with the school's handwriting policy and modelling how to identify a tricky spelling will support pupils, especially if these are taught explicitly. The transcriptional elements of writing cannot be ignored as they are essential to make writing understandable to readers, but an overreliance on these puts future writing opportunities, for both transactional and creative purposes, at risk (Gardner, 2018).

However, writing at greater depth for children requires an emphasis on the compositional aspects of writing. These are the muddy waters of the writing process – the subjective and challenging parts of putting pen to paper. The National Curriculum states that effective composition 'involves forming, articulating and communicating ideas' (DfE, 2014, p. 5) and an 'awareness of audience, purpose and context' (DfE, 2014, p. 5). This is where clarity and deeper understanding is needed. In the teacher assessment frameworks, writing at greater depth at Key Stage 1 requires 'writing effectively and coherently for different purposes' (Standards and Testing Agency, 2018a, p. 7), with Key Stage 2 adding in the need to consider 'a range of purposes and audiences' (Standards and Teaching Agency, 2018b, p. 5) in their choice of language, structure and formality. Teaching these aspects requires the teacher to be able to understand the processes needed, both cognitively and practically. Unless the knowledge of the teacher is secure about how this happens, supporting pupils can be very demanding. Therefore, becoming a writer – being a teacher who writes – will support you with these aspects.

FOCUS ON RESEARCH

The National Literacy Trust (2018) highlighted that fewer children enjoy writing than previously, and this is an increasing trend in a recent study into writing enjoyment and attitudes in 8- to 11-year-olds. There are the majority of children who believe writing is fun; however, the research suggests there are significant barriers to writing, including difficulty in deciding what to write and finding the writing process itself difficult (The National Literacy Trust, 2018). It also suggests that children who find writing difficult are also only writing when they have to.

The question that lies at the heart of this chapter is whether or not this is reflected in the teachers. If the teachers experience the difficulties of deciding what to write, identify their barriers and, most importantly, how these can be overcome, it would ensure that the pedagogical approach in the classroom is inclusive and empathetic. The notion of writing when you have to can also be addressed. Many teachers will see that this is the case in their own lives and careers; however, the evidence suggests that many teachers do not self-identify as writers (Cremin and Oliver, 2017). The concept of school and personal writing is one that challenges the teaching of writing – Gardner (2018) argues for a greater emphasis on personal literacy, with less focus on skills-based teaching and more scope for creating personal and reflective writing experiences. Therefore, if teachers are not experiencing these types of writing themselves, focusing only on the skills and restrictive models of writing, it could be argued that they are not offering the opportunities for pupils to deepen their understanding of the writing process.

CASE STUDY

MODEL TEXT

I wrote this Year 4 text based on the Greek gods. Zeus has gone away on a holiday and a replacement is needed in the meantime. This model text is a persuasive speech in role as Ares in an attempt to convince the other Greek gods that he would be a suitable replacement:

Gods and goddesses,

Finally, it is my turn to speak. How dare you keep the God of War waiting? My name is Ares, as you all know, and I believe that I can become the leader of the gods as I have all of the necessary skills to replace Zeus. There is clearly no one else that could do this as I am a proven, victorious and powerful candidate.

First, I am a natural leader. I have led the Olympians into battle many times and I always emerge victorious. If I am selected, I will guide everyone towards a better, brighter, stronger future.

As well as this, I have the strength to match any rival and squash any enemy. The last time Poseidon and I disagreed, he suffered at my hands. Would you like to get on the wrong side of me? By choosing me, you will have nothing to worry about.

Proud, loyal, trustworthy – the way they all describe me. I stand by the side of those who fight with me and I shall never let them down. If I am the new leader, I shall inspire mortals, inspire gods and even inspire Zeus, our magnificent leader.

It is clear that I am the perfect god for the job. I am stronger, smarter and more loyal than anyone else, therefore I am the best choice. Choose wisely or you will make the worst mistake of your immortal lives. Thank you!

In creating this, the processes identified that could be explicitly shared and taught to the children were as follows:

- Having an initial focus on grammar and punctuation choices prevented the writer focusing on audience and purpose. Focusing on the grammar and punctuation could take place after creating a first draft, during the editing process.
- This model was edited and rewritten many times, with paragraphs shifted for effect. Supporting the children in understanding the order in which they share information is critical in constructing a persuasive argument.
- Sentences were spoken out loud, trying out different phrases and word choices. Pupils need more time on oral rehearsal, both before writing and during writing, to judge and reflect on the effect of their phrasing and word choices.
- Creating this text would produce 'messier books' – editing and refining needed to be focused on to create the finished product.
- When it was being created, I acted it out as if in the throne room, speaking out loud to the gods and goddesses. Imagining the situation and acting it out supported the writer in understanding the audience and purpose. Children will need to talk out loud and 'perform' their speeches to improve and create them.
- After writing the first draft, the use of commas, dashes and exclamation marks could be reviewed. Additionally, conditional sentences, the rule of three (using three adjectives to emphasise an idea), and comparatives and superlatives presented themselves as the natural language features that could be developed with the children.

FOCUS ON RESEARCH

TEACHERS AS WRITERS AND READERS

Research into effective literacy teachers found that a detailed knowledge of children's literature distinguished them from others (Dombey, 2015). There is much research into teachers as readers, supported by the development of the Reading for Pleasure agenda (The Open University, 2019). Many key aspects from the research can be applied to the teaching of writing. An in-depth understanding of the writing process, its complexity and challenges, will create stronger teachers of writing. Bearne and Reedy (2018) note that when teachers write, they are demonstrating a model of what it is to be a writer. Bushnell et al. (2019) suggest that enthusiasm and eagerness to develop your own writing will help pupils become knowledgeable writers enormously. Brooks (2007) argues that it is up to individual teachers to establish their own writing and reading practices, and that a single model is not suitable. Consequently, we will explore some of issues relating to writing for children without fixating on a set method. The following aspects should be considered in forming your own practices and pedagogies for the teaching of writing.

Gardner (2018) advocates a personal literacy that can enhance pupils' identities as writers, and contends that writing is learning about the self. When writing as a teacher, this can place you in a vulnerable position. When writing, the role of emotion has a significant part to play (Baker and Cremin, 2018). It is notable that you may express or explore some deep-rooted emotions, as writing is a reflective process and your previous experiences as a writer, which may be negative, come to the forefront. Managing this is a delicate balancing act. There are two areas in which emotions may come to the surface. The first is writing *for* the class. When you create a text to use, you are offering it as an excellent example of what you expect from the pupils. It can also be used as a stimulus to provoke the children to express their own ideas. The reason this can be difficult is that you will be opening yourself up to possible criticism – the pupils may not appreciate the text and your colleagues might spot mistakes or issues with what you have created. Knowing that this might happen could put teachers off writing their own texts.

Second, writing with the children when modelling the writing can place you in an even more challenging situation. You will be required to think in the moment. You could make mistakes on the board. A senior leader could walk in and begin to judge the writing you are demonstrating to the children. There are a wide range of situations that could develop, so placing yourself in that position is not necessarily appealing. Morgan (2018) states that teachers become nervous and self-conscious, while Baker and Cremin (2018) explain that spontaneous composition offers little protection from emotional exposure. Managing emotions and being confident in the process can offer protection from these concerns. Equally, having more experience of writing in general means that these situations could happen less frequently. Korth et al. (2017) adds that the focus on specific skills and conventions mean that less time could be spent on the actual process of writing – that is, starting with a blank piece of paper and creating something from nothing.

Chamberlain (2019) notes that a child's definition of writing is a reflection of their teacher's approach. Pupils will see this approach through shared writing or modelled writing. These are two different concepts. Modelled writing is heavily teacher-led, with the teacher writing in front of the class and explaining decisions and their thought processes. Shared writing involves the children in co-creating a text with the teacher, where the teachers provides advice, recommendations and uses the children's ideas to create a text that can be used to support the children's independent writing. These forms of writing instruction have a role to play in understanding how to support pupils. Creating a sense of authenticity in these writing experiences is the challenge. Often, the focus is on the finished product. Equally, this could be said of the pupils' work. Instead, the focus needs to shift to the process of creating that text. If the text created is flawed in some aspect or lacks a 'finished' quality, it might be perfectly reasonable as long as the thought process involved was clearly explained to pupils and they can identify strategies they can use to create their own text. Many teachers would use a prepared text or avoid writing in front of the class if possible, to avoid making mistakes or producing writing that they have not experienced before. Overcoming this has the potential to impact on the progress of pupils in the class, as well as how you view yourself in the classroom and the pedagogical decisions you make.

Subject knowledge plays a significant part here. If this is not secure, it can be difficult to be confident in your ability to explain your grammatical decisions to the children you are working with. You need strong foundations in order to write for children so that you can focus on the processes. If you are overly worried about an expanded noun phrase, a modal verb or a subordinate clause, this can affect your ability to describe your thinking when modelling. Classroom management can also be an element that puts teachers off exploring this. It can tend to feel very teacher-led, yet a short burst of purposeful, clear and direct modelled writing can be completed with even the most challenging of classes. It can feel time-consuming, but if shared and modelled writing are not part of your pedagogical approach, it is hard to identify precisely how writing is taught directly to the pupils.

Modelled writing example

I recently composed this text for pupils in a Year 3 class. The theme was on creating instructions for how to capture a dragon.

Follow these instructions and you will soon be rid of the terrifying dragon.

- *Before the dragon is in sight, ensure your large net is ready and in position.*
- *If you need support with this, call on some fellow knights who will more than happily help rid you of this beast.*
- *Afterwards, call the dragon by standing on the top of the hill near to your net, yelling as loudly as possible.*
- *Watch the horizon carefully, looking for the approaching dragon.*
- *When spotted, run as quickly as possible towards your trap.*

In creating this, the processes identified that could be explicitly shared and taught to the children were:

- I said many of these sentences out loud. I often asked myself questions, placing myself in the position of the audience as a knight reading these instructions. This offered insight into the oral rehearsal the pupils would need.
- I found myself physically acting out the instructions, checking that the language made sense and was detailed enough. Storyboarding the instructions was useful. Getting the children to storyboard their instructions would support the planning process.
- Identifying a range of fronted adverbials was challenging. Having a resource bank of these was useful, beyond just having a list of adverbs. I used this resource when I was writing and it would benefit the children.
- Rereading was a key aspect here, mainly because instructions need clarity. I asked someone else to read them out loud. The process needed peer support.
- Role-playing as a knight writing meant that I felt less emotionally engaged. I felt I could take more risks when modelling because I was writing in role.

Pupil progress

To have a significant impact on pupil progress, the teacher's authenticity as a writer is critical. How the pupils view the teacher will contribute to their perceptions of what the writing process involves; what a competent and creative writer is; and the attitudes required to create a piece of text. Understanding the hurdles that need to be overcome can contribute to their progress because, as a result, the teacher can foresee these and put scaffolding or specific resources in place to address this. Identifying these may only come from completing the task yourself. Often, a model text can provide a clear goal or example to the pupils. A success criterion alongside this may focus on the grammatical features or organisational layout required to produce an effective piece of writing. Setting outcomes based on the writing process is not particularly prevalent. For example, when teaching a group of Year 4 pupils, the success criteria could read as saying your ideas out loud, reading your work back to check that it makes sense, and making five deliberate changes to your writing after working for five minutes. There might be no specific focus on grammar, no specific focus on organisation – instead, the focus could be on how to write and the skills needed as opposed to the outcomes. If the process becomes heavily focused on the spelling and grammar, this can detract from compositional process. They are essential elements, yet they do not need to be front and centre of every piece of writing.

Editing and refining text is another skill that can be difficult to teach. Writing for children allows this process to be explicit to pupils. Chamberlain (2019) notes that modelling and experiencing the emotional intelligence required to refine and edit writing is an aspect that can be very challenging. When writing, you will experience moments of self-doubt, of discomfort (Cremin, 2006) and it will appear that a finished version is some way off. Cremin (2006) argues that teachers need to engage artistically and creatively as writers, understanding the emotional capacity required to tolerate risk-taking and the ongoing insecurity. The question is: 'What do you do?' Children can be frustrated when they are engaged in creative writing, resulting in comments like, 'I don't know what to write' and 'It can't be improved'. Writing for pupils offers insight into these emotions and how best to manage these.

Editing is always a challenge. Children often see their work as finished and modelling this, with audience and purpose in mind, will exemplify how best to cope. At this point, it might be worth considering the skills that would be modelled here. You could argue that editing is the ability to see what has been committed to paper as fluid and changeable, revisiting the purpose of the writing, alongside making better word choices or decisions about the structure of a sentence. Again, completing this process will help the ability of the teacher to empathise with the children and be able to unpick what the feelings could be at the heart of pupils' responses. Adopting a learner-centred focus (Grainger et al., 2005) will support the teacher's ability to adapt to pupils' needs and understand how to support them when writing.

CASE STUDY

A teacher created this text to use with a Year 1 class based on a class mascot. Rocky the Rhino, the class mascot, is allowed to go home with the children on different weekends. However, in this situation, he has gone on a school trip with the class. He has written a recount to the class about the events of the day:

> Yesterday, we visited an animal park in Hereford to see all of the animals. When we got there, we had a delicious snack. Then we went to see the owl chicks. It was noisy because all of the chicks were screeching! After that, we went to feed the donkeys who ate some food out of my hand. Finally, it was lunchtime and I played on the slide with my friends. After lunch, we saw some happy goats who were jumping all over the paddock. Finally, it was time to go home.
>
> The trip was brilliant and my favourite part was seeing the owl chicks. I would really like to go again.

In creating this, the processes identified that could be explicitly shared and taught to the children were:

- Simplifying the language for a Year 1 class was difficult. Writing for Key Stage 1 pupils might appear easier – the expectations are lower than those of Key Stage 2 – but understanding which elements they will find need support with is problematic for the teacher. By creating this beforehand, it reinforced the thinking needed for modelled writing in front of the class. Identifying just one or two key areas to concentrate on is essential so that the children are not overloaded with information. As a result of this process, I felt that chronological order and consistent tenses would be the focus.

(Continued)

(Continued)

- The teacher had not considered the purpose behind the writing. He had not reflected on why 'Rocky the Rhino' was writing the recount. To develop greater depth writing at Key Stage 1, 'writing effectively and coherently for different purposes' (Standards and Testing Agency, 2017) is critical. The children might consider the purpose to be to write the recount for the teacher. This might be thought of as lacking purpose so, on reflection, the purpose would be to go on the school newsletter.
- Basing the writing on a real-life experience supported the writer and, therefore, the children. Using more real-life experiences with younger children would be beneficial.

Strategies to support writing for children

Writing for pupils will help develop a deeper understanding of the writing process and how best to support pupils. Below are several suggestions for activities or ideas that could support deeper writing by all pupils in your class:

- **Personal writing**
  - o   The starting point is to find time to write yourself, for creative or artistic purposes. Knowing that it serves a purpose – deepening your understanding of how it feels and what is involved in writing – will support your understanding of the children you teach. It will also help in developing your writer identify. Your perceived writer identify is not set in stone – it can be dynamic and changeable (Eyres, 2018). A reflective journal or diary is a good place to start.

- **Developing agency**
  - o   A skills-based curriculum, heavily focused on transcription and grammar, belies the broad spectrum of what it takes to become a writer. To develop both your autonomy and that of the children, it is beneficial to start writing regularly. You could begin with writing alongside the pupils. Giving modelled or shared writing a go, even with some support such as a prepared text, is a starting point, but moving on to writing with no preconceived ideas will help the children to see the writing process as it really is. After this, writing while they are working for a short period of time will help the children see you as a writer, and this modelling can provide vital support and encouragement for the class. It demonstrates the values and attitudes required – an essential part of being a writer.

- **A bank of writing**
  - o   When you have constructed and created a model text, you can begin to build up a bank of texts. Rather than searching in books, online or for other resources, you

will have discovered the best resource possible – yourself. Having 20–30 'go to texts' could be enough to last a couple of years and they could be adapted to suit different classes and year groups. The experience of writing them will also give you confidence and enjoyment.

- **Scaffolding**
  - o   Understanding how to build up children's resilience can be supported by completing similar tasks to them. As explained in this chapter, writing for children can support you in understanding how to overcome the challenges they will face. Voicing your inner talk (Cain, 2018) can support their experiences. Mistakes might happen when writing, but teaching children what to do about it will scaffold their own personal writing experiences.

- **Grammar in context**
  - o   There are many arguments suggesting that grammar is best taught in context (Myhill et al., 2012; Andrews et al., 2006). When writing for pupils, you will be making purposeful decisions about the grammar needed. This will be appropriate to the text you are creating, which should prevent 'shoehorning' grammar in, as you will know what sentence structures or word choices will be the best to model the pupils. Often, teachers believe they know the grammar that is needed but, when writing, it draws attention to the specific grammar that could be challenging for pupils that had not been thought of beforehand. Writing for children will also address the balance of composition to transcription and grammar. The last elements can often be heavily focused on, meaning that composition can get lost. The two go hand-in-hand; writing texts yourself will help model the use of grammar in context.

- **A writing community**
  - o   Establishing a school community of writers will do wonders to the profile and understanding of writing in your school. Imagine a school where everyone understands how it feels and what is needed to put pen to paper and create something from nothing. Friendship encourages creativity and risk-taking when writing (Grainger et al., 2005). Creating shared experiences between staff, teachers and children and the wider community will create a learning environment conducive to writing and the writing experience.

- **Technology**
  - o   The use of technology-enhanced learning and its links to writing are only just being realised. Composition does not necessarily involve writing with a pen; everyone is typing text messages, using social media and computers to create. Embracing this process and modelling this for pupils has real potential. It is very supportive for the editing and refining process, and does allow for a greater focus on compositional elements. This is because it can autocorrect and negate some of the challenging elements for pupils. If focusing just on the process, using technology to model the writing process could offer you a way in that you had yet to consider.

CASE STUDY

This warning tale narrative (Corbett, 2001) was created for a Year 6 class, whose topic was based on exploration and featured a new character entitled Ellie the Explorer:

Suddenly, Ellie awoke. She pulled herself out of her sleeping bag, tiptoed over to her step-brother Hunter and shook him awake.

'Come on! It's time to go,' whispered Ellie.

Grabbing their backpacks, they climbed out of their tents. Their parents' tent didn't move. Silently and slowly, they walked into the woods of the Amazon rainforest to begin their search. Ellie knew that her parents had warned her about going out into the rainforest alone, but she had to try and find it. The jewel everyone wanted – the INCA diamond!

'Ellie, I'm tired,' complained Hunter. 'Mum and dad said we shouldn't come out here without them. We're going to get into so much trouble.'

'We'll be back before they're even awake,' Ellie replied.

As they got further into the trees and undergrowth, the noises in the forest got louder and louder. Birds squawked, trees groaned, and creatures moved. Ellie began to feel nervous.

All of a sudden, something moved in the bushes in front of them. Hunter and Ellie froze. They saw it move again, then the nose and whiskers of a jaguar poked out from behind the leaves. It gave out a loud growl as it stared at the two small explorers.

'Don't move,' said Ellie, shaking with nerves.

'I can't move,' Hunter replied, 'otherwise it'll pounce on us. What are we going to do?'

Before he could utter another word, the bushes behind them rustled loudly. They turned and saw their dad appear. Bravely, their dad moved forward pointing his rifle at the jaguar.

'Ellie, Hunter – get behind me. Now!'

They slowly stepped behind him. After a few seconds, the tiger turned around and made its way back into the rainforest. Dad crouched down and Ellie and Hunter gave him a big hug.

'Now, whose idea was this early morning walk?' he asked.

Hunter pointed at Ellie and she looked at the floor.

'Well Ellie, off exploring again. Being the daughter of a famous explorer hasn't helped has it? Let's get you both back to the camp where we're safe,' Dad said.

Ellie began to walk and gave a big sigh. She'd got away with it! Maybe they could try again the next day. Then she heard her Dad's voice again.

'Oh, and Ellie?'

'Yes, Dad.'

'You're on washing up duty for the next two weeks!'

Groaning, Ellie carried on trudging back to camp. She'd have to keep her search for the diamond under wraps . . . for now.

In creating this, the processes identified that could be explicitly shared and taught to the children were:

- Planning was time-consuming. I used story-mapping to create the warning tale. The characters and their relationships had to be carefully considered. When constructing a complex narrative, children need time to create the world in which the story will be set. To expect them to generate it on the spot is unrealistic and not representative of the writing process. More structured planning time would make a difference.
- The process of deciding how the characters spoke – their levels of formality – was a challenging aspect. Shifting from narrator to character appears straightforward, but this transition is complicated if the children do not have clarity over who their characters are and the voice they use. Understanding how to switch voice from character to character with relative ease became an aspect to focus on with the children. To support this, identifying that going into greater depth about their characters was essential before writing and modelling how to 'become' each character when writing their dialogue, through the use of voices and acknowledging out loud who to write as at that moment in time, would be required to support all pupils. Writing at greater depth in Key Stage 2 requires subtle shifts in formality, but writing for the children highlighted how explaining this can be difficult.
- As this was a longer text, demonstrating a passion for the process was important (Grainger et al., 2005). Writing has its ups and downs. Managing the rollercoaster of the writing process, such as the moments where there are no ideas forthcoming or struggling to find the right words to express a particular moment, and how to work through those moments, requires enthusiasm and determination. Modelling these attributes to pupils is vital, with the reward of an engaging and successful text created at the end.

Conclusion

Deeper writing necessitates an in-depth understanding of the writing process. It requires teachers to be reflective and writing for others can be profoundly moving. This goes beyond subject knowledge such as grammar terminology and spelling strategies. Although these are integral to writing, knowing, understanding and, more importantly, experiencing the writing process through writing for pupils will immeasurably improve writing in the class for all pupils. Supporting struggling writers is problematic for teachers, who often focus on grammar and word classes to aid progress rather than the more process and creative elements of writing. Teachers can lack confidence in teaching writing, which leads them to focus on skills with pupils as these can be understood and taught more quickly (Dix and Cawkwell, 2011). To have the understanding and knowledge of how it feels to write, what has influenced you as a writer and what is involved in the process can have a powerful pedagogical impact (Räisänen et al., 2016). Deeper writing is not just about more adverbs, expanded noun phrases and spelling every single word precisely. It means becoming more knowledgeable about how to write – the attitudes, attributes and environment that supports the writer most effectively – alongside becoming knowledgeable about yourself and the world in which you live.

References

Andrews, R., Torgerson, C., Beverton, S., Freeman, A., Locke, T., Low, G., Robinson, A. and Zhu, D. (2006) The effect of grammar teaching on writing development. *British Educational Research Journal*, 32(1): 39–55.

Baker, S. and Cremin, T. (2018) Teachers' identities as writers, in Cremin, T. and Locke, T. (eds) *Writer Identity and the Teaching and Learning of Writing*. London: Routledge, pp. 98–114.

Bearne, E. and Reedy, D. (2018) *Teaching Primary English*. London: Routledge.

Brooks, G.W. (2007) Teachers as readers and writers and as teachers of reading and writing. *The Journal of Educational Research*, 100(3): 177–91.

Bushnell, A., Smith, R. and Waugh, D. (2019) *Modelling Exciting Writing: A Guide for Primary Teaching*. London: Sage.

Cain, M. (2018) *Teaching for Mastery in Writing*. London: Bloomsbury.

Chamberlain, L. (2019) *Inspiring Writing in Primary Schools* (2nd edn). London: Sage.

Corbett, P. (2001) *How to Teach Fiction Writing at Key Stage 2*. London: Routledge.

Cremin, T. (2006) Creativity, uncertainty and discomfort: teachers as writers. *Cambridge Journal of Education*, 36(3): 415–33.

Cremin, T. and Oliver, L. (2017) Teachers as writers: a systematic review. *Research Papers in Education*, 32(3): 269–95.

Department for Education (DfE) (2014) The National Curriculum in England: Framework for Key Stages 1 to 4. Available online at: www.gov.uk/government/publications/national-curriculum-in-england-framework-for-key-stages-1-to-4/the-national-curriculum-in-england-framework-for-key-stages-1-to-4#inclusion (accessed 21 March 2019).

Dix, S. and Cawkwell, G. (2011) The influence of peer group response: building a teacher and student expertise in the writing classroom. *English Teaching: Practice and Critique*, 10(4): 41–57.

Dombey, H. (2015) Creatively engaging readers in the early primary years, in Cremin, T. (ed.) *Teaching English Creatively* (2nd edn). London: Routledge, pp. 41–52.

Eyres, I. (2017) Conceptualising writing and identity, in Cremin, T. and Locke, T. (eds) *Writer Identity and the Teaching and Learning of Writing*. London: Routledge, pp. 3–18.

Gardner, P. (2018) Writing and writer identity: the poor relation and the search for voice in 'personal literacy'. *Literacy*, 52(1): 11–19.

Grainger, T., Goouch, K. and Lambirth, A. (2005) *Creativity and Writing: Developing Voice and Verve in the Classroom*. London: Routledge.

Korth, B., Wimmer, J., Wilcox, B., Morrison, T., Harward, S., Peterson, N., Simmerman, S. and Pierce, L. (2017) Practices and challenges of writing instruction in K-2 classrooms: a case study of five primary grade teachers. *Early Childhood Education Journal*, 45: 237–49.

Morgan, D.N. (2018) 'I'm not a good writer': supporting teachers' writing identities in a university course, in Cremin, T. and Locke, T. (eds) *Writer Identity and the Teaching and Learning of Writing*. London: Routledge, pp. 3–18.

Myhill, D.A., Jones, S.M., Lines, H. and Watson, A. (2012) Re-thinking grammar: the impact of embedded grammar teaching on students' writing and students' metalinguistic understanding. *Research Papers in Education*, 27(2): 139–66.

National Literacy Trust (2018) Writing enjoyment, behaviours and attitudes in 8- to 11-year-olds in 2017/18. Available online at: https://literacytrust.org.uk/research-services/research-reports/writing-enjoyment-research-2017-18/ (accessed 20 March 2019).

The Open University (2019) Reading for pleasure. Available online at: https://researchrichpedagogies.org/research/reading-for-pleasure (accessed 29 March 2019).

Räisänen, S., Korkeamäki, R. and Dreher, M. (2016) Changing literacy practices according to the Finnish core curriculum. *European Early Childhood Education Research Journal*, 24(2): 198–214.

Standards and Testing Agency (2017) Teacher Assessment Frameworks at the end of Key Stage 1. Available online at: https://www.gov.uk/government/publications/teacher-assessment-frameworks-at-the-end-of-key-stage-1 (accessed 18 March 2019).

Standards and Testing Agency (2018a) Teacher assessment frameworks at the end of key stage 1. Available online at: https://assets.publishing.service.gov.uk/government/uploads/system/uploads/attachment_data/file/740343/2018-19_teacher_assessment_frameworks_at_the_end_of_key_stage_1_WEBHO.pdf (Accessed 21 March 2019).

Standards and Testing Agency (2018b) Teacher assessment frameworks at the end of key stage 2. Available online at: https://dera.ioe.ac.uk/31092/1/Teacher_assessment_frameworks_at_the_end_of_key_stage_2_for_use_from_the_2018_to_2019_academic_year_onwards.pdf (Accessed 21 March 2019).

8
DEEPER WRITING THROUGH DRAMA

Christina Castling

KEY QUESTIONS

- How can drama be used as a means of laying the groundwork for deeper writing?
- How do I become familiar with some key drama-based activities that can be used to inspire writing?
- What is my personal attitude to drama, creativity and play?

Introduction

This chapter is going to start a little differently from the others so far in the book.

Get yourself a pen and a piece of paper. Done it? Good. Now, your challenge is to write a story beginning with: 'It was just like any other Wednesday . . . '

You've got three minutes – go!

How was that? Enjoyable? Torturous? Somewhere in between? Some of you will feel like you've missed your calling to be a novelist, while others will wonder at how a seemingly simple task can feel so difficult. How do you think the rest of your staff team, your fellow teachers, would find it?

CASE STUDY

WHEN TEACHERS WRITE . . .

At the beginning of a half-day creative writing CPD session, teachers from a primary school in Sunderland were given the same challenge: a blank sheet of paper, a pen and three minutes. Some scribbled away furiously, some stared at the blank page tapping the pen and some nervously looked at what other people were doing. When the timer stopped, there were a variety of responses:

'I didn't have a clue what to write.'

'I had loads of ideas.'

'It was horrible.'

'I was really worried you were going to ask me to read it out.'

'I kept trying to think of better adjectives and that stopped me writing.'

'I loved it.'

'The time pressure was stressful.'

And then, the penny-dropping moment and the comment accompanied by many nods of agreement:

'It made me realise what some of the children in my class feel like when I ask them to write.'

With a full-to-bursting curriculum and literacy lessons tightly packed, there is rarely a spare moment to put pencils down and head into the hall for a bit of fun with drama. Instead, the heads need to get down and complete the writing. If drama isn't simply 'a bit of fun', however, and can rather wield a striking power to unleash creativity and pave the way for deeper writing, making time for it and learning how best to utilise it is surely worthwhile. This is what the Sunderland teachers in the case study started to discover.

CASE STUDY (CONTINUED)

After a wide range of quick-fire drama activities to inspire creative ideas, to build confidence in storymaking and to enjoy shared experience, the teachers were asked, again, to write for three minutes. This time, everyone wrote immediately and some were decidedly unwilling to stop. There was eagerness to share their writing with each other and all agreed that it was easier to write, was a more enjoyable experience and yielded better results than the first writing challenge.

This chapter will explore the ways in which drama can be used to provide a firm grounding for deeper writing, offering practical suggestions of how to bed this down into your teaching practice, and will consider whether having 'a bit of fun' along the way is important.

When starting to build

In *Practice, Pedagogy and Policy: The Influence of Teachers' Creative Writing Practice on Pedagogy in Schools* (2012), Caroline Murphy provides a useful examination of how creative writing has been conceptualised in educational policy, beginning with the Newbolt Report (Board of Education, 1926). In exploring Newbolt's insights which, although written nearly 100 years ago feel strikingly contemporary, Murphy draws attention to a metaphor that is helpful in exploring deeper writing – that of erecting a building. Newbolt suggests that too great an emphasis on technical accuracy in writing at the expense of creative expression is 'criticising bricks, not architecture', and that this can lead to 'a slow but steady process of discouragement which, in the end, must subdue even the bravest spirit' (Board of Education, p. 75). His assertion that writing should, instead, be 'a genuine attempt by the pupil to express as well as he can what he is really capable of thinking and saying' (Board of Education, p. 75) is a liberating idea and one that is all too easily lost on those young writers who struggle with where to put a comma and how to use a fronted adverbial. If children can be captivated by a vision of the building they want to create, with all its beauty and individuality, the placing of the bricks suddenly feels much more important. A solitary block of clay is not particularly interesting – until, that is, you realise it can help create a palace.

The idea that having a bigger vision or purpose for writing motivates children is widely documented. What is perhaps less readily taken into account, however, is, to continue the building metaphor: how the ground should be prepared for the foundations. Before placing a single brick, the ground has to be softened, broken up, made ready. And that's where drama comes in.

Preparing the ground

It would be wonderful if deep writing came easily, flowing from the pen, or to the keyboard, with a flourish. The reality, however, is somewhat different. Even confident and skilled writers can struggle to 'get started' and, having started, to know where to turn next. When used well, a drama-based approach can get a class prepared for writing, thus enabling deeper writing to grow and develop more easily thereafter. This chapter will explore four main ways in which drama can get the ground ready:

- Saying 'yes' to ideas.
- Experimenting and experiencing through play.
- Working collaboratively.
- Having fun.

Saying 'yes' to ideas

'Yes' is arguably the most important word in creativity. It demonstrates a willingness to explore, giving ideas space to breathe before allowing the internal critic to question their validity. When encouraging children in their writing, however, it is easy to unintentionally communicate a 'Well, I guess so', rather than a 'Yes!'. By continually pushing for 'better' or 'more interesting' ideas, there is a lurking suggestion that an idea is not *quite* good enough.

Certainly, there is a need to delve into creative ideas, to inspire and empower deeper writing, but if those ideas are judged harshly at a ground-readying stage, this can easily stop the building altogether. Approaching writing with a determined attitude of acceptance and a readiness to follow ideas (however ridiculous) where they lead, may seem a frightening prospect, but it also provides opportunities for new and surprising discoveries.

A popular tweet in 2013 suggested that the 'creative process' could be described as:

1. This is going to be awesome.
2. This is hard.
3. This is terrible.
4. I'm terrible.
5. Hey, not bad.
6. That was awesome.

(www.twitter.com/boltcity/status/369484217349992448)

The first step – 'This is going to be awesome' – is a loud 'yes' to a creative idea; it's what gets the creative process going. The tweet suggests that this is followed by a realisation that it's not so easy after all, that maybe it is not going to be any good and 'Why did I think I could do it in the first place?' With a learned resilience, that doubt gives way to perseverance and ultimately the creation of something of which to be proud. The problem often faced when writing in the classroom is that if children don't begin with 'yes', if they are not invested in and excited by the starting point, they jump into the creative process at step two. Before being excited by the potential of what could be created (the beauty of a building that could be built), a child simply says, 'this is hard', moves swiftly to 'this is terrible' and even more quickly to 'I'm terrible'. Some writing might be produced, but it is unlikely to be accompanied by a 'that was awesome'. If this process is repeated often enough, we are left with children convinced that not only is writing hard, but that they are terrible at it.

A 'yes' at the beginning of writing clearly does not solve all problems. There is still work to be done in shaping ideas and, more specifically, in building confidence with struggling writers, but it certainly starts the journey in the right direction.

The following activity champions 'yes'.

ACTIVITY 1   'THIS IS NOT A . . .'

This activity celebrates imaginative ideas, promotes quick thinking and provides a useful jumping-off point for writing exercises. It demonstrates that creative ideas can spring up from the most mundane of objects (a scarf, a water-bottle, a shoe) and this can be a liberating realisation for children who have limited life experiences.

To start with, get everyone to stand in a circle. Reveal an object to the group (I often begin with a scarf) and explain that it is going to change into something new. Establish a convention for how this will happen (for young children, try blowing invisible, magic dust, and for older children, try a quick click of the fingers), then hold out the scarf to demonstrate:

'This is not a scarf, this is . . . a tail.'

Another blow of dust/click of the fingers: 'This is not a scarf, this is . . . a golf club.'

Another blow of dust/click of the fingers: 'This is not a scarf, this is . . . a slide for a teeny, tiny elephant.'

With each of your suggestions, mime the new use of the object: wiggle the scarf like a tail, swing it like a golf club, let your finger be the elephant whooshing down the slide. (Note that the freer you are with your creative ideas, the greater the licence you give the children to be free with theirs.) Once you have demonstrated, pass the object to the child next to you and, following the click or blow of magic dust, encourage him or her to do their own

'This is not a . . . ' with an accompanying mime. The object can then be passed round everyone in the class.

Enjoy listening to their ideas and praise the children for finding unexpected uses for the scarf. When silly ideas come up, say 'yes' to them as far as possible: why would the scarf not be earwax or vomit or a bogey? (Plenty of writers for children demonstrate how much fun can be had with things considered revolting and disgusting by grown ups – Roald Dahl's *Revolting Rhymes and Dirty Beasts* (2016), for example.) Accepting silly ideas begins to demonstrate that writing is an arena in which fun and laughter are allowed and where saying 'yes' can lead to exciting places.

Links to children's literature

There are many great stories that explore unexpected uses of mundane objects. This activity can provide an introduction to a deeper engagement with a variety of texts – for example:

- *No-Bot: The Robot with No Bottom* (Hendra, 2013) Bernard the Robot loses his bottom and discovers his friends had been using it all along: Bird as a nest, Bear for his drum kit and the Squirrels to build sandcastles. A picture book.
- *Jack and the Flumflum Tree* (Donaldson, 2011) Jack sets off to find the fruit of the flum-flum tree. Armed with a patchwork sack of strange items from chewing gum to tent pegs, Jack and his friends have to think creatively as they encounter all sorts of problems on the journey. A rhyming picture book.
- *The Borrowers* (Norton, 2014) The Borrowers live out of sight, tucked away in old houses. They use humans' objects for their own special purposes and, although girls aren't supposed to go borrowing, Arrietty does and soon makes friends with the boy of the house. A chapter book.

Experimenting and experiencing through play

'Play' can be a confusing term, meaning many different things in relation to exploration and creativity. Here, we will be using 'play' to refer to a realm of creativity where experimentation is characteristic and discoveries are made through experience. That is not to say that play is totally free and formless, but that it embraces freedom within the structure it is given. Anna Craft refers to play as having 'an openness to possibilities' (cited in Winston, 2004, p. 115) and it is as these possibilities are explored that they can begin to give way to more thoughtful and deeper writing.

It is a fallacy that to maintain control of behaviour, teachers must be separate from play and watching from the sidelines. In being prepared to participate in any play that is instigated, a teacher models creative freedom and will witness the joy on their children's faces as they see their teacher becoming an elephant stomping around the room or a Roman soldier marching in their ranks. As Winston claims: 'crucial to the whole mix is the teacher's willingness to play, too – not only that, but to play harder than the children themselves . . . in this way your own play can become a licence and a model for theirs' (Winston, 2004, p. 10).

Playing 'in role'

Much has been written on drama in the classroom that focuses on creating 'a drama' together – i.e. entering an imagined world as a class and making creative discoveries through that immediate shared experience. This idea is rooted in the work of Dorothy Heathcote, who developed the concept of 'teacher in role' as a way for children to deepen their learning through experience. The books of Winston (2004) and O'Neill and Lambert (1989) provide helpful structures for lessons of this style. In reading books like these, it can be tempting to assume that to use drama successfully, one must be able to convincingly adopt a character, sustaining this role for an entire lesson, and confidently guide a class through an imagined world without breaking the illusion or losing the children's focus. However, as Fleming notes: 'many students and teachers embark on simple role play with a class only to come out shell-shocked and disillusioned' (Fleming, 2017, p. 57), attributing this to pupils failing to take the drama seriously, the drama failing to materialise and control breaking down (Fleming, p. 60). When playing 'in role', it is beneficial to make good use of practical advice – for example, Fleming's *Starting Drama Teaching* – and to start small, adopting a role in just one activity (as in the case study below), to enable a growth in confidence and development of skills for both you and the class.

It is also to be remembered that as fruitful as creating drama in role can be, it is by no means the only way to experience and experiment with ideas – i.e. to play (the warm-up activities and still image detailed below led to equally valid creative discoveries). A broad attitude to play, one that encourages a continual hunting out of opportunities, however small, for a class to experiment with possibilities, inspires deeper writing, whether a teacher 'becomes' a different person in the process or not.

CASE STUDY

A WHALE WASHED UP ON BLYTH BEACH

The Year 6 class at a primary school in Northumberland took part in a drama lesson to inspire ideas for report writing. After a series of warm-up activities (including the children using their bodies to make shapes of items found in the sea), the class began to create a still image of an imagined moment: a whale being discovered on Blyth beach.

A group of children took up position as the whale and, as each child offered a suggestion of an addition to the scene, the teacher asked them to join the frozen picture.

Within a few minutes, the whole class was included. There were lifeguards, a passer-by with her dog, police officers, fire fighters, a film crew and some children on a day out. The teacher walked around the image tapping each child on the shoulder to hear their thoughts and feelings. Even the whale voiced his desire: 'I want to go back to the ocean.'

The image was given a title – a headline to be used later in report writing – and the children then split into small groups. The teacher explained that when she put on her hat, she would become a television executive and asked the children to give that character a name. On putting on the hat, 'Francesca' addressed the children as reporters in the field: before 'Right everyone, we'll be on air in 5 minutes and I expect each of you to have your reports ready. I want a description of what's happened, interviews, facts and anything else you think might work. Make sure you know who's saying what. Don't let me down. Get started . . .'

She spoke with each group to ensure they were on task and gave a two-minute warning. She also selected one of the less confident members of the class to become the cameraman and ensured all speaking was directed to him throughout the report. With a 5, 4, 3, 2, 1, the news report was live: 'Good afternoon, I am here on Blyth beach where events are unfolding at an extraordinary rate. Over to our first reporter for more information . . .' The teacher acted as a bridge between each group, providing additional support as necessary, and rounded the 'recording' up with a 'Thank you for watching and back to the studio'.

Following the workshop, the children went back to the classroom ready to write a newspaper report, armed with quotes, statistics, eye-witness accounts and a clear image in their minds of what the event looked like. This inspired and equipped them for deeper writing.

The children's evaluation of their work highlighted the benefits of playing in this way. When asked if drama was useful in their writing, they answered:

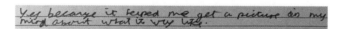

Figure 8.1   Child's evaluation of writing

'Yes because it helped me get a picture in my mind about what it was like.'

Figure 8.2   Further evaluation of the writing

'Yes, because you got to feel what the character that you were would have been feeling.'

Working collaboratively

While writing can often be viewed as a solitary pursuit – we picture an author sitting alone at a desk, poring over their words – this needn't be the case and, in fact, as is stated by Baldwin and John (2012, p. 22), 'working supportively with collaborating peers, can leave children less individually and personally exposed, with the result that they may be less fearful about the writing they are doing together'. Drama is, by its very nature, collaborative and so, by closely aligning it with writing, the way can be prepared for a less intimidating experience and the creation of work that has greater depth.

ACTIVITY 2   WALK THE STORY

Walking the story as a full class enables everyone to share in creating ideas – e.g. creating a story or location. It encourages fast thinking and relies on listening to and building on each other's ideas. While this activity can feel a little scary to begin with, once it has been practised a few times, it can lead to fruitful shared story experiences.

To start with, get everyone standing in a circle and ensure there is a gap between the two children standing opposite you.

We are going to make up a story together (or create a wonderful description of a place) as a whole class. We'll all need to join in to make it as good as it can be. The rules are: 1) you're only allowed to speak when you're walking across the circle and 2) there's only allowed to be one person in the circle at a time.

Do a quick demonstration by walking across the circle towards the gap and starting a story/beginning some description. Stop speaking when you reach the gap. Ask for a volunteer to continue the story/description and allow them to walk across the circle, saying their sentence and finishing in the gap you left in the circle. Do this slowly with volunteers a few times to ensure that everyone understands the concept, then ask for suggestions as to what will make this game work best – i.e:

- listening well to each other and building on each other's ideas;
- being brave and joining in;
- being kind and respectful of others' ideas.

Then, try doing a full class story or description. To begin with, ask the children to put a finger on their nose if they have an idea, as this enables you to choose which child enters the circle and ensures that dominant voices do not take over. For older children or those experienced in collaborative creating, removing teacher selection is a good challenge in considerate turn-taking. The children will be tempted to rush across the circle, but encourage them to take it slowly as it works best at a leisurely pace.

Coach the class as you go – for example:

- *I'd like to hear more about this creepy bridge.*
- *Who can tell us what that character's clothes are like?*
- *Let's have some more detail about that.*

Having taken part in this activity, the children are ready to tackle a story-writing task. They will already have said, or heard classmates say, sentences that could be included in their story and so, not only will the blank page be less intimidating, but having been coached in searching for more detail, they will be better equipped for deeper writing.

FOCUS ON RESEARCH

The creative energy in developing characters, locations and stories collaboratively is harnessed daily in writing centres across the world. The first of these, 826 Valencia, was started in San Francisco in 2002 by author Dave Eggers, and the idea spread internationally, with writing centres now established in the UK and Ireland – i.e. Ministry of Stories, Grimm & Co, Fighting Words and Live Tales. In these story-writing workshops, children do not write individually until they have first created characters, a location and the beginning of a narrative as a class. There is whole-group investment in this shared creativity, thus empowering the individual's writing thereafter. Not only does this provide a vibrant atmosphere in which to write, it also encourages the children to view themselves as writers.

This opportunity for identity to be recast is one of the gifts that drama offers children who may be deemed 'challenging' in other learning contexts. As Baldwin and John note, 'sometimes classmates find themselves looking at each other anew when a child who has difficulty with the process of writing comes up with the best ideas' (2012, p. 22). Winston also draws attention to this potential for transformation, referring to collaboration within in role drama work:

> *instead of being powerless, they can take on the role of someone powerful. Instead of performing a social role that they may well not be happy with – a child deemed to have special needs, for example – they can become someone who is respected and listened to.*

> (Winston, 2004, p. 12)

The opportunity that working collaboratively through drama provides to push against the restrictions sometimes holding children back was simply expressed by a Year 6 pupil from New Delaval Primary:

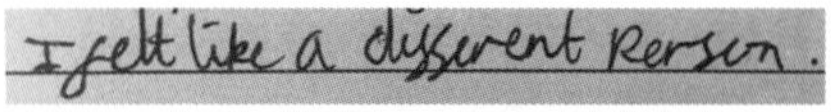

I felt like a different person.

Figure 8.3   Year 6 child's reflection on participation in a collaborative drama activity

I felt like a different person.

In the case study below, less confident members of the class were markedly keen to take on the imagined role and children who were considered 'reluctant writers' in the classroom were eager to put pen to paper.

CASE STUDY

CREATING A CLASS CHARACTER: ALLY TELLTALE

A Key Stage 2 class at a County Durham school had been working weekly with a local writer to develop skills in creative writing. In this session, they were experimenting with ideas for character.

With the children sitting in a circle, the writer carefully placed a suitcase, hat and scarf in the middle, explaining that these belonged to a character the children hadn't met yet. She asked the children, 'What questions could we ask this person to find out more about them?' Throwing a beach ball from child to child, a series of suggestions were gathered, including:

- 'How old are you?'
- 'Do you live with your family?'
- 'What makes you happy?'
- 'Do you have any pets?'
- 'Where do you go on adventures?'

'I don't know about you', said the writer, 'but I'd really like to meet this person.' The children agreed and the writer selected a child, Saafir, to become the character, asking him to put on the hat and scarf, and to hold onto the suitcase. 'Now everyone, let's look at how this character is standing and what expression they have on their face.' With an encouragement to Saafir to stand as still as he could, the class discussed what this character looked like, the writer pushing for deeper and more detailed description. After a few minutes the writer asked: 'I think it'd be good to have Saafir back in the room, wouldn't it . . . ?' and Saafir rejoined the group. 'Saafir, welcome back. Oh, we missed you. You'll never believe it, but while you were gone, we met the person who owns these objects. Could someone tell Saafir what we saw?' The children then recounted the detailed descriptions from a few minutes earlier, with Saafir eagerly listening to what he had 'just missed'.

With an, 'I don't know about you, but I'd really like to find out more about this person', the writer selected a different child to become the character (insisting they wear the costume in the same way as Saafir had). This time, the group was given opportunity to question the character, using the suggestions from earlier. The character name was established – Ally Telltale – and various details were discovered about him: he was lonely, he had never been far from home, he had a suitcase full of gadgets and he loved chicken nuggets. The writer, again, mined for detail by encouraging probing questions and, as before, after a few minutes welcomed the child back into the room with a 'We missed you. You'll never believe it, but while you were gone . . . '.

This process was repeated and as the children recognised the pattern, they fully embraced the playfulness of welcoming the child back and sharing information about Ally Telltale. The writer then explained that Ally Telltale was going to visit a new place for the first time and was nervous about meeting new people. The challenge was set for each child to write an introduction that Ally could use.

The children enthusiastically found a space of their own around the hall, some sitting on chairs, others lying on their fronts, to write their introductions. The session was drawn to a close by those who were happy to share their writing by reading their introduction as Ally Telltale while, of course, wearing the costume and holding the suitcase.

Having fun

Learning and enjoyment can sadly be placed all too easily at opposite ends of the spectrum: it would be nice if children enjoyed the task, but it's more important that they deepen their skills in writing. Within this thinking, if drama is simply about having fun, it has little, if any, place in an English lesson. If, however, fun is a deeply significant part of the writing process, drama can be seen to play an important role.

FOCUS ON RESEARCH

Using data from nearly 40,000 pupils aged 8–18, the National Literacy Trust points to a link between writing enjoyment and writing behaviour, confidence, motivation and attainment. More specifically, NLT notes that, 'eight times as many children and young people who enjoy writing write above the expected level for their age compared with those who don't enjoy writing'. Their findings highlight 'the importance of writing enjoyment for children's outcomes and warrant a call for more attention on writing enjoyment in schools, research and policy' (Clark and Teravainen, 2017, p. 15).

To return to Newbolt's metaphor, if convinced that building is going to be boring, why bother to begin in the first place? If, however, on starting to dig the ground, the process turns out to be enjoyable, placing bricks on top of each other becomes a distinctly less intimidating and disheartening task. When drama activities are used intentionally, being well-structured and integrated fully into lesson planning, they can inspire the most reluctant of writers to grab a pencil and start scribbling: '(o)nce we enjoy something, we want to do it again and we gradually get better at it (whether it be drama or writing)' (Baldwin and John, 2014, p. 20). Therefore, for 'children who are particularly struggling with writing and those who have become disaffected by failure, drama can be a lifeline for re-engagement and for building up their self-esteem and belief in themselves as writers' (Baldwin and John, 2014, pp. 21–2). Drama enables children to see that writing is not simply about putting words on a page, but instead is a means by which they can share their extraordinary ideas with others.

How to pepper your practice with drama

Having examined four different ways in which drama can be used to prepare for the foundations of deep writing, here follows three top tips for peppering your practice with drama:

1. Take time to do a quick warm-up

In a rehearsal room, there will always be a warm-up because there is an understanding that, however experienced the actors, coming 'cold' to creativity will not lead to high-quality work. The same is true in a classroom. If you are about to do some creative writing, set aside even just a couple of minutes to warm up the body and the imagination. You could try:

- a speedy physical warm-up (e.g. jog on the spot for 5 seconds, wiggle your left elbow for 6 seconds, scrunch your nose for 8.5 seconds);
- moving the body into strange positions (e.g. make your body as huge/tiny/wide/thin as possible);
- quick fire words (e.g. coming up with as many words as possible, beginning with a letter);
- tongue-twisters (e.g. she sells sea shells on the sea shore);
- asking the class for a suggestion of a 30-second warm-up (if they are familiar with these quick-fire activities, the children will have some weird and wonderful suggestions you could use).

2. Get out from behind the desk

As Baldwin and John note, 'in English lessons, too many teachers and children in classrooms remain stubbornly and unnecessarily desk-bound for much of the time' (2012, p. xii). Keep looking for ways you can get the children up on their feet, asking yourself: 'Is there a way to experience this instead of just talking about it?' If there is mention of music in a story, listen to it; if food, taste it; if you're exploring suspense, pull the blinds down and create spooky sentences by torchlight; if you're doing descriptive writing about being crammed into the hold of a ship, mark out the area with benches, sit close together and share what being squashed really feels like. Sometimes it isn't practical to re-create experiences and talking about ideas is more appropriate. In doing this, why not try moving to a different space: under a tree, in a den under the tables, lying on tummies in a circle in the school hall? You'll be surprised by the difference a change of environment makes.

3. Embrace unpredictability

An unknown outcome can be a daunting thing, but it can also lead to exciting discoveries. In the unpredictability of drama, 'motivation and understanding will be strengthened, language use extended, flexibility of mind encouraged, concepts tested, and opportunities created for creative thinking and problem solving' (O'Neill and Lambert, 1989, pp. 20–1). Ask yourself, 'If this goes wrong, what's the worst that could happen?' and accept that risk-taking can be worth it. Leave some space for the unexpected in your planning, don't answer every question and give yourself the freedom to be surprised. Teaching your children to take creative risks while in a safe and supportive space will give them the ability to push at the boundaries of their knowledge and understanding as they get older. In a quickly changing world where innovation is prized and creativity is considered the most desirable skill an employer looks for, giving your children the tools to tackle the unexpected with enthusiasm and confidence will equip them well for the future.

FOCUS ON RESEARCH

LinkedIn's Economic Graph (the global economy represented digitally, based on 590 million members, 50 thousand skills, 30 million companies and 20 million open jobs) suggests that 'creativity is the single-most important skill in the world for all business professionals today to master'. LinkedIn Learning Instructor Stefan Mumaw, who has written six books focusing on creativity, defines it as: 'problem-solving with relevance and novelty'. He claims that while some people might be naturally more creative than others, it is not an innate ability and therefore, by investing time and energy, one can learn how to be more creative.

(www.learning.linkedin.com/blog/top-skills/why-creativity-is-the-most-important-skill-in-the-world)

Conclusion

This chapter has explored how using a drama-based approach can get a class ready to put pencil to paper. By taking time to say 'yes' to ideas, to experiment and experience through play, and to work collaboratively, children not only have fun, but are being readied for deeper writing. Although it is tempting to rush the writing process, this time of preparation is crucial and yields great results.

So, to return to Newbolt's architectural image: let us empower children to become master builders and help them to ready the ground for the foundations. May they dream big dreams of what their buildings can be and, once built, be convinced that it was worth the effort of putting one brick on top of the other.

Special thanks

Special thanks to New Delaval Primary School, Blyth.

Recommended websites

For more information on how 826 Valencia came into existence, see:

www.826valencia.org
www.ted.com/talks/dave_eggers_makes_his_ted_prize_wish_once_upon_a_school?language=en#t-664653

For more information about writing centres, many of which offer free writing workshops for schools, see:

Ministry of Stories – London (www.ministryofstories.org)
Grimm & Co – Rotherham (www.grimmandco.co.uk)
Fighting Words – Dublin and Belfast (www.fightingwords.ie)
Live Tales – Newcastle (www.live.org.uk/livetales)

See also:

www.learning.linkedin.com/blog/top-skills/why-creativity-is-the-most-important-skill-in-the-world
www.twitter.com/boltcity/status/369484217349992448

References

Baldwin, P. and John, R. (2012) *Inspiring Writing Through Drama: Creative Approaches to Teaching Ages 7–16*. London: Bloomsbury.
Board of Education (1926) *The Teaching of English in England*. London: H.M. Stationery Office.
Clark, C. and Teravainen, A. (2017) Writing for enjoyment and its link to wider writing. *National Literacy Trust Research Report*.
Dahl, R. (2016) *Revolting Rhymes*. London: Puffin Books.
Donaldson, J. (2011) *Jack and the Flumflum Tree*. London: Macmillan Children's Books.
Fleming, M. (2017) *Starting Drama Teaching* (4th edn). Oxford: Routledge.
Hendra, S. (2013) *No-Bot: The Robot with No Bottom*. London: Simon & Schuster.
Murphy, C. (2012) Practice, pedagogy and policy: the influence of teachers' creative writing practice on pedagogy in schools. Doctoral thesis, Northumbria University. Available online at: http://nrl.northumbria.ac.uk/13334/
Norton, M. (2014) *The Borrowers*. London: Puffin Books.
O'Neill, C. and Lambert, A. (1989) *Drama Structures: A Practical Handbook for Teachers*. London: Hutchinson.
Winston, J. (2004) *Drama and English at the Heart of the Curriculum: Primary and Middle Years*. London: David Fulton.

9
DEEPER WRITING FOR EAL PUPILS

Kulwinder Maude

TEACHERS' STANDARDS

This chapter will help you with the following Teachers' Standards:

2d. demonstrate knowledge and understanding of how pupils learn and how this impacts on teaching;

3a. have a secure knowledge of the relevant subject(s) and curriculum areas, foster and maintain pupils' interest in the subject, and address misunderstandings;

3b. demonstrate a critical understanding of developments in the subject and curriculum areas, and promote the value of scholarship;

3c. demonstrate an understanding of and take responsibility for promoting high standards of literacy, articulacy and the correct use of standard English, whatever the teacher's specialist subject;

5. adapt teaching to respond to the strengths and needs of all pupils.

KEY QUESTIONS

- How do I control the full range of genres or text types associated with writing across the curriculum?
- How do I engage bilingual children with a range of literary resources from both languages and cultural worlds?
- How do I scaffold writing in order to enable bilingual children to move from dependent to independent learning?

Defining terms

In the UK context, Cameron and Besser (2004) define:

EAL as English as an additional language and recognises the fact that many children learning English in schools in this country already know one or more other languages and are adding English to that repertoire.

Bilingual is a term used for those children who have access to more than one language at home and at school. They may or may not be fluent in both languages. For the purpose of this chapter, the terms EAL and Bilingual maybe used interchangeably.

OFSTED terms those children as **Advanced learners of EAL** who are no longer considered to be at the early stages of English acquisition. Often born in this country, such children are considered as no longer in need of support with language acquisition especially spoken language. However, they may continue to need support in order to develop the cognitive and academic aspects of English language.

Introduction

In the absence of an explicit focus on language, students from certain social backgrounds continue to be privileged and others to be disadvantaged in learning, assessment and promotion, perpetuating the obvious inequalities that exist today.

(Schleppegrell, 2004, p. 3)

The fundamental goal of any language is to convey meaning to the intended audience. In the context of a primary classroom, children who do not have English as their first language may have limited familiarity with the dominant culture, audience and the overall purpose of communication, whether it is spoken or written. Writing is a key skill for both formal education and for life beyond school, and without good levels of writing skills in English, EAL children are likely to be at a disadvantage. Social communication often uses written English to interact with other people, often at a distance, what we have experienced, how we feel, what we know and what we think about what we know. In the academic context, writing is the medium used to record what is learnt, to explore the meanings of ideas, and to display knowledge and thinking in school.

This chapter discusses some of the challenges that EAL children may encounter in learning to write in an additional language, including issues related to language and culture; challenges that are likely to be greater for children who are not already literate in another language. Two distinct approaches to scaffold EAL children in developing writing are presented:

1. All children (not only EAL) need to be taught explicitly how to control the full range of genres, or text types, associated with writing across the curriculum (Gibbons, 2015).

2. We shall also look at how bilingual children's range of literary resources from both languages and cultural worlds could be drawn upon to express their written understandings in multiple modes, forms and styles (Dutta, 2007).

Links to the National Curriculum

The National Curriculum (2013) acknowledges that effective composition requires clarity, awareness of the audience, purpose and context, and an increasingly wide knowledge of vocabulary and grammar. Since there is no guidance on how this clarity and awareness of audience, etc., should be achieved in children who are learning to write in an additional language, this chapter argues that teachers need to understand the challenges faced by EAL children learning to write in a new language so that they can scaffold writing accordingly.

ACTIVITY 1

Before moving forward, drawing on your knowledge of children in the class, consider what effective writers are likely to do well when writing in English or any other language. Gibbons (2009) defines effective writers as ones who:

- understand the purpose of writing;
- understand what they need to do with language so that it is appropriate for the audience and purpose;
- understand how to organise and structure the overall writing and how this organisation differs according to the type of the writing;
- understand that most writing is a recursive process, which requires writers to revise, perhaps reorganise, and edit their work;
- be aware of the differences between speech and writing and understand that writing is not simply speech written down;
- draw on models of good writing and know how to go about finding out what they don't know, such as spelling of a word;
- know something about the subject they are writing about;
- make their writing explicit enough for readers to understand their meaning (for example, by anticipating what may need explanation). Anticipation of reader needs may relate to *content* (for example, defining particular technical terms or providing sufficient information) or *language* (for example, making clear what pronouns like *it, he,* and *she* refer to).
- be confident writers in English or another language.

(p. 107)

On the other hand, less effective writers tend to shy away from the act of writing itself. They may come across as lacking in inspiration, motivation, organisation and cognitive skills needed to plan their writing. You may often see such children complaining about not knowing where to start. They are often unaware of the difference between various text types, linguistic features and audience. They tend to follow formulaic methods or ways of thinking, often converting speech into writing without giving much thought to sophisticated structure or organisation. Editing or drafting doesn't mean much to these children. Needless to say, they seldom experience success at writing in class.

Learning to write in a second language presents further challenges for EAL children. As mentioned before, often our school systems assume that all children entering Reception (in the UK context) have already developed a sound understanding of the unspoken assumptions and nuances of language. Consequently, language development in school seeks to build on the foundations of early literacy absorbed from home and immediate surroundings. Now, this may not be the case for EAL children. Gibbons (2009, p. 107) aptly points out that concepts of print, such as sound-symbol relationships, directionality, and the script or writing system itself in English, may be unfamiliar to the EAL children. In a more recent publication, Gibbons (2018) vehemently argues that one of the major challenges for EAL learners is to understand the grammatical differences between spoken and written language. However, the policy stance on EAL is very different in England compared to the rest of the world. A recent report (DfE, 2012) highlights the Government's policy for children learning English as an additional language. The policy seeks 'rapid language acquisition and inclusion within the mainstream education as soon as possible' (ibid., p. 1). We argue that in the absence of explicit guidance and support, mainstream classroom teachers may find it difficult to plan targeted support for development of writing in English as an additional language.

FOCUS ON RESEARCH

WRITING IN A SECOND LANGUAGE

Research carried out by Cameron and Besser (2004) into the writing of more advanced learners of English as an additional language – i.e. pupils who had been in UK schools for at least five years – identified a number of key features of language that pupils learning EAL appeared to handle less confidently than their monolingual, English-only peers. These included the use of:

- formulaic phrases;
- prepositions;
- modal verbs;
- use of genres;

- under-development of narrative components, particularly endings, and
- the use of tense.

(p. 8)

Furthermore, Garcia (2009) argues that all learning should challenge children's thinking and develop their academic literacy at the same time. Academic literacy can be defined as children's ability to understand higher order 'textual' language in order to access the curriculum and the learning that accompanies it (Maude, 2018, p. 41). To support deeper writing for EAL children, teachers need to identify specific cultural and language features of particular genres and the corresponding academic language. Before we discuss genres, let's have a look at our own understanding of academic language and how it feeds into developing academic literacy.

ACTIVITY 2

Gibbons (2018) uses the example of five texts (below) about magnets to illustrate the difference between *academic* and *everyday* language. Before reading any further, try to order these, moving from *everyday* to *subject-specific* academic language.

1. We found out that the pins stuck on the magnet.
2. Some ferromagnetic materials that exhibit easily detectable magnetic properties are nickel, cobalt and their alloys.
3. Look it's sticking! Look at that! But that one didn't stick.
4. Magnetic attraction occurs only between ferrous metals.
5. We discovered that a magnet attracts some kinds of metal.

(p. 46)

Text 3 is an example from group talk in Year 3 science. The class knew what they were looking at and the group was presenting their findings. Note the use of words like 'it's', 'look', 'that' and 'one', which make complete sense in a shared context. Such group work is beneficial for EAL children at all stages of language acquisition.

Text 1 is also spoken, but after the group was asked to present their findings to the rest of the class. All groups were conducting different experiments and had to report their findings. The teacher had reminded the children to use some key vocabulary and show awareness of audience.

(Continued)

(Continued)

Text 5 was produced the next day when the teacher had further reminded the children to consider subject-specific vocabulary and the unknown audience.

Text 4 is from a secondary science book. Here, the verb 'attract' changes to 'attraction' (noun). This is known as 'nominalisation', a process in which verbs are turned into nouns (complex noun phrases) in academic texts. Explicit teaching of such complex constructions facilitates development of sophisticated writing in EAL children.

Text 2 is an example from a university textbook with text generally written for a specific audience in academic language and passive voice. If EAL children are unfamiliar with the context, it can hinder comprehending the main message, which in turn can impact writing.

In a nutshell, transition from everyday to academic language becomes much easier if teachers plan activities explicitly focused on collecting new information through group work, talk partners and teacher modelling. Ideas about scaffolding such learning will be discussed later in this chapter.

What is a genre (different text types and their features)?

Duke and Purcell-Gate (2003, p. 31) define 'genre' as patterns in which language is used in a particular culture or society. It refers to the linguistic features, format and purpose of the text.

Different types of genres commonly taught in school are poems, story narratives, novels, argument, recounts, etc.

The genres of school

Derewianka (1990) and other teachers and linguists (De Silva Joyce and Feez, 2004; Droga and Humphrey, 2003; Macken-Horarik, 1996; Martin et al., 1987) proposed the framework of *functional grammar* for the purpose of teaching of writing. They highlighted Recounts, Narratives, Information Reports, Procedures, Arguments, Discussions and Explanations as the genres most commonly taught in school. Although explicit teaching of the above-mentioned genres is no longer required in the National Curriculum in England, some schools still follow these as guidance to inform their writing curriculum.

ACTIVITY 3

1. Read and analyse the four text types mentioned in the tables below. Think about the implications for your subject knowledge.

2. Decide which year group (Key Stage 1 or 2) each text type may be best suited to teach.

Creative and personal genres

Type of text	Recount	Narrative	Other?
	Our class excursion.	The elephant and the mouse.	
Purpose	To tell what happened.	To entertain, teach.	
Organisation	• Orientation (tells who, what, where, when).	• Orientation (tells who, what, when).	
	• Series of events.	• Series of events.	
	• Personal comment/conclusion.	• Problem.	
		• Resolution.	
Examples of connectives (to structure ideas)	To do with time (first, then, next, afterward, at the end of the day).	To do with time (one day, once upon a time, later, afterward, in the end).	
Other language features	• Past tense tells about what happened.	• Past tense tells about what happened.	
	• 'Action verbs' – e.g., 'left', 'arrived', 'ate', 'went'.	• 'Action verbs – e.g. 'ran', 'took', 'sold'.	
	• Words to describe people, events and actions.	• 'Thinking verbs'– e.g. 'thought', 'wondered', 'hoped'.	
		• May have dialogue and 'saying' verbs – e.g. 'said', 'replied', 'asked', 'shouted'.	

Factual genres (to produce knowledge)

Type of text	Information Report	Procedure	Other?
	Insects	How to make a healthy meal.	
Purpose	To give information about something.	To tell how to do something.	
Organisation	• General statement.	• Goal	
	• Characteristics – e.g. habitat.	• Steps in sequence	
	• Characteristics – e.g. appearance.		
	• Characteristics – e.g. food, etc.		
	• May have subheadings.		
Examples of connectives (to structure ideas)	• May not be used.	To introduce each step – e.g., 'first', 'second', 'third'.	
	• Subheadings structure information.		
	• If report describes life cycles, time connectives such as 'first', 'two weeks' 'later', 'then', 'finally'.		

(Continued)

(Continued)

Type of text	Information Report	Procedure	Other?
Other language features	• Generalisations using present tense: 'it eats', 'it lives'. • Often uses 'to be' and 'to have' for descriptions – e.g. 'A fly is an insect; it has six legs.' • Specialised vocabulary about insects.		

Analytical genres (to reflect on and analyse knowledge)

Type of text	Argument	Discussion	Other?
	'Should smoking be made illegal?'	'Should smoking be made illegal?'	
Purpose	To persuade others, to take a position and justify it, showing one side of an argument.	To persuade others, to take a position and justify it, showing two or more sides of an argument.	
Organisation	• Personal statement of position. • Argument 1 and supporting points/evidence; argument 2 and supporting points/evidence, etc. • Conclusion and possible recommendation.	• Identification of the issue. • Argument 1 and supporting points/evidence; argument 2 and supporting points/evidence, etc. • Counterarguments. • Conclusion and possible recommendations.	
Examples of connectives (to structure ideas)	• To introduce each argument – e.g. 'first', 'second', 'in addition', 'finally'. • To introduce the conclusion – e.g. 'therefore', 'in conclusion'.	• To introduce each argument – e.g. 'first', 'second', 'in addition'. • To introduce each counterargument – e.g. 'however', 'on the other hand', 'nevertheless'. • To introduce the conclusion – e.g. 'therefore', 'in conclusion'.	
Other language features	• Subject-related vocabulary. • Evaluative vocabulary that indicates writer's belief ('It is extremely likely that').	• Subject-related vocabulary • Evaluative vocabulary that indicates writer's belief ('It is extremely likely that').	

(Gibbons, 2015, pp.106–7)

Awareness of the most common school genres will help you in making these explicit to EAL pupils, which in turn will help you in guiding your assessment of their writing development.

Explicit teaching about writing

All children are expected to be able to write confidently for academic purposes. But EAL children may find the task unsurmountable without explicit teaching about how language in a text is geared towards a particular purpose and audience. Derewianka (1990 in Gibbons, 2009, p. 110) took a functional approach to language, linking it with real life, and proposed the following teaching and learning cycle. The aim was to make the implicit understandings about language explicit for EAL children.

Suggested teaching and learning cycle

Stage 1: Building the field. Here the focus is on developing familiarity with the text. Teachers introduce activities that make use of speaking and listening, reading and note-taking, using technology, etc. to research the topic.

Stage 2: Modelling the genre. Here the children are introduced to the form and function of the particular genre in which the children are going to write. The teacher models an example and discusses the overall structure, purpose and linguistic features of the genre with the children.

Stage 3: Joint construction. The teacher and children attempt to write together using explicit guidance about the genre given by the teacher. This also gives children an opportunity to see how a text is constructed.

Stage 4: Independent writing. At this stage, the pupils write their own text (which may be different from the one modelled) using the scaffolding provided in the previous stages of drafting and group work.

CASE STUDY

Gibbons (2015) suggests some practical classroom-based activities that you can use in each of the above stages. Activities like researching about a particular animal to write a non-chronological report, writing a biography of a famous person, coming up with instructions for a new game or preparing a balanced argument on a current topic, etc., are some examples that lend themselves well to the strategies mentioned below. Note that this four-stage process can also be used with Activity 2 above.

STAGE 1: BUILDING SHARED KNOWLEDGE OF THE TOPIC

This can be done in a number of ways:

- Build a class *mind map* of their current knowledge of the topic. This is also useful in developing vocabulary associations between unknown words and already existing knowledge.

(Continued)

(Continued)

- Use a *wallpaper* activity to collect ideas based on the current knowledge.
- Children can prepare a list of questions that they would like to find out about the topic.
- Use shared reading or big books to read around the topic.
- Develop a *word wall/word bank* about the topic, where the topic-based vocabulary is displayed.
- Use *barrier games* such as 'find the difference' to describe the key differences or similarities.
- Watch a video and provide an *information grid* for pairs of children to complete as they watch.
- Get the children to interview an expert in the field. They can write a letter inviting the expert into the classroom and prepare appropriate questions to ask.

STAGE 2: MODELLING AND DECONSTRUCTING THE GENRE

Here are some examples of how you can build children's understanding of the *purpose, overall structure and language features* of the genre. It is important to choose a text similar to the one that children will eventually write themselves.

- Read and *show the model report* and discuss its purpose – to present factual information.
- Draw attention to the *overall structure* or 'shape' of the text, and function of each stage.
- Children in pairs do a *text reconstruction* of part of a report, reordering jumbled sentences into a coherent text.
- Use the model text as a *cloze activity*, making the gaps according to the grammatical features or vocabulary you are focusing on.
- Use part of the model text as a *running dictation*. This helps keep the majority of the text in memory, which can be used later for genuine academic conversations.
- Introduce the grammatical structures that are particularly relevant to the topic – for example, use of imperative verbs in instruction writing.

STAGE 3: JOINT CONSTRUCTION

At this stage, the children are already thinking about the writing, but not writing alone yet. The joint construction should be an example of the same genre, maybe a report on another animal. This provides the necessary scaffolding before attempting to write independently.

- *Remind* children of stages 1 and 2 and reread information gathered in both stages.
- *Model self-checking* that real writers do by asking questions like: 'Is this the best way to say it?' 'Does anything need changing?'

- Suggest appropriate vocabulary; consider alternative ways of wording an idea by *thinking aloud*.
- Remind to look at the information grid where children have gathered ideas in stage 1.
- Focus explicitly on how language is used. Discussions of grammar, vocabulary, spelling and punctuation are in the context of actual language use.
- Model the process of writing, work collaboratively with the pupils making changes, amending, adding words, etc.
- Once finished, rewrite or transfer it to a large piece of paper or type electronically so that it acts as an additional example. You can type on the interactive whiteboard directly as well.

At this stage, metalanguage (language about language) can be explicitly modelled in the context of actual language use, which encourages thinking in English while reducing reliance on translation in the first language. EAL children especially in the early stages of English language acquisition may rely on the vocabulary repertoire of their first language. They need explicit expansion of vocabulary in English in order to increase the recall of information related to school curriculum when writing in a second language.

STAGE 4: INDEPENDENT WRITING

At this stage, pupils attempt to write individually or in pairs. It is useful to remind children of the prior learning, information collected along with specific linguistic features of the language. Sometimes, early EAL learners may need further scaffolding in the form of writing frames which help in organising the form and language structure. EAL Nexus is a useful website for further information about use of writing frames.

(pp. 112–16)

Following the above-mentioned four stages, teachers can combine a product and process approach to writing, effectively signposting the different stages involved in independent writing. It should be noted that although following the process approach gives freedom to create an original writing outcome, some familiarity with the final outcome in the initial stages helps EAL children develop the necessary linguistic and content base required for original writing.

FOCUS ON RESEARCH

Continuing professional development in EAL teaching is influenced both by policy and practice (Flynn, 2018, p. 58). Although the number of children with EAL has been on the rise in general, this has not been matched with high-quality and easy-to-access training

(Continued)

(Continued)

available to teachers. However, a useful starting point is to consider some research-informed principles about EAL practice offered by Lucas et al. (2008):

- EAL learners must have opportunities to produce output for meaningful purposes (Swain and Lapkin, 1995).
- Social interaction in which EAL learners actively participate nurtures the development of conversational as well as academic English (Kotler et al., 2001; Wong Fillmore and Snow, 2005).

You can develop your understanding further by accessing freely available resources on the NALDIC (National Association for Language Development in the Curriculum) and Bell Foundation (EAL Nexus) websites as well.

EAL children and the writing process

Dutta (2007, p. 129) argues that teacher knowledge of 'how the bilingual mind works' along with 'teacher–child' and 'peer talk' are essential to the development of effective writing skills in EAL children. However, we know that children do not necessarily learn to write by being taught explicitly about language features in isolation. If these linguistic instructions are not accompanied by language-focused collaborative group work and genuine opportunities for talk where there is space for building on prior knowledge, teachers are not allowing EAL children in effect to let their bilingual identities shine through their writing.

Furthermore, Bruner (1986, p. 26) argues that it is essential that EAL children are encouraged to 'behold the world not univocally but simultaneously'. He endorses the idea of joint culture creation through not just teacher–child, but also peer talk, subsequently creating a classroom environment where teaching and learning trigger multidirectional thinking, imagination and personalised ways of responding to a best topic. The freedom to draw on their resources in both worlds is crucial for successful development of writing in EAL children (Dutta, 2007, p. 128).

As mentioned before, teacher knowledge of how the bilingual mind works also helps in encouraging teachers to allow and accept alternate and imaginative forms of writing that can be drawn upon from different cultures. This writing may also involve creating new narratives, bringing previous knowledge and experiences into the current meaning. Young children especially will often tell their stories not only through words but also gestures, play-acting and drawing that enriches, informs and strengthens their writing development (Vygotsky, 1978).

In a nutshell, Dutta (2007) surmises that for EAL children, it means accessing and including the wealth of cultural literacies, choosing the most appropriate topics and ways of making meaning in their heads (p. 129). This is best illustrated through a selection of bilingual writings that Dutta shares in her book (2007). Here, we discuss one such example.

CASE STUDY

The narrative below is written (through pictures) by 5-year-old Zubair in Reception whose love of ghost stories in Bengali exemplifies his knowledge of story grammar.

Figure 9.1   I want to write a ghost story

(Continued)

(Continued)

Figure 9.2   More from the ghost story

(Dutta, 2007, pp. 89–90)

Looking at Zubair's story, we can see that he clearly understands the morphological structure of stories. Folk stories from around the world can be surprisingly similar in their form and common themes. If we analyse little Zubair's story using Propp's (1968) idea of *moves* as a framework for writing analysis, it can look like this:

Moves	Example	Underlying meaning
Villainy (something goes wrong).	'The big ghost wanted to eat up the rabbit.'	Creates tension, disturbing the peace and quiet of a happy family.
Defeat villainy (good attempting to defeat the evil).	'The little ghosts picked up the rabbit and ran out to the police car and hid in it. When the big ghost went out the little ghosts went and hid under the big ghost's bed.'	Reaction to the first move.
Initial failure to defeat villainy.	The big ghost came back and broke his bed.'	Story reaches its climax, but a sense of failure to defeat villainy prevails.
Villainy is finally defeated.	'The little ghosts picked up the rabbit and escaped through the chimney. The rabbit ran away to the farm and lived with his friends there. The little ghosts ran away and lived with their friends in the river.'	Conclusion reached.

In Zubair's story, we see a glimpse of how a bilingual mind works. He seems to be combining his cultural and linguistic artefacts in order to produce his story in the following ways:

- The setting in his story could be Bangladesh which he regularly visits to see his extended family. The teacher knew that he had experience of listening to stories told by his aunties and uncles sitting in the courtyards and verandas during the hot, rainy season.
- On the other hand, the setting could be England – the presence of chimney and police car signify just that. His plan to escape through the chimney bears semblance to Father Christmas and Tom and Jerry cartoons.
- He also borrows words like 'farm' and 'rabbits', which could have been fresh in his mind from the recent school visit to a farm.

This is a good example of how Zubair's two worlds – languages and cultures – combined to represent his bilingual voice. It can be said that Zubair's learning to write is strongly intertwined with his bilingual identity and teachers must be aware of this in order to promote EAL children's writing development.

ACTIVITY 4

- How can you encourage children to learn through multimodal experiences?
- How can teachers make sure that the planning for writing takes into account ways of bringing such experiences into the lessons?

Conclusion

This chapter endeavours to highlight potential difficulties and linguistic challenges that EAL children might face in their development of academic writing in school. It also reminds the reader of what Gibbons has argued (2002, 2009, 2015, 2018) over a number of years that every genre occurs within a particular culture and has a distinct purpose, as well as words to represent connections between ideas, language and vocabulary. Teachers need to make sure that knowledge of particular genres is made explicit in the classroom along with providing the context of actual language use. In addition, Dutta (2007, p. 154) maintains that writing about memorable experiences provides children with a sense of pride, personal connection and a willingness to experiment with a range of vocabulary and phrases, creating unique combinations. This not only validates their culture and personal identities, but also equalises learning and writing potential. 'When writing concerned is personal it has the potential of putting the writer at centre stage' (Rosen, 1989, p. 24).

Further reading

The following texts provide information on developing writing for EAL children:

Derewianka, B. (1990) *Exploring How Texts Work*. Portsmouth, NH: Heinemann and Primary English Teaching Association of Australia (PETAA).

Gibbons, P. (2009) Scaffolding EL learners to be successful writers, in *English Learners, Academic Literacy, and Thinking*. Portsmouth, NH: Heinemann.

Humphrey, S., Droga, L. and Feez, S. (2012) *Grammar and Meaning*, Appendices 1, 2, 3. Sydney: Primary English Teaching Association of Australia (PETAA).

Recommended websites

EAL Nexus – https://ealresources.bell-foundation.org.uk/teachers/eal-nexus-resources

The site hosts high-quality resources and teaching materials, which are free-to-access for mainstream teachers and others.

National Association for Language Development in the Curriculum (NALDIC) –https://naldic.org.uk/

References

Bruner, J.S. (1986) *Actual Minds, Possible Worlds*. Cambridge, MA: Harvard University Press.

Cameron, L. and Besser, S. (2004) *Writing in English as an Additional Language at Key Stage 2*. Available online at: www.naldic.org.uk/Resources/NALDIC/Research%20and%20Information/Documents/RR586.pdf (accessed 8 May 2019).

De Silva Joyce, H. and Feez, S. (2004) *Developing Writing Skills for Middle Secondary Students: Book 2*. Sydney: Phoenix Education.

Department for Education (DfE) (2012) A brief summary of Government policy in relation to EAL Learners English as an Additional Language. Available online at: https://www.cambridgeassessment. org.uk/Images/116003-a-brief-summary-of-government-policy-in-relation-to-eal-learners.pdf (accessed 8 May 2019).

Department for Education (DfE) (2013) National Curriculum. Available online at: www.gov.uk/government/ collections/national-curriculum (accessed 8 May 2019).

Derewianka, B. (1990) *Exploring How Texts Work*. Primary English Teaching Association: NSW.

Droga, L. and Humphrey, S. (2003) *Grammar and Meaning: An Introduction for Primary Teachers*. Berry: NSW: Target Texts. Available online at: www.targettexts.com

Duke, N. and Purcell-Gate, V. (2003) Genres at home and at school: bringing the known to the new. *International Reading Association*, 57(1): 30–7.

Dutta, M. (2007) *Bilinguality and Literacy: Principles and Practice* (2nd edn). London: Continuum.

Flynn, N. (2018) Continuing professional development for EAL: mapping the field and filing in the gaps. *EAL Journal*, 5: 58–62.

Garcia, O. (2009) *Bilingual Education in the 21st Century: A Global Perspective*. West Sussex: Wiley-Blackwell.

Gibbons, P. (2002) *Scaffolding Language Scaffolding Learning: Teaching English Language Learners in the Mainstream Classroom*. Portsmouth, NH: Heinemann.

Gibbons, P. (2009) Scaffolding EL learners to be successful writers, in *English Learners, Academic Literacy, and Thinking*. Portsmouth, NH: Heinemann.

Gibbons, P. (2015) *Scaffolding Language Scaffolding Learning: Teaching English Language Learners in the Mainstream Classroom* (2nd edn). Portsmouth, NH: Heinemann.

Gibbons, P. (2018) What is academic literacy and who should teach it? *EAL Journal*, 6: 46–8.

Kotler, A., Wegerif, R. and Le Voi, M. (2001) Oracy and the educational achievement of pupils with English as an Additional Language: the impact of bringing 'talking partners' into Bradford schools. *International Journal of Bilingual Education and Bilingualism*, 4(6): 403–19.

Lucas, T., Villegas, A.M. and Freedson-Gonzalez, M. (2008) Linguistically responsive teacher education: preparing classroom teachers to teach English language learners. *Journal of Teacher Education*, 59(4): 361–73.

Macken-Horarik, M. (1996) Literacy and learning across the curriculum: towards a model of register for secondary school teachers, in Hasan, R. and Williams, G. (eds) *Literacy and Society*. Essex: Addison & Wesley Longman.

Martin, J., Christie, F. and Rothery, J. (1987) Social processes in education: a reply to Sawyer and Watson (and others), in Reid, I. (ed.) *The Place of Genre in Learning: Current Debates*. Geelong, Victoria: Centre for Studies in Literary Education, Deakin University Press.

Maude, K. (2018) Encouraging reading comprehension in learners of English as an Additional Language. *Impact: Journal of the Chartered College of Teaching*, 5: 40–3.

Propp, V. (1968) *Morphology of the Folktale*. Austin, TX: University of Texas Press.

Rosen, M. (1989) *Did I Hear You Write?* London: Andre Deutsch.

Schleppegrell, M. (2004) *The Language of Schooling: A Functional Linguistics Perspective*. Manwah, NJ: Lawrence Erlbaum.

Swain, M. and Lapkin, S. (1995) Problems in output and the cognitive processes they generate: a step towards second language learning. *Applied Linguistics*, 16(3): 371–91.

Vygotsky, L. (1978) (Cole, M. et al. (eds)) *Minsd in Society: The Development of Higher Psychological Processes*. Cambridge, MA: Harvard University Press.

Wong Fillmore, L. and Snow, C.E. (2005) *What Teachers Need to Know About Language*. Washington, DC: Center for Applied Linguistics.

10

ENGAGING PUPILS THROUGH THE USE OF DIFFERENT MATERIALS

Lucy M. Davies

TEACHERS' STANDARDS

This chapter will help you with the following Teachers' Standards:

2d. demonstrate knowledge and understanding of how pupils learn and how this impacts on teaching;

3a. have a secure knowledge of the relevant subject(s) and curriculum areas, foster and maintain pupils' interest in the subject, and address misunderstandings;

3b. demonstrate a critical understanding of developments in the subject and curriculum areas, and promote the value of scholarship;

3c. demonstrate an understanding of and take responsibility for promoting high standards of literacy, articulacy and the correct use of standard English, whatever the teacher's specialist subject.

5. Adapt teaching to respond to the strengths and needs of all pupils.

KEY QUESTIONS

- How can different types of engagement be fostered to generate deeper writing?
- Why can relying on written texts to inspire deeper writing disengage some children?
- How can I use a range of different materials in the classroom to engage children in deeper writing?

Introduction

Consider the term 'deeper writing'. What does it mean to you? Is it the same as writing at mastery level, or is it something subtly, but significantly, different? It certainly implies a level of writing that is beyond superficial in a similar way that achieving mastery level demands, but it can also mean a type of writing that can be achieved by all pupils, not only those exceeding the expected standards. The Department for Education (DfE, 2018) has recently produced an updated framework to help define the meaning of greater depth:

> *Working at greater depth the pupil can, after discussion with the teacher:*

- write effectively and coherently for different purposes, drawing on their reading to inform the vocabulary and grammar of their writing;

- make simple additions, revisions and proof-reading corrections to their own writing;

- use the punctuation taught at key stage 1 mostly correctly;

- spell most common exception words;

- add suffixes to spell most words correctly in their writing (e.g. –ment, –ness, –ful, –less, –ly);

- use the diagonal and horizontal strokes needed to join some letters.

(p. 6)

The DfE also provides exemplars of 'writing at a greater depth', with examples of writing showing how greater depth writing varies from 'expected standard' writing (DfE, 2018). These examples are useful to teachers, but this chapter seeks to provide specific ideas for engaging children in writing that can be used to help pupils who have already met the expected standard to work at greater depth, and broaden the range of writing greater depth children are already producing. However, it is also hoped that using the various materials in this chapter will result in deeper writing for children of all abilities – after all, deepening the richness of writing can be achieved regardless of academic ability.

What is engagement?

The word 'engagement' is frequently used in schools; it is widely recognised as an essential component to successful learning in any subject and is strongly linked to attainment (Kuh, 2003; Van Ryzin, 2011). Some believe it is a term used so often and without definition that is in danger of moving from a 'buzz word' to a 'fuzz word' (Vuorio, 2014). However, the lack of clarity surrounding the word engagement *can* be lessened by recognising that six main types of engagement exist – social, cultural, physical, behavioural, emotional and intellectual (or cognitive) – meaning that engagement is multidimensional (Reschly and Christenson, 2012). In terms of academic attainment, evidence suggests that it is emotional and intellectual engagement which are most important. This chapter, therefore, focuses on materials that can be used to primarily foster these dimensions.

FOCUS ON RESEARCH

Research suggests that students tend to be more engaged in non-academic subjects (Shernoff et al., 2014), perhaps because they are taught less frequently and therefore provide some novelty to pupils, but also because academic subjects can be seen as less open-ended and less creative. When pre-trainee teachers were interviewed in a study at Durham University about their views on creativity and curriculum, though most saw English as a creative subject, all saw art and drama as more creative than English (Newton and Waugh, 2012, p. 23). Yet, outside the world of primary school teaching, writers, artists and actors are often grouped together as some of the most creative professions.

Engagement in English

So, what is it about English at primary school that means it lacks the creative status of art and the performing arts? First, in English the increased focus on terminology relating to Spelling, Punctuation and Grammar (SPaG) has been criticised as not necessarily improving writing ability. Meanwhile, SATS tests in SPaG in Year 6, as well as in other areas of the English curriculum, have led to concerns that, rather than improve children's writing, they are adversely affecting writing ability. Second, it is also worth considering the amount of writing pupils do in other National Curriculum areas. As Newton and Waugh point out, 'Young learners are required to write a remarkable amount each school day, but the process of writing is often simply the medium through which other learning activities are judged' (2012, p. 26). Writing is used in almost every subject to demonstrate knowledge as evidence of learning. In order to encourage children to write at a deeper level, they need to be inspired to write and sustain motivation throughout a writing task, which may also include redrafting. The use of films, music and artefacts can appear less formal to children and take away the fear that some children associate with writing, as well as adding novelty to stimulate initial interest.

What does this mean for teachers trying to stimulate deeper writing?

There is a good deal of research on the relationship between engagement and writing, with academics and practitioners often focusing on learners who are reluctant writers (Hawthorne, 2008; Senn, 2012). However, although the current English Curriculum is challenging, children with 'writing apprehension' is not a new phenomenon and various studies predate the National Curriculum (Daly and Miller, 1975). Apprehension can range from unease to feelings of dread and panic, and, regardless of the degree of apprehension a child is experiencing, they will find it hard to emotionally engage with writing – that is, finding writing fun, exciting, enjoyable and satisfying. So, what can be done? One way to establish this connection is by giving children some choice in their learning. Choice has been found to be an effective way to engage children in their learning (Assor et al., 2002) and can help encourage independence in writing. As Adam Bushnell explains in Chapter 4, independence is vital to achieving greater depth writing. Pitching a lesson that is too easy or too difficult can disengage children (Shernoff et al., 2014). The advantage of using non-text materials is that the same stimulus allows for stretching activities for all learners, whereas weaker readers, or very able readers, can be stifled for whole-class activities using a 'best-fit' text.

In practice, using the checklists below can help reflect on whether opportunities to promote engagement have been planned for in writing lessons.

Emotional engagement checklist

- Taking risks without the fear of reprimand.
- Tasks that excite and inspire.
- Novelty.
- Relevance.
- Familiarity with material.

Intellectual engagement checklist

- Opportunities for creative thinking.
- Problem solving.
- Level of challenge.
- Curiosity.
- Independence.
- Choice.

Moving away from books as a stimulus

There is no disputing that children who read voraciously are often the most proficient writers, partly because children with less reading proficiency lag well behind their on-grade-level peers in vocabulary acquisition (Snow et al., 1998). Additionally, introducing children to a range of reading texts can help with their genre writing. For those children who already enjoy reading, stimulating their writing skills by introducing a variety of stimulus can extend their ability, and help provide a broader range of greater depth examples. The wider the variety of stimuli used, the more the chance of a teacher finding a material that genuinely motivates each child in their class. Research has shown that this intrinsic motivation fosters more interest, excitement and confidence, which can lead to enhanced performance, persistence and creativity (Deci and Ryan, 1991). At the same time, using a variety of materials ensures that children who struggle to read to the same level as some of their peers, or simply have not discovered the joys of reading, do not also fall behind in writing.

Film

Using films

A key requirement to writing at greater depth is to be able to write in different genres. An advantage of using film clips is that the genre of a film is often quickly recognised by children, particularly in Key Stage 2. The Literacy Shed (www.literacyshed.com) is a useful source of film clips compiled for use in the classroom. Clips are categorised in to different 'sheds' and include The Fantasy Shed, The Ghostly Shed, The Thinking Shed and The Fun Shed. Different sheds therefore lend themselves to different genres of writing – sci-fi, Gothic thriller and farce. Of course, it is not just animated films that can be used as a stimulus, and scenes from full-length movies can be shown in isolation (see Case study 1).

CASE STUDY 1

USING FILM CLIPS

MAIN THEMES: NARRATIVE WRITING, SLOW WRITING, DRAFTING, CROSS-CURRICULAR ENGLISH AND SCIENCE

A mixed Year 4/5 class had a half-term topic on Space. The Space theme had particularly interested the children and the teacher decided to use a scene from Apollo 13 to help structure their writing, having found that in previous weeks the children could become so enthralled with what they were writing about that the quality of their writing suffered as they tried to put their ideas to paper quickly. She decided to use a 'slow writing' approach, using the shuttle launch scene to help the children write a detailed suspenseful narrative. The whole scene was played and the teacher asked the class for their initial views on what was happening and how the characters felt. Key words from the discussion were written to a mind map at the front of the class, with the teacher asking probing questions such as, 'You've said the astronauts look scared. Can we think of any other words like scared?' In response, the children generated words, including 'terrified', 'anxious' and 'petrified'. The teacher told the class that the mind map could be used like a word bank for the next part of the lesson. The same scene was then played in stages with children having to write down a few sentences based on a specific brief, such as 'Describe the look on the astronauts' faces' and 'How do you think they are feeling?' By the end of the lesson, all children had compiled a detailed narrative in a structure that made sense. The next two lessons were spent enhancing their first draft by thinking about techniques they could use to add suspense, like parenthesis and exclamation marks. The final draft was written on Space-themed paper and displayed in the classroom.The combination of a theme the children were interested in already, the detail the scene offered and the process of 'slow writing' engaged the children so much in the initial lesson that the children took pride in redrafting their work to achieve a level of writing deeper than what they had previously been able to produce.

Making films

Film can also be used in a different way. Instead of previously made films being used as a springboard for writing, the children can make their own films. Creating a script for the film allows the teacher to focus the activity on a particular writing genre – for instance, persuasive writing if the video is to advertise a product; dialogue if the video is based on an interview; or, recount if the video is similar to an online blog or vlog. Children's main experience of film will be as viewers, which is useful as it makes them highly aware of their audience. Performing their writing allows them to see reactions from their audience in a way that written work alone does not permit. Meanwhile, making an occasion of the film screening can be extremely motivating for the children and add relevance to writing activity (see Case study 3).

CASE STUDY 2

MAKING FILMS IN KEY STAGE 1

MAIN THEMES: WRITING A RECOUNT, LEARNING TEXT BY HEART, CROSS-CURRICULAR ENGLISH AND GEOGRAPHY

A Year 1 class had spent the term learning about the countries in the United Kingdom as part of their topic. The children had shown a particular interest in London and were curious about famous landmarks and tourist spots, such as Buckingham Palace and Harry Potter World. The teacher decided that an ideal way to end the topic would be for the children to write a postcard to their family pretending they had been to London. The children were able to choose two landmarks to include on their postcard. Once the postcard text was written, the children learnt the text by heart and were filmed in front of a backdrop of London reciting their postcard. The video was then added to the school's social media account for family members to view. The teacher found that the class took more care in their writing knowing that it would be used to compile a video and that it would be viewed by others. He also found that the exercise encouraged children to learn text by heart.

The following illustrates K's postcard which was learnt by heart and then performed in front of a green screen.

LETTER

Dear Mam and Dad,

I'm having fantastic time in London. There is so much to do and there is so much to see. On Monday I have just been to Buckingham Palace but the Queen was not there. On Tuesday I went to Big Ben when it rang it was loud and it is tall and big.

Wish you were here,

K

CASE STUDY 3

MAKING FILMS IN KEY STAGE 2

MAIN THEMES: POETRY, ENVIRONMENTAL ISSUES, WORKING WITH OUTSIDE AGENCIES AND AUDIENCE

A Year 3 teacher used free Pupil Parliament planning from litfilmfest.com to inspire a range of writing. The class decided to tackle the palm oil problem as some had seen a Christmas advertisement that had used the topic as its focus. The teacher showed the class the advert, and the other children agreed it would be an interesting topic to research; they were particularly engaged by the young orangutan with the teacher noting that they were able to relate to the animal as they readily made links between their own lives and that of the young animal. The children researched facts about damage done to the orangutan's environment and adopted a baby orang-utan; as their knowledge grew, so did their engagement. Also, in adopting the orang-utan, the children felt that the issue had real relevance to their own lives. Their writing initially consisted of writing a *Newsround*-style film. Part of the film included interviews with MP James Frith, and Ed, an education officer from Chester Zoo, who were asked questions written by the pupils. Interviewing real people gave the children a real sense of purpose and sustained engagement levels, so the teacher then decided to use the topic of palm oil to generate a whole-class personification poem. The poem was then performed in front of a green screen and the class helped choose images that would reflect the themes of the poem. Both the *Newsround-style* film and the poem were then screened at a local theatre with the children's families invited to

celebrate the project. The teacher felt that knowing their writing would have an audience gave the children's writing an added sense of purpose.
The film can be viewed at:

https://drive.google.com/file/d/1KeortN6BKu32hEkqUBts2WNoDzFenC2_/view?usp=sharing

Music

Music is a medium that children are highly familiar with by the time they enter primary school. As babies and toddlers, both at home and in Early Years settings, songs and nursery rhymes form an important part of language acquisition and language skill development. Many primary aged children have already developed musical preferences and identified particular musicians and performers as their favourites. In terms of engagement, using music in the classroom is familiar, and therefore likely to raise their self-efficacy levels and create an environment where they feel comfortable taking risks. Tasks that use popular music can also be used as independent research tasks, where children examine lyrics to identify various writing techniques, such as the one described in Case study 4 (below). However, using music children may be less familiar with, such as classical music, can be an effective way to stretch and challenge them in a way that is conducive to fostering intellectual engagement (see Case study 4). The escapism music can provide can be used to help children reach what Csíkszentmihály (1997) calls a state of flow. Teachers may recognise this immersion in an activity as being characterised by children being 'in the zone'. Music, and other sound effects, can also be used to add an additional sensory layer to a narrative; rather than simply imagine the sounds, children can listen to clips. Audio resources can also be useful for teachers wanting to support children to create a particular atmosphere in their writing. Many teachers already play music during whole-class writing activities, sometimes using calming background music to block out distractions, or music that helps to evoke a particular genre.

CASE STUDY 4

USING SONG LYRICS

MAIN THEMES: CHOICE, RELEVANCE, WRITING USING VARIOUS TECHNIQUES

A Year 6 class, with almost a quarter of the class working at greater depth in English, had produced various pieces of extended writing through the year. The teacher, however, had spent a good deal of time scaffolding these pieces and wanted to encourage

(Continued)

(Continued)

the children to work more independently. He decided to allow children to choose a song of their choice written by a popular musician using BBC Music Stories to motivate them to research and write at length in an enjoyable way, having been working hard towards their SATS tests. He also hoped that the activity would result in more individualised pieces of writing. The children began by listening to the song and writing down their predictions of what had inspired the musician. They then wrote down their favourite lyrics, and identified particular techniques like similes, metaphors and adjectives that had been used. In the following lesson, the children began writing their own songs using the same techniques and spent the remainder of the week completing their songs. The teacher found that the activity had engaged all the children in the class and resulted in children of all abilities independently producing a piece of writing at a deeper level to their usual standard.

CASE STUDY 5

CLASSICAL MUSIC

MAIN THEMES: FLOW THEORY, COMPILING A FACT FILE, BIOGRAPHIES

As part of a music topic, Year 4 children were starting to look at the work of Benjamin Britten, a composer unknown to the class. The teacher decided to introduce the composer by playing a piece of music from Britten's opera, *Peter Grimes*, to the class on loop. While the music was being played, the children painted on long rolls of paper laid out across several desks. The aim of the lesson was to get children to paint in a way that emulated the emotions they felt from listening to the music and reflect the pace, tone and volume of the piece. The children were engrossed in the painting to the point where they reached a state of flow. Towards the end of the lesson, the teacher stopped the music and the class spoke about how they felt during the painting, which emotions the composer had being trying to convey and what they thought had inspired him to write the piece. In the next lesson, the teacher introduced a biography of Benjamin Britten, who composed the opera. The children were motivated to read about the composer with whom they already felt an emotional connection and were keen to meet the learning outcome of creating a fact-file about him, using not only the biography the teacher had provided, but also by undertaking their own research online. The fact file was then used to write biographies about Britten. The teacher felt that the initial lesson had enabled the children to emotionally connect to the composer and inspired them in their written work, which otherwise may have otherwise lacked relevance.

Artefacts

The use of artefacts, or objects, can stimulate both emotional and intellectual engagement almost immediately. Younger children are often encouraged to bring objects that are relevant to themselves into nursery or school for show and tell, for this very reason – they generate interest. In Key Stages 1 and 2 giving children an artefact with no information is an approach often used in enquiry-based learning activities across the curriculum and can stimulate children's curiosity and help construct questions about the object. The questions themselves can form part of a piece of writing, but they can also be used in the planning stage of a writing project. Teachers can also help scaffold children's responses to the object by asking questions that foster higher level thinking, such as, 'How do you think this was used?' and 'I wonder who this object belongs to?' These questions support children in analysing, synthesising and problem solving to generate productive thoughts that can then be used to write at a deeper level. Having something tangible that can be handled by the children can foster engagement by introducing a real sense of excitement and authenticity into a lesson.

Possible artefacts/objects

- Clothing and jewellery
- Coins (particularly replica antique coins)
- Maps and globes
- Marbles
- Message in a bottle
- Natural objects (rocks, wood, shells)
- 'Old' technology (cassettes, videotapes, pagers)
- Perfume
- Pottery
- Tickets (travel or events)
- Toys
- Writing equipment (quills, chalk boards)

FOCUS ON RESEARCH

PICTURE BOOKS AND IMAGES

Picture books are a common feature in Early Years settings, but can often be harder to find in the upper years of primary school. Research has found that teachers lack in-depth knowledge of picture books for older children (Cremin et al., 2008). Yet picture book illustrations offer a sense of immediacy (Waugh et al., 2016) and accessibility for all children, regardless of their reading ability. In many ways, this is understandable, because, as

(Continued)

(Continued)

mentioned earlier in this chapter, an appropriate level of challenge is needed to engage children. However, in recent years authors and illustrators have published some deeply thought-provoking picture books that can stimulate deeper writing among older children. Admittedly, some of these picture books do contain text, but much less so than other books. Those that do 'are dependent upon the accompanying pictures for their specific meaning and import; they often sound more like plot summaries than actual stories' (Nodelman, 1988, p. viii). Furthermore, text can be blanked out initially to provide greater scope for children to make their own predictions and narratives before being replaced, so that children can compare how their narratives vary from the author's. Viewfinders can be used in a similar way, obscuring part of an illustration so that children can make predictions based on limited information before slowly revealing the complete illustration. The open-endedness of these activities mean there is no wrong answer.

Picture books can be an excellent stimulus in engaging children in thinking about how society is changing and inspiring pieces of writing based on real-life events and historical changes.

Of course, images alone can also be used as a stimulus, and collecting a rich bank of images can prove invaluable for teachers. Both picture books and images are particularly useful in producing writing based on inference and result in imaginative texts being produced (see Case study 6).

CASE STUDY 6

IMAGES IN YEAR 6

MAIN THEMES: INFERENCE, CREATIVE WRITING, NEWSPAPER ARTICLES, EDITING AND RE-DRAFTING

The teacher started the week's English lessons by providing the children with large pictures of interesting images laid out in the classroom. The children had to circulate the room and write words based on the images, not only on what they could see, but also on what they imagined the smell, sound and touch would be. The children used these words to write a short description of the image. In the following lesson, the teacher used an intriguing image she had found on Pobble (www.pobble365.com) of girl holding a cracked eggshell entitled 'Hatched'. The class were instantly engaged by the strangeness of the picture and enjoyed sharing ideas about it. The children had previously looked at features of newspaper articles and used their knowledge to base a newspaper article on the picture. As the children could generate their own scenarios, they had a great deal of choice in terms of the content of their article, which the teacher felt engaged them in drafting and redrafting. The following day, the teacher provided the class with different images of various creatures, suggesting that the egg in the initial picture may have been laid by one of the creatures. In groups, the children then wrote words that were exciting on the images. This informed a short descriptive character description, as the one produced by Ross, below.

As the top of the egg split, an elephant-like creature bounded out of the egg. Its ears which were like radars swivelled around, presumably searching for its prey. Its silk fur rustled in the Arctic winds and it reared back to release a bellowing honk. Then it bounded away, its legs powering it away through the barriers of wheat with its tail trailing behind it.

The final task was to write a letter or diary entry in role as the girl, bringing together the previous two pieces of work (see Ross's letter below). This exercise demonstrated to the children that the same piece of writing could be adapted and used in a variety of ways. The class recapped features of diary entries and letters collaboratively, and then wrote in a way in which their 'voice' would be evident.

LETTER

Dear Dad,

How have you been without me? Bet you don't miss the messy barracks. I've had a really bizarre week, you might have seen it in the paper. So, I was with my friends and I ran ahead into Farmer Goufan's field (I know, his name is hilarious). I found this massive egg rolling abut in a clearing, just as it was about to hatch! As the top of the egg split, an elephant-like creature bounded out of the egg. Its ears which were like radars swivelled around, presumably searching for its prey. Its silky, peach fur rustled in the Arctic winds and it reared back to release a bellowing honk from its tiny trunk. Then it careered away, muscled legs powering it through the barriers of wheat with a wispy tail trailing behind it. There were loads of journalists and police there!

I can't wait to see you again. I hope this letter reaches you soon.

Lots of love,

Ross

The teacher found that the images sustained high levels of interest throughout the week, and children enjoyed refining their ideas and adding details (as seen in Ross's letter) to produce increasingly sophisticated writing as the week continued.

Visits

Often, the rationale and justification behind a school visit is to give the children an experience that is not possible in the classroom and the 'awe and wonder' evoked by a visit can be an excellent stimulus for deeper writing. School or class visits provide children with a real experience to inspire their writing. Authentic learning is widely recognised as being a highly engaging strategy for learners of all ages, but at primary school it is particularly useful, as it helps children construct knowledge. Writing about a school visit or a theme related to a school visit is relevant for children, but the visit can also provide a real sense of inspiration. As adults thinking back to our own school days, it is often visits that we remember most clearly; the immersive experiences children gain from school visits also mean writing generated from these events can be highly detailed. Writing based on visits have a clear meaning and is of immediate value to children. Meanwhile, as class visits are a collective experience, the planning stage of a piece of writing can be done collaboratively with children orally rehearsing what they plan to write.

The examples in the table below are based on popular visit types taken from the website, UK School Trips (www.ukschooltrips.co.uk).

Location type	Writing activity ideas
Castle	Non-fiction piece on the history of the castle.
	Stories with historical settings, such as a fictional recount of a siege.
	Day in the life of a soldier/royal person.
Beach	Sensory poem describing the sights, sounds, feel, smells and tastes associated with the beach.
	A newspaper report or a news broadcast about pollution at the coast.
Forrest/woods	Personification poem.
	Writing a modern fairy tale.
	Spooky stories.
Park	Letter writing: persuading local council to improve park facilities.
	Advertising: encourage local residents to use the park more frequently or create a tourist brochure on the local area.
Adventure activity	Suspense writing.
	Persuasive writing encouraging audience to take part in adventure activities
Museums	Diary entry in the role of an historic person.
	Choose an item displayed in the museum to research or use as a portal to another word.
	Stories from different cultures.
	Time travel adventure stories.

Location type	Writing activity ideas
Theatre	Play scripts.
	Day in the life of a performer.
	Play review written in character as a theatre critic.
Emergency and public services	Writing job advertisement.
	Newspaper interview with police office/firefighter/ambulance staff.
Sporting arenas	Writing a commentary for a sporting event.
	Descriptive writing focusing on atmosphere.

Conclusion

When children are engaged in their work, they persist despite challenges and obstacles, and take visible delight in accomplishing their work (Schlechty, 2001 in Saeed and Zyngier, 2012). Examples of how to use various materials included in this chapter illustrate how choosing a stimulus that appeals to a class can lead to deeper writing by generating positive emotions that often best support engagement. Once children are emotionally engaged in a writing project, they are more likely to intellectually engage, putting in more effort, generating ideas and checking their work through sustained motivation levels. Furthermore, research on engagement in writing suggests that students who are engaged writers appear to have greater self-efficacy (Hawthorne, 2008). Increased self-efficacy in writing is likely to lead to children approaching further lessons with more positive emotions, generating a positive cycle of emotional engagement, intellectual engagement, deeper writing and greater self-efficacy.

Special thanks

Year 3 pupils and staff at Tottington Primary, Bury.
Year 1 pupils and staff at St Joseph's RC Primary, Darwen.
Ross K and the Year 6 class and staff at John Emmerson Batty Primary School, Redcar.

Recommended websites

BBC Music Stories – www.bbc.co.uk/programmes/p02mp7z3
The Literacy Shed – www.literacyshed.com
Litfilmfest – www.litfilmfest.com
Pobble – www.pobble365.com
UK School Trips – www.ukschooltrips.co.uk

References

Assor, A., Kaplan, H. and Roth, G. (2002) Choice is good, but relevance is excellent: autonomy-enhancing and suppressing teacher behaviours predicting students' engagement in schoolwork. *British Journal of Educational Psychology*, 72(2): 261–78.

Cremin, T., Mottram, M., Bearne, E. and Goodwin, P. (2008) Exploring teachers' knowledge of children's literature. *Cambridge Journal of Education*, 38(4): 449–64.

Csíkszentmihályi, M. (1997) *Finding Flow: The Psychology of Engagement with Everyday Life*. New York: Basic Books.

Daly, J.A. and Miller, M.D. (1975) The empirical development of an instrument to measure writing apprehension. *Research in the Teaching of English*, 9(3): 242–9.

Deci, E.L. and Ryan, R.M. (1991) A motivational approach to self: integration in personality, in Dienstbier, R. (ed.), *Nebraska Symposium on Motivation: Vol. 38. Perspectives on Motivation* (pp. 237–88). Lincoln: University of Nebraska Press.

Department for Education (DfE) (2018) Teacher assessment exemplification: English writing working at greater depth within the expected standard: Frankie. Ref: ISBN 978-1-78644-851-4, STA/18/8103/e PDF, 2.01MB, 36 pages.

Hawthorne, S. (2008) Students' beliefs about barriers to engagement with writing in secondary school English: a focus group study. *The Australian Journal of Language and Literacy*, 31(1): 30.

Kuh, G.D. (2003) What we're learning about student engagement from NSSE: benchmarks for effective educational practices. *Change: The Magazine of Higher Learning*, 35(2): 24–32.

Newton, L. and Waugh, D. (2012) Creativity in English, in Newton, L. (ed.) *Creativity for a New Curriculum: 5-11*, p. 19. London: Routledge.

Nodelman, P. (1988) *Words about Pictures: The Narrative Art of Children's Picture Books*. Georgia, GA: University of Georgia Press.

Reschly, A.L. and Christenson, S.L. (2012) Jingle, jangle, and conceptual haziness: evolution and future directions of the engagement construct, in *Handbook of Research on Student Engagement* (pp. 3–19). Boston, MA: Springer.

Saeed, S. and Zyngier, D. (2012) How motivation influences student engagement: a qualitative case study. *Journal of Education and Learning*, 1(2): 252–67.

Senn, N. (2012) Effective approaches to motivate and engage reluctant boys in literacy. *The Reading Teacher*, 66(3): 211–20.

Shernoff, D.J., Csíkszentmihályi, M., Schneider, B. and Shernoff, E.S. (2014) Student engagement in high school classrooms from the perspective of flow theory, in *Applications of Flow in Human Development and Education* (pp. 475–94). Dordrecht: Springer.

Snow, C.E., Burns, M.S. and Griffin, P. (1998) Committee on the Prevention of Reading Difficulties in Young Children. *Prevention of Reading Difficulties in Young Children*. Washington, DC: National Academy Press.

Van Ryzin, M.J. (2011) Protective factors at school: reciprocal effects among adolescents' perceptions of the school environment, engagement in learning, and hope. *Journal of Youth and Adolescence*, 40(12): 1568–80.

Vuori, J. (2014) Student engagement: buzzword of fuzzword? *Journal of Higher Education Policy and Management*, 36(5): 509–19.

Waugh, D., Neaum, S. and Waugh, R. (2016) *Children's Literature in Primary Schools*. London: Learning Matters.

11
DEVELOPING REASONING TO ENCOURAGE DEEPER WRITING

Michaela Oliver

KEY QUESTIONS

- What does reasoning look like in English?
- How can we promote reasoning in English lessons?
- What kinds of task structure support the development of reasoning?
- How can reasoning about texts support reasoning when writing?

Introduction

Reasoning is undoubtedly an important skill to develop within children, yet knowing what this looks like in English and how this should be promoted is not always obvious. Consider the following exchange:

Student: I think having an important message or a moral is the most important feature of fairy tales.
Teacher: Why do you think that?
Student: Say, for Red Riding Hood, the mother says stick to the path but don't go off the path, otherwise you'll lose it and you might walk into strangers and you're not to talk to strangers, but Red Riding Hood went off that path and it teaches the people who read it . . . to listen to their mum and not to ignore her.
Teacher: Can you tell me why you've decided to put message and moral right at the top of the diamond ranking grid?
Student: Because the only reason why you really have a fairy tale story is to teach you a message or moral.

This example demonstrates a teacher–pupil exchange designed to elicit the child's reasoning behind particular task decisions. The group was completing a diamond ranking exercise (discussed in more detail later). Through careful questioning, the teacher was able to elicit the child's reasoning behind this assertion, as well as examples from particular texts within the fairy-tale genre.

This chapter will consider reasoning, its importance and how it might be developed within primary English lessons. It will outline what reasoning looks like in English and how to explicitly model and teach it. The chapter will also consider how promoting reasoning about texts created by others can encourage students to make more reasoned decisions when creating their own texts, thus leading to deeper writing.

Reasoning in primary education

While it is widely accepted that teaching reasoning within schools is important (e.g. Trilling and Fadel, 2009), the difficulties teachers face in this endeavour have also been recognised (Wegerif, 2010). Now often prioritised in relation to Maths and Science, as seen in curriculum priorities and CPD opportunities, reasoning does not seem to be given as much attention within English.

A major problem with teaching reasoning in English is that there is a multitude of definitions offered for reasoning, as well as a plethora of associated terms to describe (to a greater or lesser extent) practices involved within the reasoning process.

Another major issue with teaching reasoning in English is that the programme of study for English in the National Curriculum (DfE, 2014) and end of KS2 SATs do not make explicit the required reasoning practices to be developed through education. There is no clear consideration given to developing reasoning skills (i.e. the skills required during the process of forming and supporting conclusions). While elements of reasoning are implied throughout, there is no framework for progression and statements implying particular aspects of reasoning, and types of evidence, are commonly repeated across key stages. We will now move to consider what reasoning looks like in English lessons.

What does reasoning look like in English lessons?

In English lessons, what is considered to constitute evidence, and therefore the basis for reasoning differs from that within other subjects. For example, reasoning in science might require engagement with experimental data and methods to support conclusions or arguments. English requires its own forms of evidence to support inferences and conclusions made. Key elements such as genre, structure, language and the context in which a text is based and/or written (such as historical, economic or religious contexts) play an important role in providing evidence, or reasons, for inferences. Each of these elements can be used with varying effects by writers and, as a result, each of these features represent important categories for analysis and interpretation. Arguing that a happy ending would be expected in *Little Red Riding Hood*, since the fairy-tale genre typically employs this structure, demonstrates use of genre as a form of evidence to support an assertion. Explicitly focusing on key elements of genre, language, structure and context, in terms of the ways in which these aspects can represent evidence for readers' interpretations, will therefore strengthen students' capacity to reason.

It is important to consider two dimensions of reasoning within English. Reasoning processes can be drawn upon by writers when they are creating texts and they can also be drawn upon by readers when interpreting and critiquing texts written by others. The reasoning involved has the same foundations, but when critiquing the literature of others, this reasoning is taken from an analytical perspective. This is illustrated in the parallel lists below:

When *interpreting and critiquing* texts, reasoning in English draws upon:

- consideration of the genre(s) drawn upon within a text, including its associated conventions, how this is employed and to what effect;
- reflection upon the organisational devices and structural features utilised within a text to achieve a sense of unity;
- consideration of the use of analogy to create, explore and contrast images, characters and themes within and between literary texts;
- reflection upon the context – e.g. historical, social, religious, biographical – in which a text is set and was created;
- consideration of the impact/effect of particular linguistic devices and language choices.

When *creating* texts, the author:

- categorises the text into literary genres in order to draw upon or stretch genre conventions;
- makes use of and reflects upon structures in the text designed to create unity;
- uses analogy to create, explore and contrast images, characters and themes within and between texts;

- considers background contextual aspects which support the creation (and guides subsequent interpretation) of a text;
- uses language to direct and flavour text (see Oliver, 2019, for further details about the theoretical underpinnings of these suggestions).

By explicitly considering and strengthening reasoning while reading, critiquing and interpreting texts, children can be guided to practise these reasoning processes during their own writing. They will be supported to explicitly consider the potential impact of their own creative choices upon readers, thus gaining control over the potential ways in which their writing may be interpreted.

ACTIVITY 1

Recap children's knowledge of the fairy-tale genre. Discuss examples and consider typical features of texts within this genre. Next, present small groups with blank diamond-ranking templates accompanied by nine cards displaying features of fairy tales (such as hero, villain, happy ending, message/moral, magical events, and so on). Children work as a group to discuss and decide upon the placement of these features within the diamond grid. This may require teacher scaffolding, particularly if children are not accustomed to group discussion and debate. Children should be encouraged to articulate their reasons for deciding why they have chosen to place features in a particular place, and why they think some features are more or less important than others.

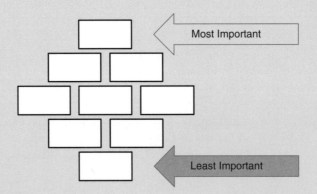

Figure 11.1 Diamond ranking grid

Once children have practised reasoning about a genre, which is largely informed by their experiences of reading within it, they can then move on to use this reasoning when writing their own fairy-tale texts. Asking children to write their own fairy tales may be a relatively common activity, yet doing this with an emphasis on reasoning development will promote writing at greater depth. Children will be able to draw upon the understandings of the genre which they developed and articulated in the group diamond-ranking exercise when they are constructing their own texts. For example, they may emphasise the importance of a message or moral in their own story planning and writing if this aspect was deemed very important in the discussion activity.

How can reasoning be promoted within the classroom?

It has been identified that focusing on reasoning while reading can develop more reasoned writing. Thus, consideration now moves to focus on ways in which reasoning can be promoted within the classroom. If we want to develop children's capacity to reason, and in turn develop the depth and quality of their writing (both fictional and non-fictional), we need to give sufficient opportunities to practise and hone these skills. The importance of language and communication are central to the development of reasoning. Dialogic approaches to teaching (e.g. Alexander, 2015) can support reasoning development by harnessing the power of talk and dialogue to further learning (remember the student–teacher dialogue presented at the start of this chapter).

FOCUS ON RESEARCH

ROBIN ALEXANDER'S FRAMEWORK FOR DIALOGIC TEACHING

Robin Alexander is a seminal figure within dialogic teaching research. He argues that 'dialogic teaching harnesses the power of talk to stimulate and extend pupils' thinking and advance their learning and understanding' (Alexander, 2015, p. 62). Alexander describes five principles which he suggests bring together the essential features of a dialogic classroom. Thus, dialogic teaching is:

Collective: teachers and children address learning tasks together, whether as a group or as a class, rather than in isolation.

Reciprocal: teachers and children listen to each other, share ideas and consider alternative viewpoints.

Supportive: children articulate their ideas freely, without fear of embarrassment over 'wrong' answers, and they help each other to reach common understandings.

(Continued)

(Continued)

Cumulative: teachers and children build on their own and each other's ideas and chain them into coherent lines of thinking and enquiry.

Purposeful: teachers plan and facilitate dialogic teaching with particular educational goals in view.

(Alexander, 2015, p. 28).

The main arguments for adopting a dialogic approach are similar to the benefits of small-group work discussed below. Thus, dialogic teaching promotes communication; develops relationships, confidence and a sense of self; develops individual and collective identities; develops spoken language and high-quality talk which scaffolds understanding; engages attention and motivation and leads to measurable learning gains; and it supports citizenship goals through a focus on reasoning, debate and argumentation skills (Alexander, 2015).

This focus on dialogic teaching illustrates the importance of talk to the development of reasoning. But this talk has to be different from the traditional modes that still dominate in some classrooms. There have been frequent reports of the limited amount of talk within classrooms, often accompanied by low-level tasks and questioning (Howe and Abedin, 2013). Alexander describes three traditional kinds of teacher talk linked to direct instruction: rote, recitation (which dominates overall) and instruction/exposition. Rote forms of talk relate to the repetitive drilling of facts, concepts or routines; recitation typically sees questions designed to test or promote recall of prior learning, or cues which enable pupils to decipher an answer from clues given in a question; and instruction/exposition involves instructing children about what to do, imparting information, and/or explaining facts, principles or procedures (Alexander, 2015).

- How many times have you observed these types of talk in classrooms?
- How often do your lessons focus solely on these types of talk?

It is not argued that teachers should abandon these forms of talk altogether, but rather, we should ensure that these are not the only ones our pupils are exposed to.

Alexander then describes two additional forms of talk which he suggests are likely to support the principles of dialogic teaching: 'discussion' and 'scaffolded dialogue'. Discussion is defined as 'the exchange of ideas with a view to sharing information and solving problems' (Alexander, 2015, p. 30). Dialogue is defined as 'achieving common understanding through structured, cumulative questioning and discussion which guide and prompt, reduce choices, minimise risk and error, and expedite "handover" of concepts and principles' (Alexander, 2015, p. 30). While offering the levels of cognitive challenge children require to achieve the highest quality learning, discussion and scaffolded dialogue require a much greater level of skill and subject knowledge on the teacher's part.

How can we harness the power of dialogue in our teaching?

The observations and arguments above in support of dialogic teaching may be fairly incontestable (particularly if one accessed the large body of research underpinning these ideas), yet actually changing the patterns of talk, or increasing the proportion of discursive or dialogic talk in our lessons, may be easier said than done. One way of promoting increased levels of discussion and dialogue may be to offer more opportunities for small group work (including times when groups are engaged in dialogue with a teacher).

Task structures to promote high-quality talk and reasoning

Each of the tasks here function as a scaffold to the development of dialogue and reasoning. Given the benefits of collaborative learning and dialogic teaching described above, they are discussed here in terms of small group tasks (of approximately two to four students), although the structures are also adaptable to whole-class or individual activities. These tasks require students to 'do' something, hopefully as a result of 'saying' and reasoning about something. Decisions are often required from students and the tasks are designed to be open-ended in the sense that a range of possibilities could be argued for. These task structures give students opportunities to put forward propositions or arguments, and to be presented with counter-arguments or alternative perspectives. Compromise and negotiation are often required to make final decisions on how the task should be completed. These demands require students to articulate their ideas and the reasoning behind them, to weigh up evidence and arguments, and to decide upon a solution as a group. They therefore meet the principles of dialogic teaching described earlier and provide an authentic context in which reasoning is required.

Role on the Wall

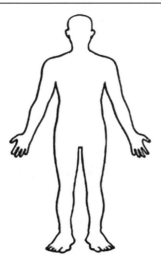

Figure 11.2   Role on the Wall outline

Role on the Wall is a strategy that presents students with an outline of a figure used to represent a particular character. The idea is that students use the spaces provided both inside and outside of the figure to record important aspects relating to the chosen character. Role on the Wall can be used in a number of ways – for example, the inside of the figure can be used to describe the thoughts, feelings, characteristics or personality of a character. This portion is often used to target the 'inner' life or qualities of a character.

The outside of the figure can be used in different ways, depending on the text, character or learning objective. For example, students could record physical characteristics of characters around the outside (perhaps considering possible tensions or harmonies between inward and outward qualities). Alternatively, the outside of the figure could be used to record the environmental sources that affect the character, particularly in terms of their inner lives – for example, life events, relationships or personal hardships/triumphs which contribute to particular emotions or personality traits. Another way to engage with the outer portion is to use this space to record descriptions of the character according to the perceptions held of them by others. Again, this may or may not correlate with what is recorded in terms of their inner qualities. Depending on the task focus, the outside of the figure could also be used as a space to record questions that readers would wish to ask a character, or that could form points for discussion within the class.

This task can be used as a whole-class activity, with a large 'role' displayed 'on the wall' of the classroom. This would be added to over the course of reading and completed as a shared class activity. Role on the Wall can also be used by individual students, pairs or groups. It can form a one-off task to reflect upon aspects of a particular character in depth. Alternatively, it can be built up over time, deepening understanding of a character over the course of reading and reflecting on what knowledge, impressions and understanding are gained over the course of a text. Additionally, multiple 'roles' or figures can be completed to compare characters according to their inward and/or outward qualities. For example, completing two 'roles' for the title characters in Mark Twain's classic tale *The Prince and the Pauper* may support a deeper understanding of some of the differences between the characters (either in terms of inward characteristics, outward features, or both).

CASE STUDY

ROLE ON THE WALL COMPARING 'HEROIC' CHARACTERS

Carolyn, a Year 5 teacher, had considered the topic of Greek Mythology during English lessons over the course of a half-term. The following four weeks were spent reading, discussing and writing about Arvan Kumar's (1988) *The Heartstone Odyssey*, a text designed to encourage greater appreciation of the need for tolerance and respect while provoking discussion about the issue of racism. The class then began to read and focus on Terry Jones's (2018) *The Saga of Erik the Viking* as the basis for English lessons. Carolyn recognised the need to make links and draw analogies between different texts, as well as to identify broader themes pervading a range of literature. She therefore planned a writing activity asking students to identify which of three selected characters was most heroic. The first character to consider, Theseus, was taken from the Ancient Greek myth, *Theseus and the Minotaur* (Ford, 2004). The second character, Chandra, is the protagonist of *The Heartstone Odyssey*, and the third character, Erik, is the leading character in *The Saga of Erik the Viking*.

Pupils were familiar with the Role on the Wall task structure. Students were asked to consider a range of texts to answer a broad question, so the single outline typical in Role on the Wall was replaced with three outlines. The three characters were compared in terms of their characteristics and personality traits which would support or refute their status as heroes.

Students were asked to complete the inner portions for each of the figures (factors that could be recorded around the outer portions were not considered within this lesson, although there may have been the potential to consider whether physical characteristics affect a person's 'heroic' stance). The teacher modelled selecting particular characteristics from a given bank of personality traits and considering which character(s) the particular trait was most applicable to. While the given word bank scaffolded consideration of 'heroic' attributes, students were free to come up with their own characteristics to describe any of the characters. Emphasis was placed on students articulating their reasons for allocating particular characters certain traits, drawing on evidence from the text of where this characteristic was displayed. Students also had to decide whether selected traits might also apply to either of the other two characters, and to what extent, if so. This activity required a continual process of comparison and reflection. Because the three characters shared much in common (and could each potentially be described as 'heroic'), the necessity of providing reasons for choosing a particular trait for a character was apparent. This meant that students were required to engage closely with the texts and then articulate their reasoning with close reference to these texts.

Figure 11.3   Y5 students' completed Role on the Wall group task

This activity required limited writing, with only short notes recorded within the figure outlines. It foregrounded group discussion and promoted a dialogic environment, aims which are valuable in themselves. Yet the activity was also used as a springboard to develop deeper writing. Arguments and evidence to support them, which were initially articulated and briefly recorded, were ultimately used to scaffold and support a written task asking students to reflect on the question 'Who was the most heroic?' Students had been given opportunities to develop their own thinking and reasoning, and to hear that of peers, through the group discussion task based on Role on the Wall. They had been required to articulate reasoning, and had most likely encountered alternative viewpoints which they then accommodated into their own views or argued against. All of these processes facilitated their writing, which essentially required transformation of their verbal reasoning into a more formal written structure. This gave students the opportunity to demonstrate one of the 'pupil can' statements for those working at greater depth at the end of KS2: 'The pupil can: distinguish between the language of speech and writing and choose the appropriate register' (DfE, 2018). While it would not have been possible for all children to work within the greater depth standards, it nevertheless provided those who might have been working within this stage with the chance to address this particular objective (see also Chapter 4). Focusing on reasoning through the task structure of Role on the Wall thus helped to promote deeper writing, where reasons for claims were made explicit and where there was close engagement with the texts and characters being compared.

ACTIVITY 2

Show the children an image of Quasimodo, taken from the 1996 Disney film *The Hunchback of Notre Dame*. Present them with an outline of this character, with space to record ideas inside and around the outside.

Ask children to work in small groups to complete the outside portion of the figure, focusing on the character's physical characteristics. This could be supplemented with a focus on adjectives and descriptive writing. Once the children have recorded observations of Quasimodo's appearance, ask them to complete the inner portion of the Role on the Wall template, focusing this time on his personality traits and characteristics. These observations should be supported with evidence from the story so that reasoning is made explicit.

Ask children to compare the inward and outward characteristics observed.

- Do they match?
- Do they usually find this pattern of contrast within fairy tales/literature in general?
- Can they think of other examples?
- Can they think of examples of characters displaying the contrasting characteristics in the opposite way – i.e. 'beautiful' on the outside, 'ugly' on the inside?

This could lead to some interesting discussion and then writing, reflecting on what constitutes 'beauty' (either in literature or more broadly), and how it can be (or is) defined. This writing could be supported with reference to examples and evidence from the completed Role on the Wall, and from discussion designed to extend consideration after the initial activity.

Other characters could be used as the basis for this activity or to extend the discussion. *Cinderella* might be interesting in terms of considering the contrast between the protagonist's initial ragged appearance and her inward beauty or goodness. Characters from transformation tales such as *The Frog Prince* might also support this reflection and comparison. Through the process of scaffolded discussion and dialogue with a focus on promoting reasoning, children should be able to produce deeper, more reflective and more considered writing.

Odd One Out

The basis of this task structure focuses on and supports students' ability to sort and classify. It requires consideration of similarities and differences between a given set of items with the goal of deciding which of a set are similar and can be grouped and which is the Odd One Out based on their dissimilarity to the other group.

There are several formats that this activity can take. In the most basic form, students are presented with three items between which they must discuss similarities and differences before deciding which one is odd. This could be developed using a more systematic approach by employing a triangle format (see Figure 11.4 below) which requires systematic recording of similarities through the use of arrows between any two items in the triangle.

Differences can also be noted around the outside of the triangle, located beside the specific item which is distinguished in some way from the other two. This format should also support students' ability to identify alternative solutions to the Odd One Out problem.

Another variation of Odd One Out is to present items in a grid (see Activity 3). This table format contains a range of items within the cells of the grid. These are then considered in terms of identified similarities and differences before students form groups from the items, based on some identified similarity which distinguishes the group from other items or groups. Again, this focuses on classification and requires students to compare and contrast items before arriving at a decision. It can be used to extend consideration from three items, of which only one is classified as 'odd', to requiring the formation of several groups, which must be distinguishable from the others, or to selecting one odd item or group from a larger set of items.

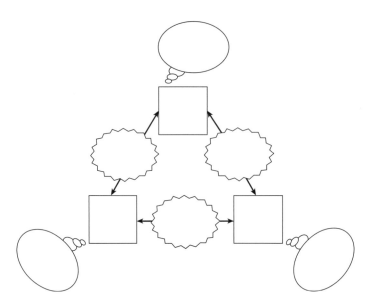

Figure 11.4   Odd One Out triangle template

Source: Higgins and Baumfield, 2001, p. 19

The basic procedure of Odd One Out, despite variations, requires the following stages, presented in Higgins and Baumfield's *Thinking Through Primary Teaching* (2001) and adapted here to apply specifically to English:

1. Present pupils with three items – e.g. characters, genres, features of a genre/text, words related to a text, linguistic features.
2. Ask them to identify similarities and differences.
3. Next, ask them to choose an Odd One Out and give a reason.
4. Encourage them to identify a corresponding similarity for each difference – e.g. if Cinderella is the Odd One Out because she is from a modest background, Snow White and Sleeping Beauty are similar in that they are both royalty.
5. Encourage a range of answers.

Step 4 is important because it requires explicit consideration and articulation from students of the similarities between the two left, rather than just a difference identified in the odd one selected. It should support them to select carefully considered 'odd' items, hopefully developing a more reasoned and justified response to the task.

Teacher modelling of what makes a good answer in terms of Odd One Out is very important. Teachers can help to steer students away from identifying superficial answers, or answers that are arbitrary in relation to the subject – e.g. an answer such as 'Cinderella is the Odd One Out because her name has only one word, whereas Snow White and Sleeping Beauty each have two words in their name' may be considered a superficial answer. This detracts from engagement with features such as character and genre, which may be more important considerations within English lessons.

The Odd One Out activity has many advantages. It requires minimal preparation time and is easy to explain to students. It encourages development of a key mode of thinking – classification – and facilitates group discussion giving a real purpose for classroom talk. The activity encourages students to develop a more precise vocabulary in English. It requires careful thinking and reasoning, both from students and teachers and, while it is open-ended, it can be approached systematically. It is suitable across the school age range and is an engaging activity.

ACTIVITY 3

Present children with a 3 × 3 grid of synonyms for 'walk'. For example:

stroll	ramble	prowl
tread	trudge	plod
hike	march	wander

Ask students to form at least two groups containing at least three synonyms each. Students should be able to articulate their reasons for grouping in this way by identifying what makes their chosen words similar to one another, as well as stating what distinguishes them from those left over. Students can then decide whether to form an additional group, add synonyms to the two groups already formed, or leave some as 'odd'.

Variation: give students three of these synonyms contained within the triangle Odd One Out format. They have to decide which two are linked in some way and which is odd. Ensure that reasoning is clearly articulated.

Although the Odd One Out activity can be treated as 'stand-alone', this task structure and the high-quality discussion that it promotes can be used as a basis for developing quality writing. For example, it could be used to structure a compare/contrast style text by scaffolding student consideration of similarities and differences between characters, texts, genres or whatever else is made the subject of an Odd One Out task. It could also support certain forms and structures of poetry writing, perhaps with a focus on grouping within stanzas or a contrast presented in the last line of each stanza.

Another way in which Odd One Out can support deeper writing is through its capacity to focus on language, as illustrated in the activity above. Vocabulary can be presented in groups of three or within a larger grid containing items that students group together based upon a shared similarity. This vocabulary might draw upon synonyms for a particular word in order to consider the nuances between definitions of seemingly similar words. This then leads to consideration and focus upon the importance of precision within vocabulary choice. A focus on language is evident within all four of the 'pupil can' statements for writing at greater depth at end of KS2. There is a need to have a rich understanding of a wide range of vocabulary and an appreciation for subtleties in meaning between synonyms to support the development of deeper writing.

Odd One Out can also be used to consider which features are important within particular genres. It could support students to appreciate the real similarities and differences between individual texts contained within a genre, or even between genre categories. This would allow them to consider which features are most important or prevalent to genre distinctions.

CASE STUDY

CONSIDERING SIMILARITIES AND DIFFERENCES BETWEEN THREE TEXTS FROM THE ROBINSONADE (OR 'CASTAWAY'/'ISLAND ADVENTURE') GENRE

Children in a Year 6 class had recently read Michael Morpurgo's (2005) *Kensuke's Kingdom*. They had read a condensed version of Daniel Defoe's *Robinson Crusoe* in a previous year group and several students offered comparisons between the two stories without being prompted to do so. This led the teacher to focus on the Robinsonade genre, or desert island story as it is commonly known. Since consideration of genre and generic structure requires children to know examples from these genres in order to analyse the commonalities and underlying genre structures and patterns, the teacher supplemented students' experience of this genre by sharing extracts from and a summary of Johann Wyss's (2004) *Swiss Family Robinson*. They also watched a film version of this story.

Children were presented with the Odd One Out triangle template containing the titles of the three Robinsonade texts listed above. They had to identify links between the texts as well as features that were distinct to one individual text. Any similarities shared between all three of the texts were recorded in the middle of the triangle. Similarities between any two of the texts (thus rendering the third text the 'odd one out') were recorded along the lines connecting the particular two texts within the triangle format. Children were encouraged to identify links that were important to the development of the particular story, to the Robinsonade genre and/or to the characters within the texts as opposed to identifying more superficial similarities which did not really engage with consideration of the genre and its features. For example, reflecting upon the importance and prevalence to the genre of an ending which sees characters escape from the island would demonstrate high-quality engagement and consideration of genre features as opposed to identification of links such as the number of words contained within the title.

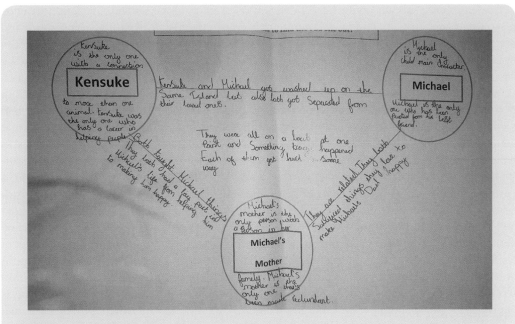

Figure 11.5 Y6 students' Odd One Out group work

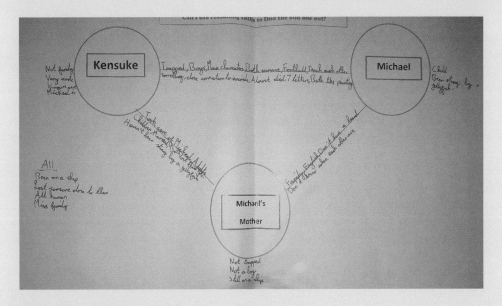

Figure 11.6 More Y6 students' Odd One Out group work

The case study above could have been left as a stand-alone activity, designed to elicit reasoning from students and to encourage rich engagement with what they have read, and the patterns and structures that they can discern within their reading. However, this activity acted as a powerful scaffold to deeper writing. Children followed this activity by creating their own narratives within the Robinsonade genre. They were able to make decisions about this writing with much greater consideration and critical reflection as a result of the discussions they had held when participating in the Odd One Out activity. They had a greatly enhanced awareness and understanding of not only the features of this particular genre, which they could then employ within their own writing, but also of the ways in which these features can differ, or even be subverted, within individual texts. The understanding, albeit probably implicit, of the ways in which a text can operate within a particular genre yet also exist as a separate and individual piece was facilitated by considering the similarities and differences between three separate texts which were all distinct and contained distinguishing features yet were still classified as belonging within the same genre category. The level of sophistication that this awareness requires and the subsequent level of autonomy that was promoted within their own writing is surely in line with aspirations to promote writing at greater depth. Indeed, the importance of independence within writing is made clear in KS2 teacher assessment guidance where it is stated that 'writing is likely to be independent if it: emerges from . . . experience in which pupils have had opportunities to discuss and rehearse what is to be written about' (2018, p. 13; this is reflected on further in Chapter 4).

Conclusion

This chapter has illustrated the importance of developing reasoning within our students. This is greatly supported by adopting a dialogic approach to teaching, in which opportunities for working in small groups are provided. Providing open-ended and engaging task structures for groups to work on not only limits behavioural problems associated with lack of structure or purely discussion-based exercises, but also requires students to demonstrate, practise and refine their reasoning processes. Making the decisions required within these task structures demands clear articulation of the reasoning behind decisions and encourages students to explicitly consider the evidence underpinning their inferences or conclusions, as well as working towards evaluating the quality and strength of this evidence (the features and importance of critical reading skills are considered further in Chapter 6). By working with others in small groups, students are also given opportunities to consider alternative ideas or counterarguments, which they can assimilate into their own ideas, or argue against.

The talk within collaborative tasks can sometimes focus upon analysing texts created by others, therefore practising reasoning *about* texts. Yet this also has value for writing. Considering authorial intentions in depth, and evaluating the effects of such decisions within the authors' texts, can help to illustrate to students the decisions involved during the writing process. It can help to make explicit the kinds of decisions that they can make about their own writing and therefore promotes a deeper engagement with their own creative choices.

Further reading

Higgins, S. and Baumfield, Viv. (2001) *Thinking Through Primary Teaching*. Cambridge: Chris Kingston Publishing.

This practical guide explores task structures that can promote and develop children's thinking skills. It applies across the primary curriculum and is supported with examples of how the tasks can be used in varying ways. Photocopiable materials are also provided.

Recommended websites

Robin Alexander – www.robinalexander.org.uk/dialogic-teaching/

Robin Alexander is a seminal figure in dialogic teaching theory and research. His website is accessible and informative and will support teachers wishing to explore the principles of dialogic teaching and learning.

References

Alexander, R. (2015) *Towards Dialogic Teaching: Rethinking Classroom Talk* (4th edn). York: Dialogos.
Defoe, D. [1719] (2007) *Robinson Crusoe*. Oxford; New York: Oxford University Press.
Department for Education (DfE) (2014) *The National Curriculum in England: Framework Document*. Available online at: www.gov.uk/government/uploads/system/uploads/attachment_data/file/381344/Master_final_national_curriculum_28_Nov.pdf
Department for Education (DfE) (2018) *Teacher Assesment Exemplification: End of Key Stage 2: English Writing: Working at Greater Depth Within the Expected Standard: Frankie*. Available online at: https://assets.publishing.service.gov.uk/government/uploads/system/uploads/attachment_data/file/655619/2018_exemplification_materials_KS2-GDS__Frankie_.pdf (accessed 26.1.2019).
Ford, J. (2004) *Theseus and the Minotaur (Ancient Greek Myths)*. Brighton: Book House.
Higgins, S. and Baumfield, Viv. (2001) *Thinking Through Primary Teaching*. Cambridge: Chris Kingston Publishing.
Howe, C. and Abedin, M. (2013) Classroom dialogue: a systematic review across four decades of research. *Cambridge Journal of Education*, 43, 325e356. Available online at: http://dx.doi.org/10.1080/0305764X.2013.786024
Jones, T. (1988) *The Saga of Erik the Viking*. London: Puffin Books.
Kumar, A. (1988) *The Heartstone Odyssey*. Derbyshire: Allied Mouse.
Morpurgo, M. (2005) *Kensuke's Kingdom*. London: Egmont.
Oliver, M. (2019) *Exploring and Developing Reasoning in Primary English*, in Shao, X. and Dobson, E. *Imagining Better Education*. Durham, England: Durham University, School of Education, pp. 137–150.
Trilling, B. and Fadel, C. (2009) *21st Century Skills: Learning for Life in our Times*. San Francisco, CA: John Wiley & Sons.
Wegerif, R. (2010) *Mind-expanding: Teaching for Thinking and Creativity in Primary Education*. Buckingham: Open University Press.
Wyss, J.D. (2004) *The Swiss Family Robinson*. London: Signet Classics.

12

USING CLASSIC TEXTS TO DEVELOP DEEPER WRITING SKILLS

Pam Vennart

KEY QUESTIONS

- How can I engage pupils in a range of classic texts that may be used to support the development of confidence in grammar, vocabulary and composition skills effectively and encourage deeper writing in the process?
- How do I support children in a range of composition skills, including poetry and description?
- How can resources such as extracts from classic texts enhance and support the development of creative writing?

Introduction

This chapter considers the role that 'classic' texts can have in improving writing in depth in primary schools. It will reflect on how teachers can develop grammatical and vocabulary choices in children's writing, as well as increase both pupil and teacher confidence in using texts that are perceived to be more challenging.

Engaging children in 'classic texts' will be explored, with the aim being to inspire and motivate children to write in greater depth, alongside a growing sense of the need to foster ambitious vocabulary and grammatical choices in creative writing. This approach was advocated in the Government document *Moving English Forward* (2012) where Ofsted praised a secondary school that had 'classic texts at the centre of the English curriculum despite the fact that many of its students had considerable difficulties with basic communication' (p. 20). This view was also supported by Pat Macpherson who wrote in Hansen (2016): 'Reading the classic stories of the past opens the window for imaginative children into whole new worlds which they can only profit from knowing' (p. 152). 'Opening windows for imaginative children' regardless of perceived ability is one of the aims of this chapter.

With the increasing focus on grammar in the primary years, it is a difficult juggling act to perform if teachers are to teach the vast terminology for the SPaG test at KS2 and not stifle creativity and fun in English in the process. A huge factor in all of this, is ensuring primary teachers themselves are not only competent in teaching grammar, but also allow for a flexible approach to lesson planning to allow time to inspire creativity in the minds of young writers. Deeper writing can be harnessed and encouraged by using more challenging texts as a model, instead of, as is sometimes the case, the teacher modelling the writing themselves; seeing and reading for themselves the impact more complex grammatical structures can have in the work of recognised classic writers often provides an excellent stimulus and support for both the teacher and the pupils.

The focus of the chapter will be to provide a series of classic text-based activities for use in the classroom which have been developed and used by experienced practitioners, in the hope it will inspire other less experienced practitioners to use classic texts more confidently. Poetry, prose and Shakespeare will be considered, with a view to supporting teachers with their planning. Reflections from professionals, including myself as an ITE English specialist, and primary colleagues, will illustrate how high-quality texts can make an impact on the composition skills of primary children.

Poetry

FOCUS ON RESEARCH

WHY USE POETRY AS A STIMULUS FOR DEEPER WRITING?

The great romantic poets write of childhood as a time of 'paradise and perfection'. Dennis Carter (1998) attributes children with the ability to 'credit marvels', interpreting this as

(Continued)

(Continued)

children's natural ability to understand language and meaning, particularly in the context of poetry. The National Curriculum guides primary teachers to use poetry for developing memory, but also advocates the following:

NATIONAL CURRICULUM – WRITING: COMPOSITION

'Pupils should be taught to develop positive attitudes towards and stamina for writing by poetry' (DfE, 2013, p. 21).

We need look no further than the still existing belief that nursery rhymes are one of the most proven and successful ways of introducing language and reading skills, enjoyment and memory to children. Goswami (1990) advocates that such early poetry offers pupils an unparalleled opportunity for creative expression, being as it is, a concise means of communication where the focus on vocabulary choices are critical.

A more recent text which considers teaching grammar through literature (Fenn and McGlynn, 2018) similarly advocates that the 'easiest way for students to become familiar and confident with new terminology is through the study of poetry, where the condensed and rich nature of the language can offer a wide range of examples' (p. 92).

With the research above in mind, the case study which follows was part of a seminar for BA students studying Education at Durham University.

CASE STUDY

CLASSIC TEXTS: PLANNING FOR DEEPER WRITING

A group of ITE students decided to teach the opening of 'The Night Before Christmas', a traditional rhyme by C.C. Moore (1839).

'Twas the night before Christmas, when all through the house
not a creature was stirring, not even a mouse.
The stockings were hung by the chimney with care,
in hopes that St. Nicholas soon would be there.
The children were nestled all snug in their beds,
while visions of sugar plums danced in their heads.
And Mama in her 'kerchief, and I in my cap,

had just settled our brains for a long winter's nap.

When out on the roof there arose such a clatter,

I sprang from my bed to see what was the matter.

The tutor read the full poem aloud and copies were given to the students. Complex vocabulary in this section of the poem (e.g. 'Twas/kerchiefs/sugar plums/ St. Nicholas) was highlighted by the students, and alternative meanings discussed. Students were asked to write a modern version of the opening lines.

The students, despite initially feeling this text was 'too difficult', gradually, through discussion and collaborative planning, came to see that there could be much mileage in considering this text as a stimulus for creative writing, grammar and vocabulary work, in line with the KS1 programmes of study.

READING: COMPREHENSION

Pupils should be taught to develop pleasure in reading, motivation to read, vocabulary and understanding by:

- listening to and discussing a wide range of poems, stories and non-fiction at a level beyond that at which they can read independently;
- learning to appreciate rhymes and poems and recite some by heart;

(DfE, 2013, p. 11)

The students then planned a range of other activities, including work on rhyme (rhyming couplets), syllables, use of iambic metre and vocabulary choices, alongside some work on historical context.

The merits of children also learning these opening lines by heart was also discussed. It was decided that this would not only be good practice, but also that learning poetry encourages a good memory and also fulfils some of the requirements of the National Curriculum.

ACTIVITY 1

Discuss what the pupils do on the night before Christmas and why we now call this time Christmas Eve. Do they have any traditions they follow on Christmas Eve?

Using a poem as a model to help them write poetry, give the first couplet to the pupils and then ask them to continue in this style. The pupils should be encouraged to

(Continued)

(Continued)

write a Christmas poem in rhyming couplets using some of the new vocabulary the poem has introduced.

Give pupils a cloze procedure with some vocabulary omitted to see what alternative vocabulary choices could be made.

Try pupils working in pairs on a couplet and writing a whole-class poem.

Another poem to encourage and foster a love of language and structure is taken from the classic text *Alice in Wonderland* by Lewis Carroll. The use of the poem 'Jabberwocky' fulfils one of the government guidelines for writing.

National Curriculum – Writing: Composition

'Pupils should be taught to develop positive attitudes towards and stamina for writing by:

writing poetry' (DfE, 2013, p. 21).

Writing poetry, then, also offers teachers an opportunity to plan for creativity alongside encouraging analysis of language and poetic techniques, which could then be embedded or used to scaffold the pupils' own writing at depth.

The following case study explores tasks that were undertaken by a Year 5 teacher with the aim of enabling pupils to create their own fantasy descriptions of an imaginary creature and write their own rhyming poetry.

CASE STUDY

JABBERWOCKY FROM *ALICE IN WONDERLAND* (1865) BY LEWIS CARROLL

Fiona, a Year 5 teacher, asked the pupils to listen to 'Jabberwocky' being read aloud. She also asked a range of questions following Bloom's taxonomy, from understanding what the poem is about, to creating one verse in this style, using A-B-A-B rhyme scheme (alternate rhyme).

Fiona read the entire poem to her pupils, but then focused on the first verse below:

Twas brillig, and the slithy toves

Did gyre and gimble in the wabe;

All mimsy were the borogoves,
And the mome raths outgrabe.

After some discussion about content, she was able to go into grammatical, structural and linguistic features in more depth.

ACTIVITY 2

Having read 'Jabberwocky' aloud, ask the following questions:

- What do you think a 'Jabberwocky' is?
- Draw one/describe one.
- Learn the first verse by heart.
- Look at rhyme and rhythm.
- How do you know which words are adjectives and which are nouns?
- Consider syntax/word order.

Some notes to support this activity for the teacher are noted below:

TEACHER GUIDE: POINTS OF GRAMMAR FOR DISCUSSION

- Contracted forms: 'twas.
- Determiners: 'the', 'a'.
- Effect of definite/indefinite article.
- Verbs 'gyre' and 'gimble' (an opportunity here to consider connotation. What do these verbs suggest? How do you gyre? Gimble?)
- nouns . . . Toves/wabe/borograves/raths/mome raths.
- Eight-syllable line.
- Ballad form and the oral tradition of poetry could be considered.

DEEPER WRITING

After sharing ideas and discussing the poetry in depth, the pupils copied the first verse and then continued one of their own which adhered to the rhyme pattern of the original. The pupils also wrote their own version by replacing Carroll's verbs, adjectives or nouns. This activity was extended by replacing the definite article with the indefinite article and discussion about what, if any, difference this makes. Pupils wrote their own 'nonsense' poem about a beast, using the word bank from this poem to support their own writing.

Poetry, then, offers endless possibilities for the primary practitioner. Embedded as it is within the National Curriculum Programmes of Study, alongside other poetry choices that are fun and more contemporary, there are equally compelling reasons to encourage pupils at primary level to engage in more demanding poetry choices.

Prose

While poetry is one area where deeper writing can be encouraged, another is using prose texts. It would indeed be a challenge beyond the reading abilities and stamina of many primary pupils in 2019 to read an entire Dickens novel. However, it is not unreasonable to use extracts from these texts to inspire writing at depth. It is also, of course, the duty of any teacher to expose all children to high-quality writing. All pupils can benefit when presented with a text that both teachers and pupils find 'hard'; exploring together the effect of vocabulary and sentence structures can offer ways into deeper writing in their own composition, too.

FOCUS ON RESEARCH

WHY USE CLASSIC PROSE AS A STIMULUS FOR DEEPER WRITING?

The word 'classic', according to Carter (2011) has to do with 'high quality' and 'tradition'. Carter goes on to remind us that historically some children used to read adult fiction because children's fiction did not exist. He also argues that children should have access to a 'full range of fiction . . . not only Roald Dahl, but also Charles Dickens' (p. 78). Cremin (2009), too, suggests that primary teachers should expand their own reading beyond the familiar and the accessible. Teacher confidence can be supported with accessible activities such as those in this chapter, so that non-specialist English teachers can expand not only their pupils' access to classic texts, but also in the process improve their own confidence and courage in this area.

Such a task is one used with a Year 6 class taking the opening paragraphs of Dickens's *Bleak House*. The aim here was to have fun trying to understand how Dickens writes, explore how London must have been in Victorian England, play a class game and hopefully end up with some deeper writing from the pupils. In this case, the pupils were to write a description of a city that used complex grammatical structures alongside ambitious vocabulary choices. The case study below was tried more recently by a colleague from St Joseph's Middle School, Northumberland, to provide examples of students' work to support this example.

CASE STUDY

CLASSIC TEXTS: *BLEAK HOUSE* BY CHARLES DICKENS

Kirsten, a Year 6 teacher, wanted to improve the variety of sentence structures the class was using, alongside trying to encourage a breadth of vocabulary in their descriptive writing. They had been working towards a longer piece of narrative writing and in this lesson they were looking at images of a city with a beach (quite a contrast from the muddy November description Dickens gives of London). She decided to use the opening lines of *Bleak House* as her model to support the pupils' writing (in Chapter 13 the value of scaffolding and providing a model for children's writing are discussed).

Kirsten explained that the class would be using Dickens's description to help them write their own. Initially, images of a beach attached to a city were shown to the pupils. A vocabulary word bank was developed, focusing on the senses. Then the opening of *Bleak House* was used with the teaching focus to push for greater depth in writing.

Kirsten read the opening paragraphs of *Bleak House* (see below) aloud and pupils were also given a copy of the text. As a class, they spent some time discussing how Dickens describes the mud and the effect of the description of the possible appearance of dinosaurs. Pupils highlighted examples of unfamiliar vocabulary and were encouraged to replace them with a more familiar word – e.g. Christmas term instead of Michaelmas term. Kirsten had paired low-ability pupils with high-ability ones, so that the task was fully differentiated. Again, with highlighters, pupils were encouraged to look at the length of sentences and whether any figures of speech, such as similes, were used.

Kirsten then told the pupils they were going to write a description of a city with a beach of their choice in the style of Dickens's description of London. They were given lined A4 paper and told to have the paper portrait style and then write the name of a city of their choice (one-word sentence). They were then told to fold the paper over so the name of the city could not be seen and the paper then passed over to the person next to them on the right. They were then told to write a series of sentences, some of which followed the Dickens model. This was then passed on and the task repeated until the pupils had written six sentences.

Throughout this task pupils were reminded to keep the picture of their city in their minds. When the pupils had passed to the sixth person the paper was opened to reveal a city and beach description. The pupils read these aloud and although many worked without any changes, pupils were able to change one thing or reword part of the description if necessary.

Here are some of the examples of the pupils' work:

(Continued)

(Continued)

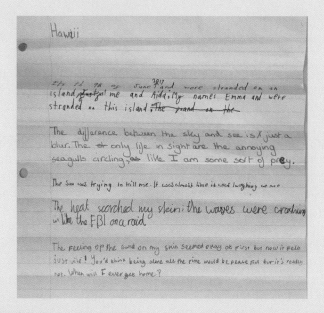

Figure 12.1   Pupils' writing on Bleak House

Of note in the example above is the use of a semi-colon and the interesting use of similes. The range of punctuation used was a feature of the writing with which Kirsten was particularly pleased.

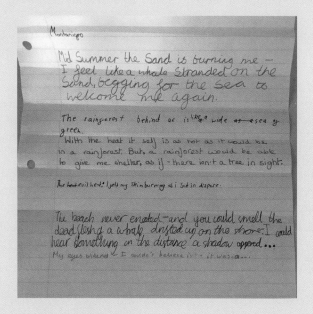

Figure 12.2   More pupils' writing on Bleak House

This example was pleasing again because of the varying use of sentences and also the effective use of personification: 'begging for the sea to welcome me'.

Kirsten had used a scaffold and model approach, but she felt the open-ended nature of the task allowed for creativity while simultaneously teaching aspects of grammar – in particular, sentence variations and vocabulary. While this had been a challenge for her mixed-ability Year 6 class, she felt the writing produced showed a great depth in terms of vocabulary and sentence constructions used by the pupils.

ACTIVITY 3

Give pupils copies of the opening paragraphs of *Bleak House*. Some discussion will be needed to explore, for example, why the streets are so muddy. How is this description of London different from London in 2019? What is a Lord Chancellor?

Revise figures of speech such as simile and personification.

Use highlighters to annotate the different sentences used here (in square brackets in the example below).

LONDON [1 word]. Michaelmas Term lately over, and the Lord Chancellor sitting in Lincoln's Inn Hall [compound]. Implacable November weather [3 words]. As much mud in the streets as if the waters had but newly retired from the face of the earth, and it would not be wonderful to meet a Megalosaurus, forty feet long or so, wad-dling like an elephantine lizard up Holborn Hill [simile]. Smoke lowering down from chimney-pots, making a soft black drizzle, with flakes of soot in it as big as full-grown snow-flakes – gone into mourning, one might imagine, for the death of the sun [complex/embedded clause/use of hyphen and personification].

The above sentence structure emerges:

1. one-word sentence;
2. compound sentence;
3. three-word sentence;
4. use of a simile/ personification;
5. complex sentence (using embedded clause/use of hyphen).

As in the case study above, pupils use A4 paper portrait style, then write the name of a city, fold over the paper and pass it to the person next to them. This is repeated five more times, with the teacher instructing what type of sentence or if a simile or personification should be used. When complete, descriptions can be read aloud. It is advisable to tell pupils they can make one change at least to help the description make sense.

Using a prose extract as a stimulus for creative writing, as well as analysis of grammatical and vocabulary choices, was made more accessible to the pupils because it was a shorter piece of text, yet it still offered challenge; deeper writing was enabled as a result. The teacher commented on the shorter nature of the text offering more scope for in-depth analysis and discussion. Using Dickens's *Bleak House* as part of a range of stimuli, including images and the 'consequences' game format, made the final deeper writing task more manageable for all pupils.

Shakespeare

Finally, this chapter will suggest some possible approaches to Shakespeare that can present a way to stimulate deeper writing. Drama is not a legal requirement of the National Curriculum and the teaching of Shakespeare is not compulsory until KS4. However, teachers should be encouraged to consider the inclusion of extracts from Shakespeare at KS2.

FOCUS ON RESEARCH

THE CASE FOR TEACHING SHAKESPEARE IN PRIMARY SCHOOLS

An introduction to Shakespeare in the primary sector has much to offer. As Seymour (2016) has asserted:

> *Pupils who struggle with literacy are suddenly as capable of succeeding as anyone else, and pupils with less confidence in English quickly discover that no-one else knows all of the words either. The same is also true of younger pupils – so much language is new to them anyway, as they encounter new words every day. In my experience, the younger the learner, the more fearless they tend to be when working with Shakespeare.*

Similarly, Michael Boyd, Artistic Director of the RSC, quoted by Curtis said:

> *Really, the right time to learn Shakespeare is when children are fearless, when they are used to trying out new language. That is very young children's daily existence, new words aren't a problem. You need to get them before they lose the habit of singing songs and have had the fairy dust shaken out of them.*
>
> (Curtis, 2008)

Purewal (2017) argues that an active experience is essential rather than the 'behind the desk, read around the class then put the film on' approach. Having fun acting and exploring words such as Shakespeare's various and colourful insults and idioms, for example, offer new and exciting ways into the language. Purewal (2017) also reminds us of the importance of teacher confidence; teachers having fun always impacts on the learning experiences for children.

When taught effectively, Shakespeare is of incontestable benefit to students: his works offer young people the chance to gain essential critical thinking skills, to develop their communication skills, and to embrace their creativity.

(p. 32)

Research, then, indicates the advantages of introducing Shakespeare at an early age. Sharing a love of new words is not restricted to those used in the twenty-first century. Children are hearing new words all the time; Shakespeare's insults, for example, are a fun way to learn about a language that was spoken by ordinary people over 400 years ago.

The following case studies offer some suggested approaches for the primary classroom, which has the additional benefit of guiding and supporting writing at greater depth. It has been argued than at the heart of good Shakespeare teaching is a confident teacher, yet confident does not mean giving pupils all the answers and reading the text yourself. It needs to be acknowledged that Shakespeare is of his time and sharing the learning is so valuable to pupils; the journey of discovery can then be one that is shared and not instructed.

CASE STUDY

CLASSIC TEXTS: *ROMEO AND JULIET* BY SHAKESPEARE

Sophie, a Year 5 teacher, had previously read Andrew Matthews's version of *Romeo and Juliet* to her class. They had then summarised the story using a six-part storyboard. Sophie reviewed this and made her own storyboard based on Shakespeare's *Romeo and Juliet* using the common six themes her class had chosen. These were displayed on the class storyboard:

1. Romeo and Juliet fall in love at a party. But they come from families that hate each other. They are sure they will not be allowed to marry.

2. Despite this, helped by Friar Laurence, they marry in secret instead. Shhh!

3. Unfortunately, that night Romeo bumps into Tybalt (Juliet's cousin). He fights with Romeo for going to the party. Romeo kills Tybalt in a duel and in the morning he is forced to leave Juliet. If he ever returns to the city, he will be put to death.

(Continued)

(Continued)

4. Juliet's parents told her she must marry someone else. Her parents don't know she is already married. She refuses in the beginning, but later agrees because she plans to fake her death and escape to be with Romeo forever, again with the help of Friar Laurence.

5. Friar Laurence designs a plan. He gives Juliet a sleeping potion. She appears to be dead and is laid in a tomb. However, Romeo does not know about the plan, visits her grave, thinks she is dead and kills himself.

6. When Juliet finally wakes up, she discovers that Romeo is dead and then kills herself too.

Sophie then asked her class who the main characters were and scribed these on the whiteboard. The class decided on eight main characters:

- Romeo
- Juliet
- Friar Laurence
- Montague Dad
- Montague Mum
- Capulet Dad
- Capulet Mum
- Tybalt

Sophie then showed the class the trailer for the 1996 Baz Luhrmann movie of *Romeo and Juliet* with Leonardo DiCaprio and Claire Danes. In it, the Montagues and Capulets are gangsters with guns in the city of Verona Beach. Despite the modern-day setting, the film retains its original dialogue. Sophie then explained that the children were to plan their own version of the play. She gave them examples of a medieval version with knights, castles and princesses, or a futuristic version with aliens, robots and space travel, or an under-sea version with pirates, mermaids and sea creatures. The class then discussed their own areas of interest, which included Fortnite, Minecraft, football, animals, manga and gymnastics. The children made notes on possible characters on whiteboards and shared these with each other.

They were then given six-part storyboards to plan their own versions using the structure of the play that was displayed in the classroom.

Once the storyboards were completed, the children added dialogue to each of the six parts. In the next lesson, they wrote the first three parts, adding descriptive detail. In the lesson after, they completed the next three parts, again adding descriptive detail.

The teacher in the case study above did not make explicit links to greater depth writing. However, when adding descriptive detail, she did encourage those children working at or towards greater depth to independently add whatever detail they would like. Greater depth children will use opportunities like this with the appropriate encouragement to show their own flair for writing.

The teacher gave examples of what genre the story might take, but gave free rein in terms of content, as long as the narrative fitted within the structure of the original play.

The play was then used for further writing opportunities, as in the activity below.

ACTIVITY 4

Read an appropriate version of *Romeo and Juliet* for your own year group, such as the 'Usborne Young Reader' version by Anna Claybourne (2006) or the comic-strip style version by Marcia Williams (2015). Once the play is familiar to your class, then writing opportunities can be explored to develop understanding of it.

- How could the children describe the fight scene between Romeo and Tybalt? How can the 'Instant Reaction' section within Part 4 of Alison Wilcox's 'Descriptosaurus' help the children to describe this scene? What further detail could be added? How can dialogue within an action scene enhance excitement and drama?
- How could the scene be described when Romeo meets Juliet? What physical descriptions could be made? How would you describe their eyes and mouths? Do these change when they first see each other? How can any of the five senses be incorporated into this writing? What adjectives could describe their feeling?

While *Romeo and Juliet* is often seen as a more accessible text for younger students, it could be argued that we underestimate what young people are both interested in and capable of considering. If we challenge ourselves to go beyond a 'romance and gang culture' play and consider leadership, power and tyranny, we can offer pupils a more ambitious diet of Shakespeare, yet still suggest subjects equally relevant to their growing understanding of the world.

CASE STUDY

TEACHING *RICHARD III* TO A YEAR 6 CLASS

Alan, a Year 6 teacher, wanted to look at aspects of leadership, tyranny and abuse of power with his class. He decided that using an extract from *Richard III* would be an ideal place to start. He introduced the topic in role as the jailer from 'the tower'. He and another colleague had made a short video in the grounds of the school following the jailer's walk

(Continued)

(Continued)

from his place of work (pretending that this was, in fact, the Tower of London). Prior to this activity, posters were placed around the area of the classroom with symbols of a wild boar and quotations from the play (some of which are listed below):

with a heavy heart,

Thinking on them, go I unto the Tower.

The bastards in the tower

Death, desolation, ruin and decay:

Bloody king

That foul defacer of God's handiwork,

That excellent grand tyrant of the earth,

But thou didst kill my children.

What news, what news, in this our tottering state?

There is no creature loves me;

And if I die, no soul shall pity me:

A horse! a horse! my kingdom for a horse!

poor England weeps in streams of blood!

Woe, woe for England!

bloody Richard! miserable England!

my accursed womb, the bed of death!

Again in role, another teacher at the school recorded a short answerphone message from Richard's mother where she disowned him, referring to her son by using some of the imagery in the play of vermin and poison (pupils were totally engrossed in the idea that William or Harry could potentially be involved in this scenario as the Tower of London still exists). Extracts of the 1995 film with Ian McKellen were shown, Richard's opening speech was read and a summary of the play was offered to set the scene for the play. Extracts from Act 1, Scene 2 were read and acted by pupils. Most pupils had the chance to read one or two of the exchanges between Richard and Anne in this scene. *No Fear Shakespeare: Richard III* was offered to the pupils, as well as the original text by Shakespeare side by side.

Much discussion took place in the course of this work about the actions of Richard, the tyrant who systematically kills his brother, friends and nephews, and, through negligence, the play suggests, his wife. He even wants to marry his own niece at one point in the play to secure his kingship.

ACTIVITY 5

With the teacher in role as the jailer from the tower, ask the following questions:

- What is 'the tower'?
- Where is it and who is being held prisoner there?
- What happens to people when they go there?
- Why is England 'miserable'? Who is Richard III?

DEEPER WRITING TASKS

Use the information gathered about Richard, which they have been keeping in notebook form, to write a short newspaper article about what was happening in England with the monarch Richard III.

Diary entries could be written after reading Act 1, scene ii with Richard and Anne; this scene was shortened, but the emphasis should be on the verbal sparring between the two characters and how Richard manages to persuade the wife of the man he murdered to marry him. The focus here is on getting the pupils to try to imagine what was going through Richard's mind and his obsession with being King of England, to the extent he would literally kill members of his own family to achieve the title.

Finally, pupils could write a short piece about the character of Richard exploring the sort of leader he had become, perhaps using some of the quotations above to support their views.

Conclusion

Developing children's ability to write in greater depth, using more ambitious vocabulary and sentence constructions, is not only a government requirement but every child's right. As stated in other chapters, the need to encourage all writers to find their own unique and individual voice of self-expression is at the heart of all outstanding English teaching. Children are uniquely placed to develop their own ideas from a range of stimulus for writing, which could also take the form of classic texts considered adult and complex. However, with thought and planning, these texts can be made accessible to pupils of all abilities and cultural backgrounds; the fact that these texts are considered 'hard' only invites challenge and creativity.

It is our duty as teachers to offer all pupils a range of experiences in the classroom; no guidance from the government states that this must be easy either for the pupils or the teachers. However, it is hoped that through the range of real activities and resources shared in this chapter, teachers will be encouraged to move out of their comfort zone and try new and more challenging poetry, prose and drama. It is hoped that teachers will ensure that the writers of the future, who may one day be considered writers of classic texts themselves, are at the very least exposed to more challenging literature and, on the way, discover the impact on meaning and content of using more complex vocabulary and grammatical constructions in their own deeper writing.

References

Carter, D. (1998) *Teaching Poetry in the Primary School: Perspectives for a New Generation*. London: David Fulton Publishers.

Carter, D. (2011) *Teaching Fiction in the Primary School: Classroom Approaches to Narratives*. London: David Fulton Publishers.

Claybourne, A. (2006) *Romeo and Juliet*. London: Usborne Publishing.

Cremin, T., Mottram, M., Collins, F., Powell, S. and Safford, K. (2009) Teachers as readers: building communities of readers. *Literacy*, 43(1): 11–19.

Curtis, P. (2008) Teach children Shakespeare at four says RSC. Available online at: www.theguardian.com/stage/2008/mar/03/rsc.schools

Department for Education (DfE) (2013) English Programmes of Study. Available online at: https://assets.publishing.service.gov.uk/government/uploads/system/uploads/attachment_data/file/425601/PRIMARY_national_curriculum.pdf

Fenn, R. and McGlynn A. (2018) *Teaching Grammar through Literature*. London and New York: Routledge.

Goswami, P. (1990) A special link between rhyming skills and the use of orthographic analogies by beginning readers. *Journal of Child Psychology and Psychiatry*. 30: 301–11.

Hansen, A. (ed.). (2016) *Transforming Primary QTS Children's Literature in Primary Schools* (2nd edn). London: Learning Matters/Sage.

Ofsted (2012) *Moving English Forward: Action to Raise Standards in English*. Ofsted: Crown copyright.

Purewal, S. (2017) Shakespeare in the classroom: to be or not to be? *Warwick Journal of Education*. 26 WJETT, vol 1.

Seymour, R. (2016) Why not to fear teaching Shakespeare to young learners? Available online at: www.britishcouncil.org/voices-magazine/why-not-fear-teaching-shakespeare-young-learners

Williams, M. (2015) *Romeo and Juliet* (Illustrated Classics). London: Walker Books.

13
REPORTING IN SCIENCE AT A DEEPER LEVEL

Catherine Reading

Introduction

Learning in science should be so much more exciting than memorising sets of facts. Fostering a sense of wonder, we can encourage children's innate curiosity to make sense of the world around us.

This chapter will explore reporting in science and how it can help support, enhance and enliven children's understanding of scientific knowledge and concepts. Writing can support the construction of scientific understanding by allowing students to articulate their thinking and communicate ideas within a meaningful context. Encouraging children to make personal connections to scientific phenomena through questions, predictions, conclusions and reflections, allows them to process their ideas, challenge misconceptions and develop their conceptual framework.

This chapter will provide you with a range of strategies to encourage effective science writing and reporting in the primary setting. Case studies will exemplify examples of deeper writing opportunities across a range of contexts.

The purpose and aims of writing in science

The National Curriculum for Science programmes of study (DfE, 2013) defines a high-quality science education as pupils building up a body of knowledge and concepts, recognising the power of rational explanation and developing a sense of excitement and curiosity about natural phenomena. Science can be used to explain what is occurring, predict how things will behave and analyse causes.

Making sense of the world involves using and developing language to communicate meaning. Writing in science, to many, is perceived to be a functional tool whereby children can consider predictions, capture observations and record data. However, the process of writing can promote the synthesis of ideas, and it can improve the clarity of thinking and aid communication with different audiences.

Traditionally, schools have considered science and literacy as different areas of the primary curriculum. It may be challenging for some to think differently about the nature of science learning alongside language acquisition and to develop new classroom practices that take advantage of the intersections. However, one of the key findings by Ofsted in 2013 (*Maintaining Curiosity: A Survey into Science Education in Schools*) was that teachers who coupled good literacy teaching with interesting and imaginative science contexts helped pupils make good progress in both subjects. Ofsted suggested that imaginative teaching allowed pupils to use their science work as content for their reading and writing, in effect doubling the time available to teach both subjects.

The Education Endowment Foundation, *Review of SES and Science Learning in Formal Educational Settings* (2017) reported an attainment gap in science at each key stage; the gap is apparent at the end of KS1 and gets wider throughout primary and secondary education. The strongest factor affecting pupils' science scores is literacy levels. Interventions, to support the development of literacy within the science context, were found to have an impact in improving attainment for low SES pupils.

Encouraging children to work scientifically

In addition to building a body of science knowledge and conceptual understanding, working scientifically is an important aspect of learning in science. Children are encouraged to develop an understanding of the nature and processes of science, to share ideas and ask questions, plan investigations, record observations, draw conclusions and evaluate practical work. Enquiry approaches can provide a multitude of opportunities to use language in authentic and meaningful ways. As children carry out scientific enquiry, they should develop a host of skills and competencies, knowledge and understanding, bringing enormous benefits. The Association of Science Education's *Guidance on Scientific Enquiry* document (2018, p. 2) states that the approach can increase children's capacity to:

- Problem-solve and answer questions – Rich opportunities are provided where children explore their ideas, develop and deepen conceptual understanding.
- Work with independence – Thinking and reasoning is nurtured alongside a host of qualities, including resilience, determination and confidence.
- 'Be a scientist' – A necessary toolkit of practical skills is developed and added to over time.
- Communicate effectively – technical and scientific vocabulary is learned, practised and used, as children communicate in a variety of ways, often with different audiences in mind.

Reporting in science

Science writing can record emerging ideas or a final product for sharing information. This permanent record can be revisited in light of new ideas. Scaffolding as a teaching strategy originates from Vygotsky's sociocultural theory and the concept of the 'zone of proximal development' (ZPD) (Vygotsky, 1978). Activities in scaffolding are just beyond the level of what the learner can do alone; as the learner's abilities increase, the scaffolding is gradually withdrawn. In the classroom setting, scaffolds may include models, cues, prompts, hints, partial solutions and think-aloud modelling (Hartman, 2002). This can enable engagement for many individuals and is essential in the development of science ideas.

As Bushnell et al. (2018) explore, scaffolding occurs in most writing lessons in a variety of ways. Supporting writing with vocabulary development, for example, can use images and multiple exposures to the words in context. It is possible to introduce specific structures and frameworks to encourage the children to imitate.

Sequencing

Supporting the development of skills such as sequencing can enable children to order events, and to prioritise and challenge ideas. Sequencing is the ability to logically order events, images and thoughts; it is a fundamental skill that allows children to recognise patterns and make the world more understandable. Sequencing events helps children to order their ideas, and asking children to sequence events challenges them to decide what are the important events or what their ideas are. There are many approaches to sequencing in science that can be used from using pictures/photographs to creating a set of instructions:

Figure 13.1   Sequencing photos of 'Making a jam sandwich'

In Early Years: sequencing photos: 'Making a jam sandwich'.

Figure 13.2   Sequencing cards using Widgit (2010) 'Cooking scrambled eggs' at https://widgitonline.com

In KS1: sequencing cards using Widgit (2010): 'Cooking scrambled eggs'.
In KS2: Observations over time: 'My bean diary' (DfE, 2018).
The DfE (2018) teacher assessment exemplification for science materials includes an example entitled 'My bean diary'. A pupil observed and described the main changes as the beans grow into mature plants over an extended period of time, using appropriate language from the National Curriculum.
In KS2: Creating a scientific method: 'Which liquid causes the most friction (drag)?' (DfE 2018).

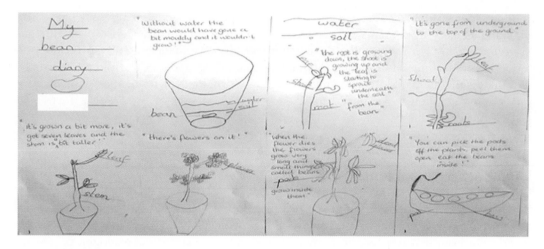

Figure 13.3   Observations over time: 'My bean diary'

Source: DfE (2018)

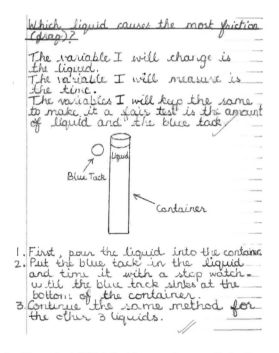

Figure 13.4   Creating a scientific method: 'Which liquid causes the most friction?'

Source: DfE (2018)

In the DfE teacher assessment exemplification (2018), an example is given of the set of instructions created by the pupil in their friction investigation. The sequencing of events gives a structure for the scientific method. The method should allow another person to be able to follow the scientific method to reproduce your investigation, rather like a recipe in cooking.

In all four examples, images are used to support the sequencing of events. The Thinking Frames Approach (AstraZeneca Science Teaching Trust website) encourages *visualisation* as a key skill in the teaching of primary science. The approach is a sequence of teaching and learning interactions that encourage and scaffold the sequence of thinking and literacy skills that children need to form their own scientific explanations. Challenging children to sequence in science is a good way of providing a focus and model for investigations.

Language development

Science writing is a mode of language use that provides students with many opportunities to express and communicate their thinking. Science writing requires a skill-set that is different from that required to communicate orally. It can be a metacognitive activity in that children must carefully choose their words, reflecting and modifying as they write. This process can contribute to language development, as they are asked to continuously refine their thinking. While children are developing these skills, perfect handwriting, spelling and punctuation may be viewed as separate success criteria from the scientific understanding.

There are a number of scaffolds and strategies that can help children to produce deeper science writing and effectively communicate their thinking:

- Interesting experiences, demonstrations and science experiments.
- The children are given the opportunity to discuss in pairs/groups and explore their thinking.
- Writing tasks that are directly related to the experiences.
- Effective modelling by the teacher.
- A classroom rich with language prompts.
- Use of everyday language in tasks for the expression of their ideas.
- Images, photos and pictures are used to support the writing.
- Feedback on the writing that develops.

Effective science writing takes practice and deeper writing requires opportunities to be given. Over time, children can develop confidence and fluidity in their writing. As science writing becomes a regular opportunity, students grow less hesitant to write – teachers can encourage this by responding to the science ideas in students' writing rather than focusing on spelling and grammatical errors.

Some everyday words have a specific meaning when used in a scientific context, which can cause confusion – for example, 'material'. Children will first relate a word to their everyday experience and the word 'material' can easily be associated with fabrics in the home or an item of clothing. It is important that children are given first-hand experience of scientific words and the new phenomenon with which they are associated; words like 'melting' and 'dissolving' are often conflated. The teacher should model correct scientific vocabulary in a range of appropriate contexts and support with images.

On research: scientific vocabulary

The introduction of scientific vocabulary requires significant contemplation. Beck et al. (2002) recommend that scientific words are first explained in everyday language in order to support the development of conceptual understanding. Barton et al. (2001) also recommend focusing vocabulary instruction on words that are critical to new content. They argue that students need to be able to construct meaning – to wrestle with their understanding of a word's meaning in terms of their prior knowledge and in terms of how the word 'fits' into, or relates to, other academic content they are learning.

Vocabulary can be introduced by differentiating between procedural and conceptual vocabulary. Procedural and conceptual vocabulary are described by the Exploratorium (2014). Procedural vocabulary is defined as vocabulary that students will need to use during an investigation and it is introduced during a classroom activity to provide students with the necessary terms to engage. Conceptual vocabulary is introduced after the children have engaged in an activity. These words can often be abstract and difficult for children to understand. Once children have an idea about the context, the introduction of this vocabulary can help them make connections between everyday language and the language of science. Strategically incorporating procedural and conceptual vocabulary at the appropriate moment in an investigation allows children to make language associations with concrete experiences.

Making science vocabulary visible

The use of vocabulary in the Working Scientifically strand is highlighted in the National Curriculum for Science (2013), from 'beginning to use some science words' in Year 1 to 'confidently using a range of scientific vocabulary and language' in Year 6. The acquisition of the language within the science context takes time to develop and must be supported by multiple opportunities to engage with scientific enquiry.

One of the factors that can promote the development of science vocabulary and language is a classroom rich with language prompts. There are many ways to increase the utilisation of science language in your classroom setting – from resources to colourful displays. The table below illustrates some of these.

Table 13.1   Using language prompts in the classroom: making science vocabulary visible

Strategy	Explanation	Ideas
Word banks	Create a bank of scientific vocabulary for each science topic.	Velcro wall display Laminated table cards Topic boxes Word wall Word bank sheets Mobiles Science dictionaries

(Continued)

Table 13.1   (Continued)

Strategy	Explanation	Ideas
Word games	Design a range of 'games' to practise vocabulary use.	Guess my word Pictionary Definition match Spelling bee Longest list of topic words Crosswords Word searches
Display	Arrange opportunities for children to display their own work and use of vocabulary.	Scientist(s) of the week Science magazine Use Art and Design/ Technology opportunities to create science-themed displays.
Concept map	Opportunities for children to produce a concept map in order to elicit language and assess their understanding.	Model with a familiar word. Scaffold using everyday terms until children become confident. Allow children to revisit the concept map at the end of the topic. Use the concept map to check for misconceptions.

ACTIVITY 1

- How visible is science vocabulary and language in your classroom?
- What resources/activities could you draw upon to support your next science topic?

Making the science language of reporting explicit

The language in science reporting records the different stages of the enquiry, from prediction and planning through to the conclusion. Children can find it difficult to generate openers and connectives in science writing. The correct use of tenses is significant when a child is reporting in science and this should be considered in generating suitable openers. The teacher can create a bank of resources and display openers and connectives around the room. For a prediction, this should be written in the present tense. For planning, the tense changes as children think ahead to what they will do, and for describing, children must recall what they have done.

ACTIVITY 2

Consider each phase of an investigation and complete the table below with appropriate openers and connectives to support report writing.

Phases of an investigation	Openers	Connectives
Prediction		
Planning		
Describing		

Construction of scientific understanding (working scientifically)

Writing that takes place in the context of a hands-on experience provides children with the opportunity to articulate their thinking while constructing new scientific understanding. Interesting phenomena draw out students' curiosity and are a catalyst for conversation. Many concepts in primary science can be explored through enquiry-based experiences and a range of activities. Through working scientifically, it is hoped that children will develop the skills to:

- ask questions;
- make predictions;
- decide how to carry out an enquiry;
- observe, record and present data;
- answer questions using data;
- draw conclusions;
- evaluate their enquiry.

One of the key components of effective problem-solving involves learning how to ask the right kind of questions. Cognitive researchers claim that there are much richer stores of knowledge and reasoning skills than would be predicted in young children. Michaels et al. (2008) suggest that scaffolding can be used to develop these areas in the primary context. The findings of the EEF Review (2017) suggest that language and children's writing play an important role in learning science; it is critical that we develop the opportunities for deeper learning, even from a very young age.

CASE STUDY

FORCES IN YEAR 3

Mark, a Year 3 teacher, had taught a science lesson on forces; the children were engaged, sharing ideas and asking questions. They were making detailed observations and drawing conclusions verbally. As he reviewed the children's written work that afternoon, Mark felt frustrated that most did not capture the experiences earlier that day. He was aware that not all children have writing skills that match their science skills. However, he felt that more could be done to capture the richness of the ideas and model report writing.

Mark decided to trial using a Primary Science Teaching Trust 'floorbook' – a large book for recording children's science learning, individually and collaboratively. Floorbooks can be used as a strategy for developing and assessing children's understanding of science. Floorbooks can include photographs, children's comments, drawings, tables, graphs, annotated diagrams, classification keys and writing.

The following week, Mark introduced the lesson on friction. It was a cold January morning and the frost had made the paths into the school slippery. He started the lesson by asking the children about their experience of walking into school. He asked the children to talk in pairs to share their ideas at the start of the lesson; the conversations elicited knowledge and insights that the children had about friction. While the children were talking, he captured their ideas on notes and stuck them into the floorbook. The children were delighted to see that their ideas had been captured in the book.

Mark asked the children to investigate surfaces for new flooring for the school hall. The children discussed their predictions and how they could investigate this question, recording their thoughts on whiteboards. Mark photographed the whiteboards and collated the images for the floorbook.

To support the children, he collated a vocabulary list on the interactive whiteboard and displayed a series of openers for the enquiry process, including the correct use of tense for each stage of the enquiry. During class discussion, Mark was able to annotate the floorbook creating a reference point for the children and provided opportunities for students to work in groups to communicate their investigations and findings.

The children were asked to produce a recommendation letter addressed to the headteacher, suggesting which material should be used for the new flooring in the school hall. Mark reviewed the children's work at the end of the investigation and found that there was a significant improvement for most children in the quality of their reporting.

Discussion

In this case study, the teacher has utilised a floorbook to audit initial ideas and capture predictions, to record group work and to scaffold the writing during the investigation. The use of photos and the 'live' annotation by teacher resulted in a rich reference point for the children. The clear scaffolding provided has been explicitly linked to the enquiry process, allowing the children the opportunity for discussion and peer review. The recommendation letter encourages the children to draw on their findings in order to support their proposal.

This approach reinforces learning in science while developing literacy and communication skills; it develops children's skills of summarising through a familiar context. The children need to understand the science in their investigation in order to explain their ideas clearly.

Ofsted's report, *Maintaining Curiosity: a Survey into Science Education in Schools* (2013), identifies that many outstanding schools have a programme of monitoring, evaluation and intervention of science that was as robust as it was for the other two core subjects. The use of the floorbook gives the opportunity to evaluate all core subjects in one area. The literacy, numeracy and scientific knowledge are woven together in a meaningful context. This opportunity could save time and gives a holistic overview of the child's progress.

To make a valid assessment of the Working Scientifically strand, a teacher needs to draw upon a range of evidence collected over time. Over the course of an academic year, children will carry out several investigations that involve different types of enquiry skills: observing over time, identifying and classifying, pattern seeking, research, comparative and fair testing. The advantage of the floorbook is that it captures the ideas of all children, even if their literacy skills do not yet match their science skills.

CASE STUDY

WORKING NOTEBOOKS WITH YEAR 2

In September, Yasmin, a Year 2 teacher, began the year with a new approach to her science teaching. Every child was given a science notebook alongside the launch of 'How to be a scientist'. Yasmin wanted to promote a different feel to her science lessons with a significant move away from the 'perfect' record of an investigation after the event. She wanted the children to have more freedom in exploring their thoughts and ideas, and felt that a 'working' science notebook could support this. The 'working' notebook could provide an on-going record of the 'thinking behind the doing' of scientific enquiry (Roberts and Reading, 2015) and would record the personal story of a child's development of scientific observations and reasoning.

The purpose of the notebook is to record a child's observations over time, to capture the refining of ideas and to identify where any new questions arise. The approach appealed to Yasmin, as a notebook can function as:

- a chronological record and can help children to understand the sequencing of events;
- a written record of an investigation: both the doing and the thinking;
- a clear, detailed and structured report;

(Continued)

(Continued)

- a reflection of all of stages of the enquiry process – to document, reflect on, and review work in progress.

Yasmin introduced the topic of plant growth; she had planned a task to observe the growth of seedlings over time. As the children first explored the idea, Yasmin encouraged them to make lists of words, drawings, and record what they knew and what they would like to find out. Children used their notebooks to write their questions and predictions, present a plan, record data and make observations. Yasmin provided scaffolding for the enquiry framework in terms of openers and connectives.

Many children provided detailed and accurate drawings alongside their observations. The notebook provided an observation sequence that was easy to follow and the children were able to revisit their initial ideas and comment or amend. After discussion with each child, Yasmin added annotations or suggestions to the notebook. The children's reflections were recorded alongside the enquiry.

Following the activity, Yasmin asked the children to produce a set of instructions of 'How to plant a bean'. The children drew upon the notebook to produce a more formal writing approach to the whole experience. This piece required the children to reflect on their understanding of the needs of plants to grow and the growth sequence.

Discussion

In this case study, Yasmin used a science notebook as a tool for supporting children's reasoning and deepening their conceptual understanding. When children make a prediction, they are required to use their knowledge and prior experiences. As children plan and decide how to answer the question, they must think about their predictions and how to record that evidence. Writing a reflection pushes students to think about the original question in relationship to new information. Making a claim requires carefully considering data and connecting evidence to the claim. Proposing explanations pushes students to bring their ideas together and to consider their knowledge and understanding (Roberts and Reading, 2015). In the case study, the opportunity for reflective writing promotes the link between observations and developing possible explanations. This generates deep learning of science content that can go beyond the minimum requirement of the National Curriculum.

Using science notebooks effectively requires many different skills; children need to develop literacy skills and adopt certain habits for science notebooks to become an integral learning tool in science. Writing skills can be modelled through literacy tasks, but do need to be reinforced in the context of science. Effective use of notebooks requires that teachers provide regular feedback to students about their notebooks and provide opportunities for authentic use. The notebook provides a valuable resource for children when planning other formal writing opportunities. The opportunity to develop a set of instructions significantly draws upon the claim, evidence, explanation and conclusion of the scientific enquiry. This activity develops the skill of identifying a chronological sequence while refining the elements of effective report writing.

Connections to scientific phenomena

Science writing can support the construction of new scientific understanding: it gives students the opportunity to articulate their thinking as they engage in science. The writing takes place in the context of hands-on activities, meaning that children can draw from direct experiences that are interesting, meaningful and shared. Understanding in primary science is developed through substantive ideas and opportunities for children to work scientifically.

Science writing can be shared with others, become part of the display in the classroom or provide a venue for written conversations between teacher and student. A piece of writing can be a repository for emerging ideas or result in a final product for sharing knowledge. A primary timetable can allow the timing to be flexible, to be able to continue activities at an appropriate moment. It is important that children have a range of experiences and carry out a range of enquiries. It creates a record that can be returned to, responded to, and revised.

FOCUS ON RESEARCH

HOW CAN SCIENCE PROMOTE OPPORTUNITIES FOR DEEPER WRITING?

Extended oral and written interactions require students to think about what they are saying and writing, which involves a deeper processing of language. The expression of ideas makes students' thinking visible, giving the teacher insights into students' understanding of science concepts, what language they have to communicate their thinking and the supports that they might need to further both. A reporting task requires a significant amount of weaving between the two domains in the sense-making process. Engagement in this practice involves both scientific sense-making and language use. This sense-making is a key endeavour for students as it helps them transition from their naive conceptions of the world to more scientifically based conceptions (Quinn et al., 2012).

Planning hands-on activities in primary science requires further consideration beyond the engagement of the class. Roberts and Reading (2015) claim that it is very difficult (for teachers and pupils) to focus on developing an understanding of both substantive ideas and evidence at the same time. Illustrating ideas of science differ in nature depending on whether the focus is the pupils' understanding of the substantive ideas of science or the ideas of evidence. The National Curriculum (2013) states that 'Working scientifically' should be taught with clear links to the substantive content. This statement provides the following challenges to teachers:

- to plan a curriculum that enables a progression in pupils' understanding of the ideas of evidence;
- to 'map' this across the progression planned for the substantive content and the school's teaching sequence;
- to include practical activities within this sequence that have as their focus the illustration or application of the ideas of evidence.

(Roberts and Reading, 2015, p. 38)

CASE STUDY

SEPARATING MIXTURES

The Year 5 class were revisiting 'separating mixtures' and the class teacher, Kirsty, was struggling with how to deliver one advanced separating technique – i.e. chromatography. Kirsty had visited the Royal Society of Chemistry, Learn Chemistry site, and had found some exciting resources that she wanted to put into practice. The Learn Chemistry site had an array of activities to choose from, but she focused on 'Crime Scene Chromatography'.

An area in the library provided the perfect space in which to begin creating the crime scene. A large square area was cordoned off by tape, with 'CRIME SCENE' labels attached. Kirsty prepared police warnings about not tampering with evidence and laid these around the outside. Inside the scene, tulip victims were laid out haphazardly on the floor. She drew a chalk line around each victim and each with a numbered card. For the final part of the set-up, Kirsty prepared a piece of evidence: a written note in black ink to be found by the children.

THE SET-UP

Kirsty started a lesson with the children, as normal, and acted surprised when the class was interrupted with some 'urgent' news. The children were asked to take a 'crime scene investigator oath' to remind them of how they needed to behave out of the classroom. On arrival to the scene, the children made observations and recorded their initial thoughts. The note was spotted and the children decided that this was a significant clue.

In groups, the children worked together to make sense of evidence left by the criminal. Kirsty set up five (one per group) for five different suspects. For each suspect, she planted a range of items to build a profile of each suspect, the items including a black-ink pen used by the criminal. The objects were random to give the children space to generate their own ideas and make their own connections.

Kirsty supported the children in setting up the chromatography technique for the five different pens belonging to different suspects. The five black inks separated into several different colours and the children compared each result with the black ink on the note. The children identified the likely criminal from their results and produced a police report of their investigation and findings.

Discussion

In this case study, the teacher has used an exciting and meaningful context in order to illustrate the use of chromatography. This practical activity is focused on the illustration of the substantive idea of mixtures and a separation technique. The working scientifically component has low demand and the method can be followed as a procedural technique.

The teacher provided a stimulating, real-life scenario to frame a report-writing task. The children were encouraged to develop their writing by producing a police report, drawing upon the results of their chromatography. The scenario provides a 'hook' to promote engagement to produce this non-fiction report. This task draws upon many skills – sequencing, planning, presenting evidence – and crucially requires the child to make an evaluative judgement to identify the criminal. The promotion of deeper thinking within a science context supports the quality of writing output.

There are many other ways the task could be developed to stimulate further writing opportunities, for instance:

- Children could create wanted posters, film television appeals, write news reports.
- If the suspect was caught, they could script and role-play the interview.
- If charged, the suspects would be taken to court. Children could script and role-play the court scene, including an expert witness, a defence and a prosecution statement. A judge and jury may also be required – after all, the destruction of innocent tulips cannot be taken lightly!

Conclusion

Science can offer rich opportunities for developing writing at a deeper level by organising the approach to teach content and develop language concurrently. This process provides an authentic and meaningful context for children to develop the more academic vocabulary of science (Gibbons, 2002).

It is critical that children have an opportunity to have a hands-on, meaningful and engaging approach to science learning. By adopting a range of strategies, teachers can provide a framework to meet the science content and the writing needs (Jimenez-Silva and Gomez, 2014). There are a number of components required to ensure that these needs are met:

- Children must have an opportunity to work co-operatively to develop social and science language skills.
- Tasks are scaffolded to promote the development of enquiry.
- Effective modelling by the teacher and use of everyday language in tasks for the expression of their ideas.
- Images, photos and pictures are used to support the writing.
- Feedback on the writing that develops.

Recommended websites

Association Science Education – www.ase.org.uk

Chemistry for Primary Schools, Warwick University – https://warwick.ac.uk/fac/sci/chemistry/about/schools/primary/candychromatography/

Learn Chemistry – Royal Society of Chemistry – www.rsc.org/learn-chemistry

Primary Science Teaching Trust – Floorbooks – https://pstt.org.uk/resources/curriculum-materials/scientific-enquiry-skills

STEM Teaching – www.stem.org.uk

Thinking Frames – AstraZeneca Science Teaching Trust – https://pstt.org.uk/resources/cpd-units/the-thinking-frames-approach

Widgit 2010 – https://widgitonline.com

References

Association of Science Education (ASE) (2018) *Scientific Enquiry in the UK*. Primary Committee. Available online at: www.ase.org.uk/system/files/Scientific%20Enquiry%20in%20the%20UK%20V2.pdf

Beck, I. L., McKeown, M.G. and Kucan, L. (2002) *Bringing Words to Life: Robust Vocabulary Instruction*. New York: Guilford Press.

Barton, M.L., Heidema, C. and Jordan D. (2001) *Teaching Reading in Maths and Science*. Available online at: https://pdo.ascd.org/lmscourses/PD11OC133/media/Science_Literacy_M3_Reading_Teaching_Reading.pdhartman 2002

Bushnell, A., Smith, R. and Waugh, D. (2018) *Modelling Exciting Writing: A Guide for Primary Teaching*. London: Sage.

Department for Education (DfE) (2013) *The National Curriculum in England: Key Stages 1 and 2 Framework Document*. Available online at: www.gov.uk/government/publications/national-curriculum-in-england-primary-curriculum

Department for Education (DfE) (2018) *Teacher Exemplification Science: Key Stages 1 and 2 Framework Document*. Available online at: www.gov.uk/government/publications/teacher-assessment-exemplification-ks2-science

Education Endowment Foundation (EEF) (2017) *Review of SES and Science Learning in Formal Educational Settings* (London: Education Endowment Foundation): Available online at: https://educationendowmentfoundation.org.uk/public/files/Review_of_SES_and_Science_Learning_in_Formal_Educational_Settings.pdf

Exploratorium, Institute for Inquiry (2014) *Developing Language in the Context of Science: A View from the Institute of Inquiry*. Available online at: www.exploratorium.edu/education/ifi/inquiry-and-eld/educators-guide/science-writing

Gibbons, P. (2002) *Scaffolding Language, Scaffolding Learning: Teaching Second Language Learners in the Mainstream Classroom*. London: Heinemann.

Hartman, H.J. (2002) Scaffolding and cooperative learning, in Hartman, H. (ed.), *Human Learning and Instruction* (pp. 23–69). New York: City College of City University of New York.

Jimenez-Silva, M. and Gomez, C. (2010) Developing language skills in science classrooms. *Science Activities: Classroom Projects and Curriculum Ideas*, 48(1), 23-28.

Michaels, S., Shouse, A.W. and Schweingruber, H.A. (2008) *Ready, Set Science!: Putting Research to Work in K-8 Science Classrooms*. Board on Science Education. Center for Education. Division of Behavioural and Social Sciences and Education. Washington, DC: The National Academies Press.

Ofsted (2013) *Maintaining curiosity: science education in schools*. Manchester: Crown copyright.

Quinn, H., Lee, O. and Valdés, G. (2012) *Language Demands and Opportunities in Relation to Next Generation Science Standards for English Language Learners: What Teachers Need to Know*. Stanford, CA: Stanford University, Understanding Language Initiative at Stanford University.

Roberts, R. and Reading, C. (2015) The practical work challenge: incorporating the explicit teaching of evidence in subject content. *School Science Review*, 96(357): 31–9.

Vygotsky, L.S. (1978) *Mind in Society: The Development of Higher Psychological Processes*. Cambridge, MA: Harvard University Press.

14

DEEPER WRITING: A CREATIVE MASTERY APPROACH

Lisa Baldwin

KEY QUESTIONS

- What do we mean by mastery in the context of the English curriculum?
- What does mastery of writing look like?
- What are the links between mastery and creativity?
- How can we teach writing to support mastery and creativity?

Introduction

This chapter explores connections between mastery, creativity and writing. It explores definitions of mathematics mastery to provide a more distinct understanding of mastery in the context of English. The chapter illustrates teaching approaches that foster pupil creativity and support children's mastery of writing, exemplifying a mastery approach through case studies.

What does mastery mean for the English curriculum?

The notion of mastery is a powerful one: the idea that, if taught appropriately, anyone can master important ideas. This is an inspiring sentiment and one echoed in debate about whether creativity is an innate talent or a skill that can be developed. The National Advisory Committee on Creative and Cultural Education (NACCCE, 1999) proposed the democratisation of creative skills, stating: 'all people are capable of creative achievement in some area of activity, provided the conditions are right and they have acquired the relevant knowledge and skills' (NACCCE, 1999, p. 29). Similarly, schools that invest in a mastery approach embody the philosophical belief that mastery is possible for *all* their pupils and have the ambition for the majority of children to achieve at least age-related expectations and most to achieve greater depth.

While all schools might strive to achieve mastery, there is a lack of guidance as to what mastery teaching entails or what English mastery is (NACE, 2017). Consequently, mastery means different things to different schools, particularly in the realm of English learning (Didau, 2017; Jolliffe and Waugh, 2017). In contrast, the definition of mathematics mastery is more distinct, with clear principles provided by The National Centre for Excellence in the Teaching of Mathematics (NCETM, 2014). Working from mathematics principles it is possible to gain greater clarity of both a definition of mastery and mastery teaching in the context of primary English.

A definition of mastery

Mathematical language to define mastery includes the terms 'procedure', 'instant recall', 'fluency', 'knowledge of rules and algorithms', 'application' and 'problem solving' (DFE, 2013). While this language describes progressive mathematical skills, the terms also have connections to competencies synonymous with English learning. Children need to develop their *recall* of phoneme–grapheme correspondence, recognition of common exception words by sight, and an understanding of the *procedural* process of segmenting, blending and counting phonemes to support both reading and spelling.

In mathematics, the term 'fluency' is characterised by flexibility: the children's ability to adapt skills to a variety of contexts through accurate and efficient means. In relation to writing, the term 'fluency' might relate to concepts of automaticity in spelling and handwriting, as well as developing familiarity with narrative structure and story language in the context of written composition. *Knowledge of rules* links to children's understanding of how language works, the grammar of both spoken and written language, and conventions of punctuation and spelling. *Application* of knowledge can be interpreted as the process of reading accurately with meaning, and as the ability to meet the demands of written composition.

Due to the interdependence of language development, mastery of writing cannot be achieved in isolation from mastery of spoken language and reading. Successful writing requires pupils to combine their knowledge and understanding of interconnected language skills. Drawing on the NCETM definition for mathematics (2014), English mastery might therefore be summarised as a child's ability to comprehend, respond to and compose language in both spoken and written forms, and to secure the skills necessary to do so in line with age-related expectations.

FOCUS ON RESEARCH

ASSESSMENT WITHOUT LEVELS

There is limited research into mastery of English learning. In 2015, some guidance on mastery was provided in a report by a government body, The Commission on Assessment without Levels. The report contains general definitions in relation to three areas of mastery learning: children's performance, teaching approaches and philosophical belief. The report states the following:

- Mastery learning is 'deep' and 'secure'.
- Mastery teaching is 'a specific approach in which learning is broken down into discrete units and presented in logical order'.
- Mastery is underpinned by the belief 'that all pupils will achieve this . . . if they are appropriately supported. Some may take longer and need more help, but all will get there in the end'.

(The Commission on Assessment without Levels, 2015, p. 17)

The meaning of mastery in relation to primary English is beginning to emerge. Jolliffe and Waugh (2017) made the first significant contribution in their book *Mastering Primary English*. The book explores current practice in schools and changes in approach. Their work explains English mastery as:

Deeper understanding demonstrated through confident, flexible, independent reading, writing, speaking and listening skills across increasingly challenging contexts.

(Branson and McCaughan, 2016, cited in Jolliffe and Waugh, 2017, p. 21)

Mastery is more than the sum of component parts

Currently, practice in writing lessons seeks to emphasise the use of grammar, language features and punctuation. Curriculum appendices (DFE, 2013) assign explicit detail of components of language to each year group. Schools sometimes use the term 'mastery' when children achieve specific learning objectives based on children's understanding of these component skills. However, measuring mastery as understanding of the component parts of the English appendices means writing development is reduced to the procurement of discrete skills rather than holistic proficiencies (Richmond, 2017). Activities supporting children's *procedural* understanding of language use and skills are certainly of value, but mastery should be underpinned by children's *fluency* in using language skills. *Fluency* is achieved through the application of age-appropriate knowledge and skills in different writing contexts. It is not the skills themselves that are the end game to mastery; it is the child's ability to apply them in a variety of meaningful writing tasks to 'communicate their ideas and emotions to others' (DfE, 2013, p. 3).

Having attempted to define mastery, the next step is to consider what mastery of writing looks like. In the case study below, one child's writing sample offers an example of mastery at Year 6.

CASE STUDY

THE TEMPEST

An inner city London school held a whole-school writing week based on *The Tempest* by Shakespeare. Various activities were planned throughout the school, from Reception to Year 6. The Year 6 teacher read from *The Tempest* and explored the play at key points, discussing different points of view and becoming familiar with the genre of the play script. The final writing task was a culmination of the week's teaching and provided the class with an opportunity to retell the scene when Prospero conjures the storm and Ferdinand's boat sinks. The learning objective was 'to rewrite the storm as a narrative text told from a different point of view'. The success criteria were to vary sentence structure and to include features of language and punctuation from all previous teaching. Below is an example of Year 6 writing:

As the boat glided closer, the storm grew. Tossing and turning, the ashen sea threw their dilapidated boat dangerously off course, lashing out and laughing maliciously. Flapping his elegant emerald green wings, Ariel stood firmly beside me, staring fixedly at the convulsing wooden ship. Smirking, I raised my sweating palms to the sky and instantaneously – like an untamed beast – the malevolent waves brutally chewed at their flailing vessel. Clouds merged into twisting, coal black tornados: encircling the boat barbarically. Footsteps. Frantically, Miranda scampered up to me and shook my arm fiercely. 'Father no! All those people will drown!' She was shaking ferociously, gasping with huge, heaving sobs. I smirked, and with all the force I had, I slammed my smooth, polished staff down onto the sandy banks of the island. 'I have my reasons.'

In this piece of writing, the child has used similes, alliteration, personification, challenging and interesting vocabulary such as 'instantaneously' and 'malevolent'. The child has punctuated

(Continued)

(Continued)

speech correctly, employed fronted adverbials and used exclamatory sentences. The child makes use of dashes to mark boundaries and cohesive devices ensure the text flows. The sentences vary between long complex structures, to the dramatic impact of a single word. Yet, despite this significant list of techniques and skills the key point about the writing is the appropriate use of these features and the effect the child's choices have on the reader. Overall, the composition demonstrates that this child can consider a different point of view from the original story and recraft the scene to alter the reader's understanding of the storm scene. The child makes creative decisions about how to apply their skills in language, drawing on their knowledge of authorial effect and their understanding of effective composition. The child's mastery relates to the art of effective, creative composition.

Supporting mastery learning

To gain knowledge of effective language application in writing, children need to learn from reading. Knowledge of how to apply taught skills comes through the exploration of authorial voice, analysis of texts and understanding how a writer's language choices impact on the writing. Only by developing this area of children's understanding will they progress to successful *application* of their knowledge and skills to communicate effectively to their readers. It is at this point in the child's learning that the link between mastery and creativity is made. The higher the child's level of creativity, demonstrated through successful *application* of knowledge *about* language and skills *in* language, the deeper the child's progress in achieving written mastery.

Deep and rich learning

The above writing sample is a small excerpt from a text that exemplifies writing at greater depth. It therefore represents a level of mastery learning beyond age-related expectations. Mastery learning requires teachers to support writing achievement at different depths. Previous models of planning have accommodated children's wide-ranging needs through differentiated learning. Mastery learning replaces differentiation of task design with rich learning tasks that enable all children to demonstrate age-appropriate levels of writing skill through varied levels of support. It is possible to explore this idea further, drawing on concepts of mastery teaching in mathematics.

In mathematics, 'deep understanding' (Branson and McCaughan, cited in Jolliffe and Waugh, 2017) comprises procedural fluency, conceptual understanding and reasoning skills. In order to unpick what this means for primary English, it is helpful to imagine deep and rich learning as different layers in a bottomless pond. The demonstration of age-related skills, as detailed in the curriculum (DFE, 2013), makes up the first surface layer of *procedural* learning. *Procedural* practice is exemplified by tasks such as highlighting word classes or language features in a given text, practising the use of newly taught punctuation skills in sentence exercises, or transforming sentences from active to passive voice. The next layer in the pond might include short composition exercises provided to consolidate new learning. This layer of learning supports a child's *fluency* of a newly taught skill and also repeated opportunity to make use of previously taught language knowledge and skills. The next layer of learning is the *application* level, when children are given opportunity to try out their new skills and knowledge in a meaningful composition task.

The depth of challenge in the task comes from the level of creative autonomy the child demonstrates when applying their new knowledge to the writing. Creative autonomy depends on children's attitude to writing and their willingness to take risks (creative dispositions are discussed later). Autonomy in *application* of learnt skills and language techniques also depends on the child's knowledge about how to write a meaningful text. Some children will need support to appropriately and accurately *apply* newly taught skills, while children capable of greater levels of autonomy will need further challenge and freedom.

FOCUS ON RESEARCH

RICH ENGLISH TASKS

Piggott (2011) states that mastery of mathematics relies on the development of deep understanding through the provision of rich tasks in a variety of contexts. She describes a rich task as having 'a range of characteristics that together offer different opportunities to meet the different needs of learners at different times' (Piggott, 2011). Her list of key requirements is adapted below to fit an English task context.

Rich English tasks:

- are relevant to children;
- are accessible and extendable;
- provide opportunities for first-hand experience;
- allow learners to make decisions;
- are organised to allow independence;
- involve learners in testing, proving, explaining, reflecting and interpreting;
- can involve learning inside and outside the classroom;
- promote discussion and communication;
- encourage children to work at length and depth;
- encourage originality and invention;
- provide opportunities for observation-led assessment;

(Continued)

(Continued)

- encourage 'What if?' and 'What if not?' questions;
- are enjoyable and contain the opportunity for surprise.

(Adapted from Piggott, 2011)

Many elements in the above list are familiar, key pedagogical approaches that support success in writing composition. Whenever teachers plan for quality writing opportunities they will consider audience and purpose, ways to make writing meaningful and engaging and ensure opportunities for talk (Chamberlain, 2018; Bearne, 2002).

Having explored the concept of deep and rich English learning, it is important to consider what this means in practice. The case study below provides one illustration of a rich writing task.

CASE STUDY

THE FIRST WORLD WAR

The case study school focused on marking the centenary of the First World War. In Year 2, children were asked to research and discover stories from the war that involved their families. Family and friends shared stories of their relatives' lives. Teachers provided opportunities for the children to retell their stories to each other in class. Some relatives visited the class and gave children the opportunity to hear a different family story and ask questions. The children's experiences of talking to their families and sharing their newfound tales permeated the writing. Recounts, diaries and biographic accounts were generated in response to this experience and the children's engagement with the task was evident in the pride displayed sharing their unique story. The school stressed the significance of remembrance, and this was magnified by the fact this included their personal history. Below is one example of Year 2 class writing:

*My great, great Grand father name was ****** ******. He was born in the east Dereham area of the country of Norfolk. His Father was a Policeman when the First World war started. My great great Grand ***** volunteered to join the British Army so that he could go to France when and Belgium to take part in the fighting. When he went to war he lied about his age, he was only 15 years old. The army did not ask many question so it was not a problem. He joined the sufflok Regiment. My great*

great granedad took part in many battles including ypes and the Battle of the somme. He was wounded in one of the battle when a piece of a shell fragment went through his leg. Geart Geart Gradnad ****** survived the war and came home to England and and marred my great grand mother ******. He never talked about the War. He brought back a German Lugel pistol trophy and an American colt pistol. He later became special constable in the Norfolk police force. He died in the 1960's and is buried in ******* church yard in Norfolk.

The children's writing was displayed in the classroom alongside photographs of relatives or mementos. At the end of the topic the school published a book of their writing and gave it to parents and carers as a commemorative keepsake. Every child had a piece of work published.

The case study school planned and delivered learning and teaching with the belief that all pupils were capable of achieving creative and expressive pieces of writing. The subject of the First World War was challenging and remote from the children's own experiences, but was made meaningful through the link to family histories and visiting speakers. The way in which the teacher approached the writing task made the children active constructors of knowledge (Piggott, 2011) and therefore the task became rich in terms of purpose and meaning. Throughout the case study, it is evident that there were many opportunities for speaking and listening to develop children's language skills. Storytelling, retelling and oral composition occurs repeatedly throughout the process, supporting to the final writing task. Through this approach, all children have the opportunity to collaborate and develop language skills through peer working.

Scaffolds and supports

Deep and rich writing tasks consider the degree of scaffolded support that children require to achieve mastery in writing. Supports should be varied to ensure that the teacher's role encourages children towards creative autonomy. The creative apprenticeship model (QCA, 2004) puts the teacher as expert and the child as the novice, yet the process should progress towards the child becoming an expert. This means that support is gradually withdrawn (Jolliffe and Waugh, 2017). The child's progression to expertise occurs through increased ownership over their work. Children should be supported to take increasing creative responsibility for the direction of their writing. But, at the point of independent writing, where can children maintain some creative control over their writing if they need support to achieve mastery?

Imitation as a scaffold for mastery writing

Corbett and Strong's (2011) *Talk for Writing* process encompasses three stages of writing: imitation, innovation and invention. These three stages translate to varying levels of challenge in terms of the creative risks that children are encouraged to take when writing. Imitation is an important first step in achieving mastery. Imitation provides a supported level of creativity that enables a child to master the required writing skills with the support of familiar narrative, vocabulary and patterns of language (Myhill et al., 2016). Support and scaffolds are provided by the original text, yet imitation still requires writerly decisions to be made, which enables the child to develop ownership at a simple level. When imitating writing, the child is developing *fluency* in the use of new skills, repeating and replicating language through the re-creation of writing similar to the way in which the language was first introduced. Through imitation, the *fluency* of the child's writer's voice is practised, honed and developed.

FOCUS ON RESEARCH

IMITATION

Myhill et al. (2016, 2018) focus on the imitation (the re-creation) of story and texts. The work explores how imitation offers children a scaffold to support understanding of grammar, language choice and writing. The literature describes the process of imitation in the following terms:

- 'Imitation is not the same as copying – it involves some kind of re-creation of grammatical patterns or ideas, rather than a direct duplication'.
- When imitating children directly imitate 'the style of the author but' use 'their own ideas to develop independent descriptions. Direct imitation is something which can help children to find their own written voice'.
- The process of imitation is 'a powerful tool to support initial learning about a text'.

(Myhill et al., 2016, pp. 6–7)

Myhill et al. (2016, 2018) emphasise how writers use imitation as the foundation on which to learn how to make decisions about language. This affirms that creative skills are involved in the composition of text through imitation, while accepting that 'it is not always evident that imitation leads to invention' (Myhill, 2018, p. 6). In the most recent work, Myhill draws on classical rhetorical traditions to further affirm the importance of this technique in learning composition.

Critical thinking and creativity

Research into mathematics explores the creative habits of mind that successful learners embody (Cuoco et al., 1996). Cuoco describes creative learners as 'pattern sniffers', 'experimenters', 'describers', 'tinkerers', 'inventors', 'visualisers', 'conjecturers and guessers'. Creative learners are capable of divergent thinking (Razouminkova, 2000, cited in Copping, 2016) and Craft describes this attribute as 'possibility thinking' (Cremin et al., 2006, p. 2; Craft, 2002). Cremin et al. (2015) links this to children's ability to engage critically with texts, to consider and explore different perspectives and possibilities other than those presented by the author. To support children to develop greater levels of creativity in their writing, they need to be encouraged to foster such creative habits in their language learning. Creative thinking occurs when children are encouraged to challenge, question and explore the possibilities presented by a text.

The case study below illustrates how one school supported Year 2 children with 'possibility thinking' (Burnard et al., 2006, p. 2; Craft, 2002) by encouraging them to become 'inventors', 'visualisers', 'conjecturers and guessers' when reading a text.

CASE STUDY

LITTLE RED RIDING HOOD

A Year 2 class was studying fairy tales and the story of *Little Red Riding Hood*. The teacher encouraged them to think critically about the text, exploring alternative points of view. She asked them to challenge the idea that the wolf was a bad character, and the children discussed possibilities why Little Red Riding Hood might not be an innocent victim. They explored scenarios where the wolf felt bad about events and the teacher posed 'What if?' and 'Why is it?' questions. The children debated different viewpoints and she supported them to justify their thoughts and ideas. Through whole-class discussion, vocabulary was developed to include language such as 'guilty', 'regret' and 'conscience'. Next, they completed a short writing task that asked them to mind map responses to the following questions:

- Why did Little Red Riding Hood blame the wolf?
- Why might she have lied about what happened?
- How might the wolf feel?
- What was the result of her lies?

The final writing task asked the pupils to assume the role of Little Red Riding Hood. They had to write a letter in response to the wolf's letter below.

(Continued)

(Continued)

LETTER

Wolfie Cottage
Deep Dark Wood
Storyshire
SL2 WOL

Miss Red Riding Hood
97 Blackwater Road
Bluebell Village
Storyshire
SL2 RRH

Dear Little Red Riding Hood,

I am writing to you to apologise for my behaviour last week. Sneaking into your Grandmother's house and attempting to eat you both was unforgivable. The only explanation I can offer you is that I forgot my morning snack which led to my blood sugar becoming low. In a moment of panic, eating you seemed like my only option. However, I can now see how inappropriate my behaviour was and how scared and upset both of you must have been.

In the future I have every intention of ensuring I always carry multiple snacks with me to avoid this happening ever again. I would like to take this opportunity to ask to meet with you to discuss this incident further and apologise face to face.

Yours sincerely,
Mr Big Bad Wolf.

After the form and structure of a letter was introduced, the children began to compose their replies to the wolf. They had to decide if they would agree to meet the wolf, consider if they could trust him and give reasons for their decision in the written response. This final writing task provided the children with freedom to choose a viewpoint, encouraging them to have ownership over their writing. The teacher enabled achieve-ment of all pupils through the articulation of 'possibility thinking' and supposition about the wolf's character. The teacher asked 'What if?' and 'Why is it?' questions to enable children to investigate new and imagined perspectives. Discussion and debate supported language, vocabulary, phrases and thoughts about the wolf. When completing the writ-ing task, all children could draw on scribed notes from the class discussion and the mind map work. Some children required further support and were provided with a letter struc-ture that included sentence starters.

Critical exploration into texts offers many creative possibilities, which provide the basis for new, unseen events, and dialogues only alluded to by the text. When teachers encour-age children to hone critical skills, the result is fuel for creative, innovative writing. This accords with the deeper levels of Corbett and Strong's (2011) writing stages: invention and imitation. At these stages the writer draws on their understanding of the original text in order to create something new and original. A child can display a deeper level of mas-tery and creativity through the application of language skills in new contexts. Contexts might include the invention of new characters, scenarios and writing events from a differ-ent perspective. It can also entail the re-creation of a known text in a different writing form or genre.

Research into creativity considers the habits of mind listed below to be important tools for mathematics learning. These habits of mind are also exciting avenues to consider when plan-ning creative English tasks. Children should be encouraged to be:

- pattern sniffers
- experimenters
- describers
- tinkerers
- inventors
- visualisers
- conjecturers
- guessers

(Cuoco et al., 1996)

Creativity, risk and freedom

The ability and willingness to take risks is an attribute credited to creative dispositions (Lucas and Spencer, 2017). A mastery approach should foster risk taking in writing because this will encourage the child to take greater ownership over the direction of their writing. To encourage risks, some schools provide opportunities for children to engage in creative writing without fear of judgement. Children are being freed from the constant scrutiny of being held to account for everything they have written. Real authors know that writing begins as a very shoddy set of scribbles, poorly spelt, poorly conceived and containing underdeveloped ideas. Encouraging children to know that a writer's initial ideas are expanded upon, improved, restructured or edited out completely is essential to their understanding of the writing process.

FOCUS ON RESEARCH

TEACHERS AS WRITERS

The 'Teachers as Writers' research was a two-year project involving university researchers, authors and teachers (Cremin et al., 2017). During the study, authors provided mentoring advice to teachers with the aim of developing their writing skills. This process enabled teachers to learn first-hand what good writing entails. Teachers and researchers then drew on their personal learning experience to consider what pedagogical approaches children needed to be successful at writing. Findings from the project have suggested that the following opportunities will support children:

- Increased choice and independence in writing tasks.
- Opportunity to play with writing styles.
- Time and space for creativity through 'free writing'.

(Cremin et al., 2017)

ACTIVITY

The 'Teachers as Writers' (Cremin et. al., 2017) study re-examines the writing process, based on authors' experiences. Watch the short video of the poet Joseph Coelho talking about his writing process: *www.youtube.com/watch?v=86MxYOtthRE*
  Consider the important things to note about this author's needs:

- What conditions does Joseph Coelho need to be able to write and compose?
- How does this insight into the writing process relate to provision in the classroom?
- What steps could you take to create similar opportunities that would support children's creative composition?

The idea that creativity in writing is something that children are able to perform at a certain points in the school day is being reconsidered in some schools, resulting in space and resources to support the notion of children as writers throughout the school day. Children are provided with a writer's notebook for their ideas and encouraged to add words and images, anything that provides creative inspiration for writing. Writing takes place throughout the day, and time is given to discussing what interests and motivates children to want to write. In one case study school, the focus for Year 5 writing has developed from the children's interest in strike action taken by many children as part of global protests over climate change. By harnessing children's desire to communicate something meaningful and of importance to them, pupils are encouraged to develop their writing.

Editing, mastery and perseverance

The editing stage of the writing process supports children to achieve deeper mastery of writing, through the close consideration of transcriptional accuracy and the effectiveness of the composition. To support the editing process, schools currently employ a range of techniques to engage children: 'polishing pens' (coloured pens to annotate and amend writing), writing slips (sections of paper that cover certain paragraphs that require revision), specific lesson time to edit and review work against success criteria, and the development of children's ability to critique their own and their peers' writing. Opportunities to edit take place as part of a single writing lesson or at different points in the final written independent writing task. However, there are two barriers to the editing process that commonly impede the validity of editing time in an English lesson. Revisiting writing is challenging to pupils. Those with higher levels of ownership and engagement over writing will be better motivated, but for many children editing seems a pointless task, attempted with lacklustre spirit. Second, it is difficult to edit your own writing when you are close to the original composition. Ideas need time to settle and editing is often more fruitful with greater perspective.

FOCUS ON RESEARCH

MASTERING WRITING

In *Mastering Primary English*, Jolliffe and Waugh (2017) explore current practice in schools that have adopted a mastery approach to writing. They suggest that the following editing practices support a mastery approach to writing:

> *Extended writing is developed through a number of sessions each week. This is done alongside regular peer critique and feedback.*

> (p. 28)

> *(Continued)*

(Continued)

Jolliffe and Waugh also stress the importance of ensuring that 'sufficient time is given to writing' (2017, p. 29) and this is echoed in the recent Teachers as Writers project (Cremin et al., 2017). The research project stresses the importance of:

- Time to write longer extended pieces of writing.
- Peer review to enable them to assess the quality of writing.

(Cremin et al., 2017)

Some schools are now giving children time and space between the original writing composition and the revisit and review stage of writing. In one case study, school children achieve high levels of success in writing because pupil writing from across the year is revisited in the summer term. At this point in the year, children's understanding has developed to encompass further skills and knowledge in terms of refining the punctuation and grammatical requirements of the National Curriculum. Also, time passed gives children distance to be more critical of their overall writing composition and consider what steps need to be taken to develop and improve ideas. If schools want pupils to achieve mastery in writing, children need both distance and time to create and shape their compositions.

At the editing stage of writing, children's attitudes are as important as their skill and knowledge. Children need to understand that good writing requires effort. To foster an attitude of perseverance in writing requires the child and the teacher to view writing as a process that entails multiple opportunities to improve the quality of the written communication and the development of ideas. Tenacity and persistence is widely thought to be a key trait of creative learners (Lucas and Spencer, 2017) and the revision of writing undoubtedly requires these skills. When a class teacher recently asked her Year 2 class, 'What makes a good writer?' one child replied, 'Courage to keep going and believe in yourself'. Thus, this discussion leads finally to the importance of children understanding that writing is a creative process, rather than an end in itself, and that it is the process that makes a good writer, not innate skill or talent.

Conclusion

This chapter aimed to clarify the term 'mastery' in the context of primary English teaching. Sound pedagogic approaches to writing remain central to good practice. Scaffolds provided by talk, models provided by high-quality texts and purposeful contexts remains vital to children's success in writing. A mastery approach aims to build on this through the provision of deep and rich learning tasks. The richness and depth of writing comes from an emphasis on critical thinking, the creative application of skills, and the development of creative habits in meaningful and challenging writing contexts.

Further reading

The following texts provide guidance on creative English teaching:

Bushnell, A., Smith, R. and Waugh, D. (2018) *Modelling Exciting Writing: A Guide for Primary Schools*. London: Sage.
Chamberlain, L. (2018) *Inspiring Writing in Primary Schools* (2nd edn). London: Sage.
Copping, A. (2016) *Being Creative in Primary English*. London: Sage.
Cremin, T., Dombey, H. and Reedy, D. (2015) *Teaching English Creatively*. Oxford: Routledge.

The following text explores mastery learning and current practice in schools:

Jolliffe, W. and Waugh, D. (2017) *Mastering Primary English*. London: Bloomsbury.
The following texts explore habits of creative learners and pedagogic approaches that support the development of creative dispositions:
Lucas, B. and Spencer, S. (2017) *Teaching Creative Thinking: Developing Learners who Generate Ideas and Can Think critically*. Wales: Crown House Publishing.
Wilson, A. (ed.) (2015) *Creativity in Primary Education* (3rd edn). Exeter: Learning Matters/Sage.

Recommended websites

Mastery and English: National Association for Able Children in Education – www.nace.co.uk/blog/6-reasons-bring-mastery-primary-english
Mastery and mathematics: *National Centre for Excellent Teaching of Mathematics* – www.ncetm.org.uk/resources/47230

References

Bearne, E. (2002) *Making Progress in Writing*. London: RoutledgeFalmer.
The Commission on Assessment Without Levels (2015) *Final Report of the Commission on Assessment Without Levels*. Crown Copyright: Government Publications. Available online at: https://assets.publishing.service.gov.uk/government/uploads/system/uploads/attachment_data/file/483058/Commission_on_Assessment_Without_Levels_-_report.pdf (accessed 11 March 2019).
Chamberlain, L. (2018) *Inspiring Writing in Primary Schools* (2nd edn). London: Sage.
Copping, A. (2016) *Being Creative in Primary English*. London: Sage.
Corbett, P. and Strong J. (2011) *Talk for Writing across the Curriculum with DVD: How to teach non-fiction writing 5-12 years*. Maidenhead: Open University Press.
Craft, A. (2002) *Creativity and Early Years Education*. London: Continuum.
Cremin, T., Burnard, P. and Craft, A. (2006) Pedagogy and possibility thinking in the early years. *International Journal of Thinking Skills and Creativity*, 1(2), 108-119. Available online at: https://ore.exeter.ac.uk/repository/handle/10036/41676 (accessed 25 March 2019).
Cremin, T., Myhill, D., Eyres, I., Nash, T., Open University, Wilson, A., Oliver, L. and University of Exeter in Partnerhsip with Arvon (2017) *Teachers as Writers: A Report for Arts Council England on the Value of Writers' Engagement with Teachers to Improve Outcomes for All Pupils*. Available online at: www.teachersaswriters.org/wp-content/uploads/2017/12/Teachers-as-Writers-Research-Report-2017-FINAL-.pdf (accessed 25 March 2019).

Cremin, T., Dombey, H. and Reedy, D. (2015) *Teaching English Creatively*. Oxford: Routledge.

Cuoco, A., Goldenberg, E.P. and Mark, J. (1996) Habits of mind: an organizing principle for mathematics curricula. *Journal of Mathematical Behaviour*, 15: 375–402.

Department for Education (DFE) (2013) *National Curriculum in England: English Programmes of Study*. Available online at: www.gov.uk/government/publications/national-curriculum-in-england-english-programmes-of-study/national-curriculum-in-england-english-programmes-of-study (accessed 21 March 2019).

Didau, D. (2017) Why 'mastery learning' may prove to be a bad idea. Available online at: https://learningspy.co.uk/learning/why-mastery-learning-may-prove-to-be-a-bad-idea-2/ (accessed 11 March 2019).

Jolliffe, W. and Waugh, D. (2017) *Mastering Primary English*. London: Bloomsbury.

Lucas, B. and Spencer, E. (2017) Teaching Creative Thinking: Developing Learners Who Generate Ideas and Can Think Critically. Wales: Crown House Publishing.

Myhill, D.A., Jones, S. and Lines, H. (2018) Texts that teach: examining the efficacy of using texts as models. *Educational Studies in Language and Literature*, 18: 1–24.

Myhill, D., Jones, S., Watson, A. and Lines, H. (2016) *Essential Primary Grammar*. London: Open University Press.

National Advisory Committee on Creative and Cultural Education (NACCCE) (1999) *All Our Futures: Creativity, Culture and Education*. London: DFEE.

National Association for Able Children in Education (NACE) (2017) *6 Reasons to Bring Mastery to Primary English*. Available online at: www.nace.co.uk/blog/6-reasons-bring-mastery-primary-english (accessed 6 March 2019).

National Centre for Excellence in the Teaching of Mathematics (NCETM) (2014) Teaching for Mastery. Available online at: www.ncetm.org.uk/resources/47230 (accessed 31 March 2019).

Piggott, J. (2011) Rich tasks and contexts. Available online at: http://nrich.maths.org/5662 (accessed 21 March 2019).

Qualifications and Curriculum Authority (QCA) (2004) *Creativity: Find it, Promote it*. London: QCA publications. Available online at: www.literacyshed.com/uploads/1/2/5/7/12572836/1847211003.pdf (accessed 1 April 2019).

Richmond, J. (2017) *Curriculum and Assessment in English 3 to 11: A Better Plan*. Oxford: Routledge.

INDEX

academic and everyday language 145–6
ADD LO(v)E 75
Advanced learners of EAL 142
agency 120
Ahlberg, J. & A. 51
Alexander, R. 58, 177–8
Alice in Wonderland case study 194
analogy 175–6
analytical genres 148t
Andrews, R. 99, 106, 107
application of knowledge 228, 229
apprehension 160–1
Apthorp, H. 89
argument writing 106–7
arguments genre 146
Armitage, R. 51
art and design 100
artefacts 167–70
assessment without levels 226
Association of Science Education 209
autism case study 94–5

Baker, S. 116
Baldwin, P. 134, 135, 138
bank of writing 120–1
Barton, M.L. 213
BBC Music Stories 166
Bearne, E. 116
Beck, I.L. 213
Bettelheim, B. 12
bilingualism 142
Bleak House (Dickens) 196–200
The Bloody Chamber (Carter) 13

Bog Baby (Willis) 50
The Borrowers (Norton) 131
Boyd, M. 200
Brien, J. 82
Britten, Benjamin 166
Brooks, G.W. 116
Brothers Grimm 13
Bruner, J.S. 152
Bunting, R. 82–3
Bushnell, A. 8, 116, 161, 210

Cappelli, R. 105
Carroll, Lewis 194
Carter, A. 13
Carter, D. 191–2, 196
Chamberlain, L. 117, 118
Chapman, J.W. 90
character creation case study 136–7
Chekov, A. 64–5
children as authors 56–7
Christmas Eve activity 193–4
classic texts
    overview 191, 205–6
    plays 200–5
    poetry 181–96
    prose 196–200
classical music case study 166
classroom audit activity 95–6
classroom design 19–21
Claybourne, Anna 203
Coelho, J. 236
Cole, B. 16
collaborative working 134–7

collective teaching 177
Commission on Assessment 226
composition 113–17
    National Curriculum 192, 194
    supported composition 41
compositional processes 83–4
conceptual vocabulary 213
concision, importance of 2
conscience alley 86
constructionism 26–7
constructions 9
constructivism 26–7
Corbett, P. 44, 232, 235
Craft, A. 131, 233
creative mastery 225
creative writing *see also* drama
creativity
    creative and personal genes 147t
    creative apprenticeship model 231
    critical thinking and 233–5
    risk and freedom 235–7
Cremin, T. 46, 57, 116, 118, 196, 233
Crime Scene Chromatography 220
critical reading 102–3
critical thinking and creativity 233–5
critiquing texts 175
cross-curricular opportunities
    film clips case study 162–3
    non-fiction writing 100
    outdoor play 48
Csíkszentmihály, M. 165
cumulative teaching 178
Cuoco, A. 233
Curtis, P. 200

Daffern, T. 84
deep understanding 228
Defoe, Daniel 186
Department for Children Schools and
    Families (DCSF) 88
Derewianka, B. 146, 149
describers 233, 235
description generators 65–6, 68
desert island story case study 186–8
design and technology 100
DfE
    greater depth writing 7, 63, 75, 159
    independent writing 74
    KS2 assessment guidance 68–9, 74
    more flexible approaches 78
    non-independent writing 74
dialect, intuition for 2
dialogic teaching
    Odd One Out 183–8
    overview 186–8
    Role on the Wall 179–83

dialogic teaching framework 177–9
dialogue in short narrative stories 75–7
Dickens, Charles 196
discussion 178
discussions genre 146
Donaldson, J. 28, 36, 50, 131
Dorfman, L.R. 105
drafting 107–8, 162–3
drama
    case study 127–8
    character creation case study 136–7
    collaborative working 134–7
    conscience alley 86
    experimenting through play 131–2
    having fun 137–8
    links to literature 131
    overview 139–40
    playing in role 132–3
    preparing the ground 129
    saying yes to ideas 129
    starting to build 128–9
    'this is not a' activity 130–1
    top tips 138–9
    walk the story activity 134–6
    whale washed up case study 132–3
    working collaboratively 134–7
Duff, D. 89–90
Duke, N. 88, 146
Dutta, M. 152, 156
dyslexia 78

EAL (English as an additional language)
    case study 149–51
    explicit teaching about writing 149–52
    genres 146–9
    grammar case study 153–5
    National Curriculum 143–4
    overview 142–3, 156
    resources 152
    teacher training 151–2
    terminology 142
    writing in a second language 144–5
    writing processes 152–5
Early Years 8–12
    constructions 9
    play 9
    role play 9
editing and perseverance 237–8
editing texts 118–19
Education Endowment Foundation 106, 209, 215
effective writers 143–4
Eggers, D. 135
Elhert, L. 36, 46–8
emotional engagement 161
engagement
    apprehension 160–1

artefacts 167–70
   emotional 161
   in English 160
   film clips case study 162–3
   intellectual 161
   making films 163–5
   moving away from books 161
   music 165–6
   overview 171
   types of 159–60
   using film 161–3
   visits 170–1
enjoyment from writing 137–8
envoying 106
Erika's Story (Vander Zee) 76–7
everyday language 145–6
EXIT model 101
experimenters 233, 235
explanations genre 146
Exploratorium 213
explorer case study 122–3
Eyres, I. 113

factual genres 147t
fairy-tale activity 176–7
fake news 102–3
fantasy character activity 23–4
Fantasy Name Generator website 65–6, 68
Ferrara, R. 79
film clips case study 162–3
films 161–5
First World War case study 230–1
Fleming, M. 132
flexibility 225
flint and steel poems 34
floorbooks 216–17
fluency 225, 227, 229
focused play 21–2
food descriptions 69–73
forces case study 216
Ford, J. 181–2
forest descriptions case study 65–8
Forest School
   alternatives to 35
   exploring and writing in ITE 33–5
   KS1 case study 29–33
   nursery case study 27–8
   overview 29
   planning for 33
formality
   case study 14–15
   levels of 7, 123
   speech 87
forward planning 2
free play and writing opportunities 19–21
free play case study 20–1

freedom 235–7
functional grammar 146
Funnybones (Ahlberg) 51

Garcia, O. 145
Gardner, P. 114, 116
genres 146–9
   interpreting and critiquing 175
   types of 146–9
geography 100
German House Book 13
Gibbons, P. 143–4, 149, 156
Gleitzman, M. 77–8
Goldilocks 13, 42
Goswami, P. 192
Gough, P.B. 83
grammar
   case study 153–5
   in context 121
   direct teaching 82–3
   functional grammar 146
   instruction in 84
   non-fiction writing 108–10
Gravett, E. 51
greater depth writing
   components 2
   DfE 7, 63, 159
   indicators of activity 93–4
   modelling and scaffolding 79
   overview 16, 40–1
Greek gods case study 114–15
guessers 233, 235
Guidance on Scientific Enquiry (Association of
      Science) 209
guided writing 41
Guinee, K. 41

handwriting 84, 87
Hansen, A. 191
Hargreaves, R. 48
Harris Burdick 4–7
The Heartstone Odyssey (Kumar) 180–2
Heathcote, D. 132
Hendra, S. 131
heroic characters case study 180–2
Higgins, S. 54, 184
holistic approach 35–6
Holocaust case study 76–7
hook stimulus case study 46–8
hooks 45–9, 50–1
hot-seating 86, 106
The Hunchback of Notre Dame (film) 182–3

Ideas Alchemy Consultancy 22
images
   activity 8

case study 168–9
picture books 167–8
resources 4, 8
imitation as scaffold 232
independence 161
independent play 9
independent writing 74
    resources for 3
    STA 3
    stimuli for 3–4
independent writing case study 76–7
informal/formal speech 87
information gathering 100–5
information reports genre 146
innovation 232
instruction/exposition 178
intellectual engagement 161
interpreting texts 175
invention 232
inventors 233, 235
ITE providers
    outdoor learning 33–5
    use of hooks and writing 50

'Jaberwocky' (Carroll) case study 194–5
Jack and the Flumflum Tree (Donaldson) 131
Jeffers, O. 51
jigsawing 106
John, R. 134, 135, 138
Jolliffe, W. 35–6, 42–3, 45, 226, 237–8
Jones, T. 180–2

Kensuke's Kingdom (Morpurgo) 186
Key Stage 1
    creating and embedding depth 53
    Forest School case study 29–33
    high-quality books 45
    hook stimuli 45–9
    hook stimulus case study 46–8
    Leaf Man activity 48
    Lighthouse Keeper case study 58–60
    making films case study 163–5
    National Curriculum 113
    nouns and noun phrases 56
    overview 41, 59
    planning using high-quality text 43
    predicting story content 53–6
    subsequent sequence of learning 48–9
    Take One Book 42–5
    Thought Shower 48–9
    vocabulary 51–3
    writing strategies 44
Key Stage 2
    assessment guidance 68–9, 74, 75
    class writing independently case study 76–7
    dialogue in short narrative stories 75–7

food descriptions 69–73
food descriptions case study 70–3
forest descriptions case study 65–8
making films case study 163–5
National Curriculum 113–14
overview 78–9
pupil can statements 64
show but don't tell descriptions 64–9
tv adverts activity 74
keyboard skills 87
kinaesthetic learning 29
King, Stephen 4
Korth, B. 116–17
Kumar, A. 180–2

Lambert, A. 132
language
    academic and everyday 145–6
    developing knowledge 82–5
    formality 7, 14–15, 123
    National Curriculum 85
    strategies for 85–7
Leaf Man (Elhert) 36, 46–8
Learn Chemistry 220
learning difficulties 78
Learning through Landscapes 12
LEGO® SERIOUS PLAY® 22–3
    activities 23–6
    constructivism and constructionism 26–7
    core process and etiquette 23
letter writing
    example of 58–9
    hook stimulus 47
    personal experiences 99
    in a role 169
    WAGOLL 42
*Letters from the Lighthouse Scheme
    of Work* 70–3
Lewis, M. 101, 110
The Lighthouse Keeper's Lunch (Armitage) 51
    case study 58–60
    predicting story content 53–6
LinkedIn's Economic Graph 139
Lipman, M. 105
Literacy Shed website 8, 162
litfilmfest.com 164
Little Rabbit Foo Foo (Rosen) 12–16
Little Red Riding Hood 13
Little Red Riding Hood case study 233–5
love of language activity 95–6
Lucas, T. 152

magpie words 91
Maintaining Curiosity (Ofsted) 217
making films case studies 163–5
Mastering Primary English (Jolliffe) 226, 237

mastery
  creativity, risk and freedom 235–7
  critical thinking and creativity 233–5
  deep and rich learning 228–31
  definition of 225–6
  editing and perseverance 237–8
  example of 227–8
  First World War case study 230–1
  imitation as scaffold 232
  Little Red Riding Hood case study 233–5
  more than the sum of component parts 226–8
  overview 225
  scaffolds and supports 231
  supporting 228
  teachers as writers 235–7
  The Tempest case study 227–8
mathematics
  mastery 225–6, 228
  rich tasks 229
Matthew effect 90
Matthews, A. 201
McEwan, I. 76–7
Medwell, J. 84, 87
Meerkat Mail (Gravett) 51–3
mentor texts 105–6
metaphors 2, 66, 128–9, 138
Michaels, S. 215
Mizen, B. 22
model-building 22–3
  fantasy character activity 23–4
  mysterious journey activity 25
  perfect day activity 25–6
model text case study 114–15
modelled writing 41
  example 117–18
Moore, C.C. 192
Morgan, D.N. 116
morphemes 91
Morpurgo, Michael 186
Moses, A. 88
moves analysis 154–5
Moving English Forward (Ofsted) 191
Mr. Men (Hargreaves) 48
Mumaw, S. 139
Munsch, R. 16
Murphy, C. 128
Murray, R. 29
music 165–6
Myhill, D.A. 82–3, 232
The Mysteries of Harris Burdick case study 4–7
mysterious journey activity 25

narratives genre 146
  film clips case study 162–3
National Advisory Committee on Creative and Cultural
    Education (NACCCE) 225

National Curriculum
  composition 192, 194
  drafting 108
  EAL 143–4
  informal/formal speech 87
  Key Stage 1 113
  Key Stage 2 113–14
  language 85
  narratives about personal experiences 99
  poetry 193, 194
  science 208, 213, 219–20
  transcription and composition 113–17
  vocabulary development 87–8
  writing poetry 194
National Literacy Strategy 101
National Literacy Trust report 103, 114, 137
National Reading panel's review 88–9
Nazi films 13
Newbolt Report 128
Newton, L. 160
'The Night Before Christmas' (Moore) 192–3
No-Bot (Hendra) 131
non-fiction writing
  content of information writing 103–5
  cross-curricular opportunities 100
  design and technology 100
  drafting 107–8
  gathering information 100–2
  insufficient emphasis on 99
  oral rehearsal 106–7
  overview 110
  persuasive writing case study 104–5
  planning for 107
  preparation for 105–6
  spelling, punctuation and grammar 108–10
  text box activity 102
non-independent writing 3, 74
Norton, M. 131
nouns and noun phrases 56
novel case study 92–4
nursery
  free play case study 20–1
  outdoor play case study 27–8

O'Brien, E. 29, 35
Odd One Out 183–8
Ofsted 142, 191
  science 208–9, 217
Oliver's Vegetables (Jeffers) 51
Once (Gleitzman) 77–8
onceuponapicture website 8
O'Neill, C. 132
oral classroom activities 106–7
outdoor play
  activities 11–12
  cross-curricular links 48

Nursery case study 27–8
opportunities 35–6
Reception Class case study 10–11
Oxford Language Report 82

The Paper Bag Princess (Munsch) 16
Papert, S. 27
pattern sniffers 233, 235
Percy Jackson and the Lightning Thief 13
perfect day activity 25–6
perseverance 237–8
personal writing 120
persuasive writing 104
Peter Grimes (Britten) 166
Philosophy for Children 105
physical skills 20–1, 35
Piaget, J. 26–7
picture books 167–8
Piggott, J. 229
play *see also* outdoor play
    Early Years 9
    experimenting through 131–2
    overview 36
    playing in role 132–3
play dough 21
plays 200–5
Pobble 168
poetry
    flint and steel poems 34–5
    National Curriculum 193, 194
    as stimulus 191–2
polishing pens 237
Practice, Pedagogy and Policy (Murphy) 128
predictions 86–7
prefixes/suffixes 91
Primary Science Teaching Trust 216
Princess Smartypants (Cole) 16
procedural understanding 227, 229
procedural vocabulary 213
procedures genre 146
Propp, V. 154
punctuation
    instruction in 84
    non-fiction writing 108–10
    speech and writing 7
    used for effect 2
    using range 7
pupil can statements 64, 78
Pupil Parliament planning 164
Purcell-Gate, V. 146
Purewal, S. 200–1
purposeful teaching 178
purposes of writing 59, 113, 120
Puss in Boots 13

quality literature 2
Quasimodo activity 182–3

reading
    critical reading 102–3
    vocabulary development 89–90
Reading, C. 219
reading dialogue 86
reading for pleasure 193
Reading for Pleasure (OU) 116
reading to children 85–6
    vocabulary cards 90–1
reasoning *see also* dialogic teaching
    in the classroom 177–9
    evidence of 175–7
    fairy-tale activity 176–7
    overview 174
    philosophy approach 105
    primary education 174–5
    task structures 179–83
Reception Class case study 10–11
reciprocal teaching 177
recitation 178
recounts genre 146
Reedy, D. 116
refining texts 118–19
relevance 56–7
reporting 214–15
resources
    bank of writing 120–1
    EAL 152
    focused play 21
    images 8
    for independent writing 2–8
    non-fiction texts 102
    Talk for Writing 44
*Review of SES and Science Learning in Formal
    Educational Settings* (EEE) 209
Reynolds, O. 29, 35, 59
rich tasks 229–30
Richard III case study 203–5
risk 235–7
Roach, T. 2, 82
Roberts, R. 219
Robinson Crusoe (Defoe) 186–8
Robinsonade genre case study 186–8
Role on the Wall 179–83
role play 9, 19–20
Romeo and Juliet case study 201–3
Rose Blanche (McEwan) 76–7
Rose, J. 83
Rosen, M. 12–16
rote learning 178
Roth, K. 41

Safford, K. 83
The Saga of Erik the Viking (Jones) 180–2
SATs 85
scaffolding 79, 121
    dialogue 178

imitation as 79
    mastery 231
school genres 146
science
    connections to phenomena 219–21
    film clips case study 162–3
    forces case study 216
    language development 212
    making vocabulary visible 213–14
    National Curriculum 208, 213, 219–20
    non-fiction writing 100
    overview 221–2
    purpose and aims of writing 208–9
    reporting 214–15
    reporting in 209–10
    separating mixtures case study 220–1
    sequencing 210–12
    vocabulary 213–14
    working notebooks case study 217–19
    working scientifically 209, 215–16, 217
Second World War case study 76–7
self-editing 2
separating mixtures case study 220–1
sequencing 210–12
Seymour, R. 200
Shakespeare, William
    case for teaching 200–1
    Richard III case study 203–5
    Romeo and Juliet case study 201–3
shared writing 41, 87
show but don't tell descriptions 64–9
Shrek! activity 15
Shrek! (Steig) 14
similarities and differences case study 186–8
similes 65
simple view of writing 83–4
slow writing 162–3
small-world play 9
snowballing 106
song lyrics case study 165–6
SPaG test 83, 85, 160
speech 2, 7
    formality 7, 14–15, 87, 123
spelling
    instruction in 84
    non-fiction writing 108–10
Sprigg, P. 33
Standards and Testing Agency (STA)
    independent writing 3
    non-independent writing 3
Starting Drama Teaching (Fleming) 132
Steig, W 14
Stick Man (Donaldson) 28, 36, 50
Strong, J, 232, 235
subject knowledge 117
suburban area case study 109–10
Sunday's news letter 99

supported composition 41
supportive teaching 177
SVOR (simple view of reading) 83
Swiss Family Robinson (Wyss) 186–8
synonyms 91
synonyms activity 185–6

Take One Book 42–5
'take one book' principle 35
talk see dialogic teaching
Talk for Writing approach 44, 105–6
Talk for Writing (Corbett) 232
Talk for Writing programme 44
teacher in role 132–3
teachers as writers
    case study 122–3, 127–8
    for children 120–4
    formality 123
    importance of 41
    overview 113, 124
    planning 123
    project 236
    pupil progress 118–20
    and readers 116–17
technology 121
The Tempest case study 227–8
text box activity 102
The Gruffalo 12–13
Theseus and the Minotaur (Ford) 181–2
Thinking Frames Approach 212
Thinking Through Primary Teaching (Higgins) 184
'this is not a' activity 130–1
time for writing 237–8
tinkerers 233, 235
topic knowledge 149–50
traditional tales
    alternatives to 16
    case study 12–16
    criticisms of 16
    importance of 12–16
transcription 113–17
transcriptional skills 83–4
triadic structures 13
Tunmer, W.E. 83, 90
tv adverts activity 74

UK School Trips 170
USA 88–9
'Usborne Young Reader' 203
The Uses of Enchantment (Bettelheim) 12

Van Allsburg, C. 4
Vander Zee, R. 76–7
visits 170–1
visualisation 212
visualisers 233, 235
vocabulary

in action 2, 89–90
developing 87–9
high-quality books 51–3
importance of reading 89–90
key elements 89
lack of 82
National Curriculum 87–8
science 213–14
sorting into word types 55
strategies for developing 90–2
types of 213
underdeveloped 85, 90
vocabulary cards 90–1
vonjecturers 233, 235
Vygotsky, L. 56, 209

WAGOLL (What A Good One Looks Like) 41, 42
walk the story activity 134–6
Waugh, D. 35–6, 42–3, 45, 160, 226, 237–8
whale washed up case study 132–3
Wiersum, G. 12
Williams, Marcia 203
Williamson, H. 29–33
Willis, J. 50
Winston, J. 132, 135
word games 88

word of the day 92
word windows 91
working notebooks case study 217–19
Wray, D. 84, 87, 101, 110
writing
    automaticity 87
    effective writers 143–4
    genres 63
    moves analysis of 154–5
    processes 83–4, 123, 152–5
    purposes of 59, 113, 120
    in a second language 144–5
    skills 83–4
    support strategies 44, 120–4
writing areas 19–20
writing centres 135
writing communities 121
writing slips 237
Wyss, Johann 186

Year 4 formality case study 14–15
Year 6 case study 4–7
yes to ideas 129

Zipes, J. 16
zone of proximal development 209